Pluma Brown

Song-hymnal of praise and joy

A selection of spiritual songs old and new

Pluma Brown

Song-hymnal of praise and joy
A selection of spiritual songs old and new

ISBN/EAN: 9783337266271

Printed in Europe, USA, Canada, Australia, Japan

Cover: Foto ©Thomas Meinert / pixelio.de

More available books at **www.hansebooks.com**

SONG-HYMNAL
OF
PRAISE AND JOY.

A SELECTION OF SPIRITUAL
SONGS, OLD AND NEW.

EDITED AND PUBLISHED BY
PLUMA M. BROWN,
JACKSON, MINNESOTA.

Anderson Bros., Music Typographers.

PREFACE.

—•—

In this collection endeavor has been made to provide a large number of hymns and songs that may be of special service in promoting the higher Christian life.

The aim has been to retain original versions as far as possible, omitting entire stanzas rather than making changes. Some of the hymns have been recently altered by their authors; and in a few instances a word, or line, has been changed to better suit the metre, or the needs of worship.

Most of the beautiful old tunes, so endeared by association, have been included. Many arrangements from foreign sources, and many tunes from the best English composers, meriting greater attention from both choir and congregation, will be found.

Grateful acknowledgment is made to the authors, composers, and owners of copyright whose kindly permissions have enriched this work.

The Editor.

CONTENTS.

SONGS AND HYMNS.

1 Holy, Holy, Holy. P. M.

Nicæa.—J. B. Dykes.

1. Ho-ly, ho-ly, ho-ly, Lord God Al-might-y! Ear-ly in the morn-ing our song shall rise to thee; Ho-ly, ho-ly, ho-ly, mer-ci-ful and might-y. God in three per-sons, bless-ed Trin-i-ty!

2 Holy, holy, holy! all the saints adore thee,
    Casting down their golden crowns around the glassy sea.
Cherubim and seraphim falling down before thee.
    Which wert, and art, and evermore shalt be.

3 Holy, holy, holy! though the darkness hide thee,
    Though the eye of ignorance thy glory may not see:
Only thou art holy; there is none beside thee.
    Perfect in power. in love. and purity.

4 Holy. holy. holy! Lord God Almighty!
    All thy works shall praise thy name. in earth, and sky. and sea:
Holy. holy. holy! merciful and mighty;
    God in three persons. blessed Trinity!

R. Heber.

2 The Herald Angels.   7 D.

C. WESLEY.
Mendelssohn. - Arr. fr. MENDELSSOHN.

1. Hark! the her-ald an-gels sing,   Glo-ry to the new-born King:
2. Hail! the heav'n-born Prince of Peace!   Hail! the Sun of Right-eous-ness!

God's good-will to man, and peace Which shall ev-er-more in-crease.
Light and life to all he brings, Risen with heal-ing in his wings.

Joy-ful, all ye na-tions, rise. Join the tri-umph of the skies:
Mild he lays his glo-ries by, Born that man no more may die:

With th'an-gel-ic hosts pro-claim, Christ is born in Beth-le-hem!
Born to raise the sons of earth, Born to give them sec-ond birth.

Hark! the her-ald an-gels sing Glo-ry to the new-born King.
Hark! the her-ald an-gels sing Glo-ry to the new-born King.

Organ pedal.

3 Truth's Advent. 7 6 l.   *Theodora.—Arr. fr.* Handel.

1. Years a - go a Child was born: 'Twas a bright ce - les - tial morn

When the shepherds sought the Child, Guarded by a vir - gin mild,

Cradled on her heart of love, Watched by an - gels from a - bove.

2 Wondrous mission had the Child,
'Mid the shades of earth beguiled;
Whispered he of peace and love,
Taught the Father's power to move
All things to his holy will,
Bidding discord's waves "be still."

3 Quietly he walked abroad,
Strewing blessings where he trod;
'Mid the haunts of fear and wrong,
Seeing only Truth's fair form;
Healing, blessing all the way,
Thus he went from day to day.

4 Lingered by the bed of pain,
Raised the dead to life again;
Made all burdens roll away,
Cast out demons by the way;
Healed the blind in every throng,
Taught forgiveness of all wrong

5 Knowing naught of space or time,
Knowing well that Life Divine
Shines in every human heart;
Still he bore the human part,
Living like the Son of man,
Loving only as God can.

6 Suddenly he went away
From the world he loved so well,
Promising to come again,
Evermore with us to dwell.
All who will, behold him now:
All who will, before him bow.

7 Jesus Christ has come again.
Saving Truth has come to men:
Angels, chant your hymns of praise,
Sons of men, your voices raise:
Shout the tidings far and near,
Christ, the blessed Truth, is here.

Sarah E. Griswold.

4   Joy to the World.   C. M.

Antioch.—Arr. fr. Handel.

1. Joy to the world, the Lord is come! Let earth receive her King: Let
ev - 'ry heart pre-pare him room, And heav'n and na-ture sing. And
And heav'n and nature
heav'n and na-ture sing, And heav'n. And heav'n and na - ture sing.
sing............
And heav'n and na-ture sing.

2 Joy to the world, the Savior reigns;
  Let men their songs employ;
While fields and floods, rocks, hills,
    and plains
Repeat the sounding joy.

3 He rules the world with truth and
  grace,
And makes the nations prove
The glories of his righteousness,
And wonders of his love
                   I. Watts.

5   The Savior's Advent.

1 Hark the glad sound! the Savior
  comes,—
The Savior promised long;
Let every heart prepare a throne,
And every voice a song.

2 He comes, the broken heart to bind,
The bleeding soul to cure;
And, with the treasures of his grace,
T' enrich the humble poor.

3 Our glad hosannas, Prince of Peace!
  Thy welcome shall proclaim,
And heaven's eternal arches ring
With thy beloved name.
                 P. Doddridge.

6   Sing to the Lord.

1 Sing to the Lord, ye distant lands!
  Ye tribes of every tongue!
His new-discovered grace demands
A new and nobler song.

2 Let heaven proclaim the joyful day;
Joy through the earth be seen;
Let cities shine in bright array,
And fields in cheerful green.

3 Let an unusual joy surprise
  The islands of the sea;
Ye mountains, sink! ye valleys, rise!
Prepare the Lord his way.
                 I. Watts.

7 The Advent. C. M.

Zerah.—L. Mason.

1. "Glo-ry to God!" this ad-vent morn, My soul ex-ult-ing sings,
To - day of old on earth was born The glo-rious King of kings.
To-day of old on earth was born The glo-rious King of kings.

2 Let every idle folly fall,
  And every discord cease;
He reigns in heaven the Lord of all;
  O'er all the Prince of Peace.

3 Glory to God! in Christ the Lord
  We own his name divine;
Earth, heaven, the Spirit and the Word
  Robed in his beauty shine.
          T. L. HARRIS.

8   *Christ in the Heart.*
1 Still, still 'tis ours the hymn to hear
  That swept o'er Israel's plain;
Loud swells the anthem;—sphere to
  In joy repeats the strain. [sphere

2 Where'er thy Spirit, Lord, is shrined,
  The inward Christ is born;
The angel-strains in heart and mind
  Proclaim the advent morn.

TUNE—*Mendelssohn.* p. 6.

9   *The Wonderful.*
1 Bright and joyful is the morn,
For to us a Child is born;
From the highest realms of heaven,
Unto us a Son is given.
On his shoulder he shall bear
Power and majesty, and wear
On his vesture and his thigh,
Names most awful, names most high.

2 Wonderful in counsel he,
Christ, the incarnate Deity;
Sire of ages, ne'er to cease;
King of kings, and Prince of Peace.
Come and worship at his feet;
Yield to him the homage meet;
From the manger to the throne,
Homage due to God alone.
          J MONTGOMERY.

10 Christmas Carol. C. M. D.

Carol.—R. S. Willis.

1. It came up-on the mid-night clear, That glo-rious song of old,

From an-gels bending near the earth To touch their harps of gold.

D. S.—world in sol-emn still-ness lay To hear the an-gels sing.

"Peace on the earth, good-will to men, From heav'n's all-gracious King:" The

2 Still through the cloven skies they
  come
  With peaceful wings unfurled,
And still their heavenly music floats
  O'er all the weary world:
Above its sad and lowly plains
  They bend on hovering wing,
And ever o'er its Babel sounds
  The blessed angels sing.

3 For lo! the days are hastening on
  By prophet-bards foretold,
When with the ever-circling years
  Comes round the age of gold;
When Peace shall over all the earth
  Its radiant splendor fling,
And the whole world give back the song
  Which now the angels sing.
          EDMUND H. SEARS.

11   Christmas Anthem.

1 Calm on the listening ear of night.
  Come heaven's melodious strains,
Where wild Judea stretches far
  Her silver-mantled plains;
Celestial choirs from courts above
  Shed sacred glories there;
And angels, with their sparkling lyres,
  Make music on the air.

2 The answering hills of Palestine
  Send back the glad reply.
And greet from all their holy heights
  The Dayspring from on high:
O'er the blue depths of Galilee
  There comes a holier calm;
And Sharon waves in solemn praise
  Her silent groves of palm.

3 "Glory to God!" the lofty strain
   The realm of ether fills;
How sweeps the song of solemn joy
   O'er Judah's sacred hills!
"Glory to God!" the sounding skies
   Loud with their anthems ring:
"Peace on the earth; good-will to men,
   From heaven's eternal King."

4 This day shall Christian tongues be
   And Christian hearts be cold? [mute
O catch the anthem that from heaven
   O'er Judah's mountains rolled!
When nightly burst from seraph-harps
   The high and solemn lay,—
"Glory to God; on earth be peace;
   Salvation comes to-day!"

EDMUND H. SEARS.

12 The Children's Song. c. m.

Christmas.—Arr. fr. HANDEL.

1. Hosanna! be the children's song, To Christ, the children's King; His praise to whom our souls belong. Let all the children sing, Let all the children sing.

2 Hosanna! sound from hill to hill,
   And spread from plain to plain,
While louder, clearer, sweeter still.
   Words echo to the strain.

3 Hosanna! on the wings of light.
   O'er earth and ocean fly.
Till morn to eve, and noon to night.
   And heaven to earth reply.

4 Hosanna! then, our song shall be;
   Hosanna to our King!
This is the children's jubilee;
   Let all the children sing.

J. MONTGOMERY.

13 Hail to Messiah.

1 Messiah! at thy glad approach
   The howling winds are still;
Thy praises fill the lonely waste,
   And breathe from every hill.

2 Renewed, the earth a robe of light.
   A robe of beauty wears;
And in new heavens a brighter sun
   Leads on the promised years.

3 Let Israel to the Prince of Peace
   The loud hosanna sing:
With hallelujahs and with hymns.
   O Zion, hail thy King.

M. BRUCE.

14   O Blessed Time.   P. M.

WM. BRIGHT.
A. SULLIVAN.

1. Once a - gain, O bless - ed time, Thank-ful hearts em - brace thee;
2. Once a - gain the Ho - ly Night Breathes its bless-ing ten - der;
3. Yea, if oth - ers stand a - part, We will press the near - er;
4. So we yield thee all we can, Wor-ship, thanks, and bless - ing;

If we lost thy fes - tal chime, What could e'er re - place thee?
Once a - gain the Man - ger Light Sheds its gen - tle splen - dor;
Yea, O best fra - ter - nal Heart, We will hold thee dear - er;
Thee, true God, and thee, true Man, On our knees con - fess - ing;

Change will dark - en many a day, Many a bond dis - sev - er;
Oh, could tongues by an - gels taught Speak our ex - ul - ta - tion,
Faith - ful lips shall an - swer thus To all faith - less scorn - ing,
While thy birth - day morn we greet With our best de - vo - tion.

Many a joy shall pass a - way, But the "Great Joy" nev - er.
In the Vir - gin's Child that brought All man-kind sal - va - tion!
"Je - sus Christ is God with us, Born on Christ-mas morn - ing."
Bathe us, O most True and Sweet! In thy mer - cy's o - cean.

15 Joy in Heaven. P. M.

1. There is joy in heav'n, There is joy in heav'n, Joy..... in heav'n!
Sons of men, be-hold from far, Hail the long-ex-pect-ed Star!
Star of truth that gilds the night, Guides bewildered men a-right.
Guides bewildered men a-right.
Glo-ry to God in heav'n! Glo-ry to God in heav'n!"

2 There is joy in heaven,
Joy in heaven!
Nations all, remote and near,
Haste, to see your Lord appear;
Haste, for him your hearts prepare.
Meet him manifested here!—Cho.
Glory to God in heaven.

3 There is joy in heaven,
Joy in heaven!
Now behold the Day-spring rise,
Pouring light on mortal eyes;
See it chase the shades away,
Shining to the perfect day!—Cho.
Glory to God in heaven.
C. WESLEY.

16 There was Joy.

1 There was joy in heaven,
Joy in heaven!
When this goodly world to frame,
The Lord of might and mercy came;
Shouts of joy were heard on high.
And the stars sang from the sky:
"Glory to God in heaven!"

2 There was joy in heaven,
Joy in heaven!
When of love the midnight beam
Dawned on favored Bethlehem.
And along the echoing hill
Angels sang. "On earth good-will.
Glory to God in heaven."

17 Song of Christmas. 7. 6 l. D.

AMELIA Y. COLE.
PLUMA M. BROWN.

1. Chil - dren, lo, the days are here Of the joy - ous Christmas cheer!
2. Guid - ed by his sa - cred star, Came the wise men from a - far;
3. Tell them in your sweet-est song "To the Fa - ther you be - long;

List - en, how each sweet chime swells From the the swift - ly clashing bells;
Roy - al gifts their hands un - fold, Myrrh and frank-in-cense and gold;
Love is wait - ing at your door, Wait-ing now and ev - er - more:

Bells that peal a - long the morn Of the day when Christ was born.
Glo - rious grew that sta - ble dim, When they knelt and worshiped him.
Still for you the star doth glow, Flam-ing o - ver night and snow.

He the Life, the Truth, the Way, Once in Beth-le-hem's man-ger lay.
While your hearts are filled with love, This di - vin - est tale a - bove,
In the beau - ty of its ray Clouds and dark - ness flee a - way:

cal

Song of Christmas—Concluded.

Near the herdsmen and their kine—He, the Heavenly, the Di - vine;
There are some in lone - ly ways, In these hap - py Christmas days:
Love and joy are in its light, Fade-less, deathless, ev - er bright;

Show- ing that the low - liest heart May with him have lot and part.
Earth - ly shad - ows round them fall, Yet the Fath - er loves them all.
Let no fear your hearts ap - pal, God, the Fa - ther, lov - eth all."

TUNE—*Mendelssohn.* p. 6.

18   *Songs of Praise.*

1 Songs of praise the angels sang,
Heaven with hallelujahs rang,
When Jehovah's work begun,
When he spake, and it was done.
For he spake, and forth from night
Sprang the universe to light;
He commanded—nature heard,
And stood fast upon his word.

2 Songs of praise awoke the morn,
When the Prince of Peace was born;
Songs of praise arose, when he
Captive led captivity.
Heaven and earth must pass away;

Songs of praise shall crown that day;
God will make new heavens and earth;
Songs of praise shall hail their birth.

3 Praise him, all ye hosts above,—
Spirits perfected in love!
Sun and moon! your anthems raise;
Sing, ye stars! your Maker's praise.
Heralds of creation! cry,
"Praise the Lord—the Lord most
      high!"
Heaven and earth obey the call,
Praise the Lord—the Lord of all.

J. MONTGOMERY

19   Holy Night.   P. M.

F. GRUBER.

1. Ho-ly night! peace-ful night! All is dark save the light

Yon-der, where they sweet vig-il keep O'er the Babe, who, in si-lent sleep.

Rests in heav-en-ly peace. Rests in heav-en-ly peace.

2 Holy night! peaceful night!
Only for shepherds' sight,
Came blest visions of angel throngs,
With their loud Alleluia songs,
    Saying, Jesus is come.

3 Holy night! peaceful night!
Child of heaven! oh, how bright
Thou didst smile on us when thou
    wast born;
Blest indeed was that happy morn,
Full of heavenly joy.

J. MOHR.

20   Worship With Joy.   7. 6 l.

Eltham.—L. MASON.

FINE.

1. As with glad-ness men of old Did the guid-ing star be-hold:
D. C.—So, most gra-cious Lord, may we Ev-er-more be led to thee.

D. C.

As with joy they hailed its light. Lead-ing on-ward, beam-ing bright;

21 Songs of Praise. 6.4.

1. Sing ye the songs of praise; Je - sus is come! High your glad
2. This day in Beth - le - hem, Je - sus was born! King of Je -

voi-ces raise; Je - sus is come! Cast world - ly cares a - way,
ru - sa - lem, Je - sus was born! Sun of all right-eous-ness,

Wor-ship and homage pay, Wel-come the bless-ed day, Je - sus is come!
Shin-ing with bless-ed-ness, Heal - ing our wretchedness, Je - sus was born!

3 Cleanse us from sense of sin,
Savior Divine!
Make our thoughts pure within,
Savior Divine!
Lo! now the herald sound
Carols the love profound,
Telling of Jesus found,
Savior Divine!

4 Save through thy merit,
Great Prince of Peace!
Give thy good Spirit,
Great Prince of Peace!
Thy love can ne'er depart,
But holy gifts impart,
Born into every heart,
Great Prince of Peace!

TUNE—*Worship with Joy.*

2 As with joyous steps they sped
To that lowly manger-bed.
There to bend the knee before
Him whom heaven and earth adore;
So may we with willing feet
Ever seek the mercy-seat.

3 As they offered gifts most rare
At that manger rude and bare,
So may we with holy joy,

Pure and free from sin's alloy,
All our costliest treasures bring,
Christ! to thee, our heavenly King.

4 In the heavenly country bright.
Need we no created light;
Thou its Light, its Joy. its Crown,
Thou its Sun which goes not down,
Here forever may we sing
Hallelujahs to our King.

W. C. DIX.

22 Holy Voices. 8. 7. 4.

1. { Hark! what mean those ho - ly voi - ces, Sweet-ly sound-ing thro' the skies? }
   { Lo! th'an-gel - ic host re-joi-ces, Heav'n-ly hal - le - lu-jahs rise. }

Hal - le - lu - jah! hal - le - lu - jah! Ech-oes back from earth and skies.

2 Listen to the wondrous story
  Which they chant in hymns of joy;
··Glory in the highest, glory!
  Glory be to God most high!"
      Thus they praise him,
  With their songs of holiest joy.

3 Christ is born, the great Anointed,
  Heaven and earth his praises sing;
Glad receive whom God appointed

For your Prophet, Priest, and King.
    Sweetest anthems
Through the heaven's high arches ring.

4 Let us learn the wondrous story
  Of our great Redeemer's birth;
Spread the brightness of his glory
  Till it cover all the earth.
      Till salvation
  Shall be known in all the earth.

The Advent Music. H. M.

Darwall.—J. Darwall.

23 Come and Worship. 8. 7. 4.

J. MONTGOMERY.
Regent Square—HENRY SMART.

1. An - gels, from the realms of glo - ry, Wing your flight o'er all the earth;
2. Sa - ges, leave your con - tem-pla-tions, Bright-er vi-sions beam a - far;

Ye who sang cre - a - tion's sto - ry, Now pro-claim Mes-si-ah's birth:
Seek the great De - sire of na - tions: Ye have seen his na - tal star:

Come and wor-ship, come and wor - ship, Worship Christ, the new-born King.

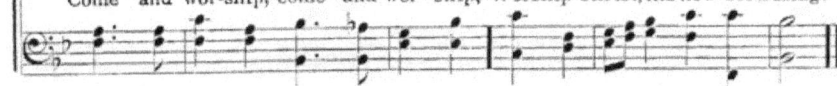

TUNE—Darwall.

24   The Advent Music.
1 Hark! what celestial sounds,
    What music fills the air!
  Soft warbling to the morn,
    It strikes the ravished ear;
Now all is still; |In tuneful notes,
Now wild it floats|Loud, sweet and shrill.

2 "Glory to God on high;
    Ye mortals, spread the sound,
  And let your raptures fly
    To earth's remotest bound;
For peace on earth. | To man is given,
From God in heaven | At Jesus' birth."

25   The Notes of Joy.
1 Hark! hark!—the notes of joy
    Roll o'er the heavenly plains.
  And seraphs find employ
    For their sublimest strains:
Some new delight in heaven is known:
Loud sound the harps around the throne.

2 Strike—strike the harps again.
    To great Immanuel's name:
  Arise, ye sons of men!
    And all his grace proclaim:
Angels and men! wake every string.
'Tis God the Savior's praise we sing.

A. REED.

26   Christmas Morning.   8. 7. D.   *Smyrna.*—Arr. fr. Mozart.

1. Now the joy-ful Christmas morning, Breaking o'er the world be-low,
2. Out of ev-'ry clime and peo-ple, Un-der ev-'ry ho-ly name,
3. Sing a-loud, then, hearts and voi-ces! Shout, O new world, free and strong!

Tells a-gain the won-drous sto-ry Of the Christ-Child long a-go.
Is the ev-er-last-ing gos-pel Good and glad for aye the same:
Hail of Light the death-less tri-umph, Join the old world's birthday song.—

Hark! we hear a-gain the cho-rus Echo-ing thro' the star-ry sky
So we, in our hap-py Christmas, Breathe the u-ni-ver-sal creed.
"Glo-ry be to God the High-est! Peace on earth, good-will to men!"

And we join the heav'n-ly an-them, "Glo-ry be to God on high!"
Clasping hands with dis-tant a-ges In a broth-er-hood in-deed.
'Twas the morn-ing stars that pealed it.— Let the world re-spond a-gain.

27 The Cherubic Pilgrim. P. M.

JOHANNES SCHEFFLER.
Arr. fr. MENDELSSOHN.

1. God's Spir - it falls on me as dew - drops on a rose:
2. Lo! in the si - lent night a child to God is born:
3. Tho' Christ a thou - sand times in Beth - le - hem be born:
4. In all e - ter - ni - ty no tone can be so sweet.

If I but like a rose my heart to him un - close.
And all is brought a - gain that e'er was lost or lorn.
If he's not born in thee, thy soul is all for - lorn.
As where man's heart with God in u - ni - son doth beat.

The soul where - in God dwells,—what church can ho - lier be?—
Could but thy soul, O man! be - come a si - lent night,
Hold there! where run - nest thou? know heav - en is in thee:
Ah, would the heart but be a man - ger for the birth.

Be - comes a walk - ing tent of heav'n - ly maj - es - ty.
God would be born in thee. and set all things a - right.
Seek thou for God else - where, his face thou'lt nev - er see.
God would once more be - come....... a Child on earth.

28 A Christmas Hymn. 10.

Manchester—English.

1. Dost seek the Christ? know he is not a-far. Perchance he walk-eth in yon crowd-ed street; Still thro' each night flames forth his sa-cred star, And in all path-ways thou the Christ may meet.

2 As thou hast min'stered to another's needs,
   Or smoothed a weary way with thorns beset,
 Or bound with gentle hand some heart that bleeds,
   There in thy pathway thou the Christ hast met.

3 Still through each winter's gloom a carol swells,
   And chiming bells ring out in joyance free;
 'Tis not alone above the stars he dwells,
   But in the heart of our humanity.

4 Let the good-will which man to man should bear
   Shine forth in deeds more nobly than of old;
 Sweet as the song that stirred the Judean air,
   And roused the shepherds watching by the fold.

5 Now let the gospel of his life abide,
   As in that far-off country 'twas begun;
 Until, amid time's all-evolving tide,
   Christ and humanity indeed are One.

AMELIA V. COLE.

29 Thou Life Within. 10.

ELIZA SCUDDER.
Ellerton.—E. J. HOPKINS.

1. Thou Life with - in my life, than self more near! Thou veil - ed
2. How can I call thee who art al - ways here,— How shall I

Pres - ence in - fi - nite - ly dear! From all my name - less
praise thee who art still most dear,—What may I give thee

wea - ri - ness I flee, To find my cen - ter and my rest in thee.
save what thou hast given,—And whom but thee have I in earth or heaven?

30   *With Faith.*

1 Forth from the shores of self my spirit sails,
  My boat is launched upon an unknown sea,
  With faith for pilot—faith that never fails,
  The faith that sounds my soul's infinity!

2 As lesser sights are left behind, and fade
  In mists that shadow earth and earthly things,
  So upward leaps the light—I'm not afraid—
  My soul is strong, my soul has found its wings!

3 Silent and still, I drift on waters clear.
  And drink with joy the cup of being's truth.
  Close as my thought is God—he speaks: I hear,—
  I know that life is one unending youth!

4 Boundless and spaceless life I now behold—
  Nor age nor time can bar its shoreless sea.
  Wave upon wave its tide is still unrolled;
  I sail with faith through soul's infinity!
                                    ELLA DARE.

31   Within.   S. M.

Serenity.—C. Bryan.

1. In thine own be - ing, thine, Not else - where, search for his:

Not in some out - er heaven and earth; With-in, he speaks and is.

2 No voice can speak his voice,
No words his essence tell;
Felt beyond feeling's conscious verge
Is he in whom we dwell.

3 Enough to know him here,
Far, near, within, around:—
The heavenly treasure swiftly flies
Before the touch of sound.

4 In silence hold thy faith,
Unspeakable, alone;
The unknown future ever lies
Hid in the God unknown.
F. T. PALGRAVE.

32   Harmony.

1 Be healed, O world! be healed;
In understanding come
To Christ, the Way, the Truth, the Life,
The one eternal Son.

2 He giveth words of grace
That quickly sets us free
From all entanglements of sense,
And brings us harmony.

3 Our dear Christ, unto thee
We look, with unveiled sight,

And find that thou and we are One,
Viewed in the Spirit's light.

4 Thus sing we with delight
Of Omnipresent Good,
Which giveth power to demonstrate
That we are sons of God.

33   With Christ in God.

1 I bless the Christ of God,
I rest on love divine;
And with unfaltering lip and heart
I call this Savior mine.

2 His cross dispels each doubt;
I bury in his tomb
Each thought of unbelief and fear,
Each lingering shade of gloom.

3 I praise the God of grace,
I trust his truth and might;
He calls me his, I call him mine,
My God, my joy, my light.

4 My life with him is hid,
My death has passed away,
My clouds have melted into light,
My midnight into day.
H. BONAR.

34 Before Thee. 7.   *Aletta.*—WM. B. BRADBURY.

1. Lo! we stand be-fore thee now. And our si-lent, in-ward vow
Thou dost hear in that pro-found, Where is neith-er voice nor sound.

Used by arr. with The Biglow & Main Co., owners of copyright.

2 Not by any outward sign
Dost thou show thy will divine;
Deep within thy voice doth cry
And our quickened souls reply.

3 Thou dost hear, and thou wilt bless
With thy strength and tenderness:
Lo! we come to do thy will;
With thy life our spirits fill.
J. W. CHADWICK.

35   *Visited.*
1 Sweetest Joy the soul can know,
Fairest Light was ever shed,
Who alike in joy and woe
Leavest none unvisited!

2 Spirit of the Highest God.
Who upholdest everything.
Thou from whom my life has flowed,
To my life thy gladness bring!

3 For the noblest guest thou art
That a soul e'er sought or won:
Have I wished thee to my heart,
Then my wishing all is done.
Tr. fr. P. GERHARDT.

36   *Christ in His New Church.*
1 Here shall Christ be all in all;
None shall to his brother call.
Saying, "Know the Lord," for he
Shall appear in charity.

2 Holy hands to lift the weak,
Hearts by love made pure and meek.
Souls that burn with mercy's flame.
Shall the inward Christ proclaim.

3 Break the bonds of party strife
Own the Savior in the life;
Nearest to the Lord are those
Who his perfect love disclose.

4 Faith, that soars from things of sense,
By an inward evidence,
And attains to joys above,
Lives within the heart by love.

5 Faith that smites the tempter down.
Faith that grasps the martyr's crown.
Faith in Christ to do or live,
Christ within can only give.
T. L. HARRIS.

37   O Heart of All.   c. m.   Bernard.—W M. GARDINER.

1. O Heart of all the shin-ing day, The green earth's still de - light;

Thou Freshness in the morn-ing wind, Thou Si - lence of the night,

2 Thou Beauty of our temple-walls,
    Thou Strength within the stone,
  What is it we can offer thee
    That is not first thine own?
                        W. C. GANNETT.

3 We bless thee for the skies above,
    And for the earth beneath,
  For hopes that blossom here below,
    And wither not with death.

4 But most we bless thee for thyself,
    O heavenly Light within,
  Whose dayspring in our hearts dispels
    The darkness of our sin.
                        F. L. HOSMER.

38   God with the Heart.
1 It is a harp of many strings,
    This human heart of ours;
  In every chord an angel sings,
    'Tis wreathed with spirit flowers.

2 It stands beside the golden door
    Where all God's tho'ts come forth,
  And all those tho'ts their music pour
    Thro' all its chords to earth.

3 God's harp of many strings! no hand,
    Of act or wish profane;—
  No breath from sin's delusive land
    Can jar its mystic strain:

4 But, deep on every quivering chord,
    In love's immortal bars,
  Now thrills the one eternal Word
    That woke the morning stars.
                        T. L. HARRIS.

39   God Dwelleth in Us.
1 Our God is never so far off
    As even to be near;
  He is within; our spirit is
    The home he holds most dear.

2 To think of him as by our side
    Is almost as untrue
  As to remove his throne beyond
    Those skies of starry blue.

3 So all the while I thought myself
    Homeless, forlorn and weary,
  Missing my joy I walked the earth,
    Myself God's sanctuary.
                        F. W. FABER.

40 Listening. C. M. D.

Leonard.—H. HILES.

1. I hear it oft-en in the dark, I hear it in the light,—
Where is the voice that comes to me With such a qui-et might?
It seems but ech-o to my thought, And yet be-yond the stars!
It seems a heart-beat in a hush, And yet the plan-et jars!

2 Oh, may it be that far within
  My inmost soul there lies
A spirit-sky, that opens with
  Those voices of surprise?
Thy heaven is mine,—my very soul!
  Thy words are sweet and strong;
They fill my inward silences
  With music and with song.

3 They send me challenges to right,
  And loud rebuke my ill;
They ring my bells of victory;
  They breathe my "Peace, be still!"
They ever seem to say: "My child,
  Why seek me so all day?
Now journey inward to thyself,
  And listen by the way!"

W. C. GANNETT.

41   Be Still, and Know.   L. M.

Arr. fr. MENDELSSOHN.

1. Be still! my feet: why rove in vain? In God thy paths shall be made plain,

And ev'ry way in which ye tread Are paths of peace, when by him led.

2 Be still! my mind; put by thy care,
The hand of God is everywhere;
Thy way, his guiding hand directs,
And all thy interests he protects.

3 Be still! my heart; what is thy cry?
Be still! and know that God is nigh,
That thy pulsations are his love,
Alone in him ye live and move.

4 Be still! my soul; thy wings are here
Thro' boundless ether thee to bear;
Thro' heights of transport to God's throne,
For thou art God's, and God's alone.
                                    DAVID H. PAGE.

42   The Inward Witness.
1 A voice is on the Sabbath air,
A voice within us while we pray;
Dear Lord! it bids our hearts prepare,
The Inward Witness to obey.

2 O cleanse us by thy sovereign love,
Till we our selfhood all resign;
Our hearts are fixed on joys above,
Our spirits own thy will divine.

43   "My Words are Life."
1 Guide me, O Lord, thy one right way,
In faith and joy, and love, I pray!
Thy precious word of saving power
Gives light and clearness every hour.

2 Now as the shadows lift for me,
Thy glorious way I plainer see;
And thus, as I commune with thee,
Thy "word" alone hath set me free.
                                    SARAH WILDER PRATT.

44   The Regenerate Life.
1 Help us, our Father, still to prove
Thy promised grace, thy perfect love;
In us thy soul's desire fulfill,
Make us the workers of thy will.

2 Fain would we think thy tho't divine,
And have no other will but thine;
Our hearts, O Lord! from self set free,
Give us love's perfect liberty.

3 With thee within, how sweet to find
Our constant guide, thy perfect mind;
While deeds of purest love declare
Thy Holy Spirit's presence there.

45 Very Near. L. M.
Seasons.—I. Pleyel.

J. Oh, sometimes comes to soul and sense The feeling which is ev - i - dence
That ver-y near a-bout us lies The realm of spir-it-mys-ter-ies.

2 The low and dark horizon lifts,
To light the scenic terror shifts;
The breath of a diviner air
Blows down the answer of a prayer.

3 Then all our sorrow, pain, and doubt
A great compassion clasps about;
And law and goodness, love and force
Are wedded fast, beyond divorce.

4 Then duty leaves to love its task,
The beggar self forgets to ask:
We feel, as flowers the sun and dew,
The One True Life our own renew.
J. G. Whittier.

46 Our Kinship.
1 Lord, when thou mak'st thy presence felt,
And when the soul has grasped thee right,
How fast the dreary shadows melt
Beneath thy warm and living light.

2 In thee I find a noble birth,
A glory o'er the world I see,
And paradise returns to earth,
And blooms again for us in thee.

3 Thou open'st heaven once more to men,
The soul's true home, thy kingdom, Lord,
And I can hope and trust again,
And feel myself akin to God.

47 Christ, our Savior.
1 I own my Savior all divine;
He lights the sacred fires that shine
To guide me to the thoughts above;
He is the all of truth and love.

2 Forevermore, forevermore,
My heart recalls his mercies o'er,
But, while I count, they multiply,
Like milky spaces in the sky.

3 His mercies roll beneath my feet;
Where heaven and earth within me meet
I take my place, and gaze abroad,
And find my spirit-life in God.
T. L. Harris.

Not farther off, but farther in,
Such is the nature of your quest;
They heaven find who heaven win,
The one true Christ is in your breast.
J. W. Chadwick.

48   The Voice of Silence.   7. 6. D.

Aurelia.—S. S. WESLEY.

1. We feel the heart of silence Throb with a soundless word, And by the inward
ear alone A spir-it-voice is heard. The spo-ken word seems writ-ten On
air and wave and sod, The bending walls of sapphire Blaze with the tho't of God.

2 O blind ones! outward groping.
   The idle quest forego,
Who listens to his inward voice
   Alone of me shall know;
Climb not the holy mountains.
   Their eagles know not me:
Seek not the blessed islands.
   I dwell not in the sea.

3 The eye shall fail that searches
   For me the hollow sky;
The far is even as the near.
   The low is as the high;
A light, a guide, a warning.
   A presence ever near,
Through the deep silence of the soul
   I reach the inward ear.
                J. G. WHITTIER.

49   *The Heavenly Atmosphere.*

1 Oh, let us on the mountain
   Forevermore abide,
Bathed in its radiant sunlight,
   From error purified:
Imbued with Christ-like Spirit.
   With whom we are allied.
And knowing Love's sweet ministry,
   Greater than all beside.

2 Abiding on the mountain.
   How blest our company;
We see ourselves transfigured
   By Truth's rare alchemy;
From mortal to immortal,
   As all in him shall be,
Who know their true inheritance
   Is from Divinity.
                SARA P. ROSE.

50 The Indwelling God. C. M.
Holy Trinity.—J. Barnby.

1. Go not, my soul, in search of him, Thou wilt not find him there,

Or in the depths of shad-ow dim, Or heights of up-per air.

2 For not in far-off realms of space
The Spirit hath its throne;
In every heart it findeth place,
And waiteth to be known.

3 Thought answereth alone to thought,
And soul with soul hath kin;
The outward God he findeth not
Who finds not God within.

4. And if the vision comes to thee
Revealed by inward sign,
Earth will be full of Deity,
And with his glory shine.

5 Thou shalt not want for company,
Nor pitch thy tent alone;
The indwelling God will go with thee
And show thee of his own.

6 Then go not thou in search of him,
But to thyself repair;
Wait thou within the silence dim
And thou shalt find him there.

F. L. Hosmer.

51 *The Inward Witness.*

1 O thou whose Spirit witness bears
Within our spirits free
That we thy children are, and heirs
Of thine eternity,—

2 Here may this simple faith sublime
O'er-arch us like the sky;
Secure below the drift of time
Its firm foundations lie.

3 Our thought o'erflows each written scroll,
Our needs, they rise and fall;
The life of God within the soul
Lives and outlasts them all.

4 Here may that witness clearer grow
Each waiting heart within,
The way of filial duty show,
And glad obedience win.

5 Here be life's sorrows sanctified,
Here truth her radiance pour;
While hope and faith and love abide,
Forever more and more!

F. L. Hosmer.

25   **The Inmost One.**   L. M. D.

Lucy Larcom.
Arr. fr. Klein.

1. How near to me, my God, thou art! Felt in the throbbing of my heart;
2. With fev'rish rest-less-ness and pain, We strive to shut thee out, in vain;
3. With-in me,—near-er far than near, Thro' ev-'ry thought thy voice I hear;

Near-er than my own tho'ts to me: Nothing is re - al with - out thee!
To darkened heart and reb - el will, Thou art the one clear Dayspring still;
My whole life welcomes thy con - trol, Im - man - u - el! God with my soul!

Thy per-fect light makes morning fair; Thy breath is freshness in the air;
Eyes art thou un - to us, the blind; We turn to thee, our-selves to find;
Thou fill'st my being's hid- den springs; Thou giv'st my wishes heav'nward wings;

The glo - ry thou of star and sun, Thou Soul of souls, thou In - most One!
We set a - jar no door of pray'r But thou art wait-ing entrance there.
I live thy life, I breathe thy breath: Nor part nor lot have I with death.

53 I Am. P. M.

Arr. by A. S. Sullivan.

1. I am strong-er than my fears, I am wis-er than my years.

I am glad-der than my tears, For I am his im-age.

2 I am greater than my pains,
I am higher than my gains,
I am purer than my stains,
For I am his image.

3 I am grander than my names,
I am broader than my claims,
I am nobler than my aims,
For I am his image.

4 I am better than my deeds,
I am holier than my creeds,
I am wealthier than my needs,
For I am his image.

5 I am truer than I seem,
And more gracious than I deem,
And more real than I seem,
For I am his image.

6 I have naught with death or birth,
I encompass heaven and earth,
Marvelous my power and girth,
For I am his image.

7 He whose image thus I bear,
And whose likeness I shall share,
All his glory will declare,
Through the "I"—his image.

HANNAH MORE KOHAUS.

TUNE—Aurelia. p. 30.

54 Indwelling.

1 The heavens thy praise are telling.
The earth declares thy might,
But naught save thine indwelling
Can show thee, Lord, aright.
Where'er our eyes are turning,
Thy footprints we can see,
The light within us burning
Alone revealeth thee.

2 We know no life divided.
O Lord of life, from thee;
In thee is life provided
For all humanity.
We know no death, O Spirit.
Because we live in thee.
And all our souls inherit
Thine immortality.

55   **The Father.**   8. 7. D.

Vokes.—J. BARNBY.

1. On the bos-om of the Fa-ther Have I dwelt for aye and aye:
In his lov-ing arms en-fold-ed, All un-con-scious-ly I lay,
Till his gen-tle voice a-woke me, Say-ing soft-ly, "Child, a-rise!
Turn thy face; cease now thy dream-ing; Know the pow'r that in thee lies."

2 Then, at first with fear and trembling,
  Slowly did my senses wake,
And life's idle, listless fancies
  Gladly did my soul forsake.
Then I caught a glimpse of glory
  Passing splendor of the sun,
And I heard the same voice whisper,
  "Learn, my child, that we are One."

3 Soon the voice grew strong and strong-
  And familiar accents bore;   [er.
And its tones grew sweet and sweeter,
  Listening to it more and more.
Thus he told me he had given
  All he was and had to me;
Seamless robe of righteous beauty,
  And the crown-ring. victory.

HANNAH MORE KOHAUS.

56 In the Silence. 8. 7. D.

Arr. fr. H. Richards.

1. In the si - lence, O my Fa - ther, I am wait - ing here a - lone;

In the si - lence, in the si - lence, Since the day's last beam has flown.
D.S.—And my soul's deep.calm e - mo - tion O - ver- flow - eth pure and free.

In the si-lence. Ho - ly Spir - it, Filled with love I come to thee:

2 In the silence. Holy Spirit.
 All alone I come to thee,
 And to those who sit in darkness
  Speak the words that set them free.
 In the silence, in the silence.
 In thy love so kind and true.
 In the living, throbbing silence
  Find the work I have to do.

3 As I wait on thee, my Father.
 Nevermore am I alone;
 In the silence, Holy Spirit.
  All thy truth to me is shown.
 In the silence, in thy presence,
  Close to thee, so close to thee.
 In the dim and mystic silence
  I commune, my God, with thee.
      J. GILBERT MURRAY.

57   *The Temple.*

1 God is in his holy temple:
 Earthly thoughts be silent now.
While with reverence we assemble.
 And before his presence bow.
He is with us now and ever.
 When we call upon his name.
Aiding every good endeavor.
 Guiding every upward aim.

2 God is in his holy temple.—
 In the pure and holy mind,
In the reverent heart and simple.
 In the soul from sense refined.
Then let every low emotion
 Banished far and silent be.
And our souls in pure devotion.
 Lord. be temples worthy thee.

58   O Resurrection Morn.   P. M.

PLUMA M. BROWN.

1. O res - ur - rec - tion morn, The wea - ry world is shorn

To - day of all its gloom! For truth has rolled a - way

The stone from fear's ar - ray, And emp - ty is the tomb.

Copyright, 1896, by Pluma M. Brown.

2 Now is death's problem solved.
The day of days evolved
  Out of its fleshly guise;
The Son of Righteousness
Hath rent his earthly dress,
  That Christ might thus arise.

3 No longer can the walls
That dreamily enthrall
  Man's glory, hide from sight;
For one with God-like mien
(Back of the prism seen)
  Hath pierced them thro' with light.

4 Yet through the shadowy deep,
Up Calvary's rocky steep
  His soul hath surely trod;

For dead and buried he
From sense of self must be
  Who knows his Father—God.

5 O day of days complete,
Odorous with victories sweet,
  And crowned with tender grace!
The diadem of thorns
Majestically adorns
  The well-run, patient race.

6 O Christ, the perfect Whole,
Thou resurrected soul,
  The glorious conquest done!
Thou Truth, and Life, and Way
To immortality
  With God, th' eternal One!

HANNAH MORE KOHAUS.

59 Resurrection Stillness. 7.6. D.

Greek Melody.

1. { For res - ur - rec - tion still - ness There's res - ur - rec - tion pow'r; }
   { And prayer and praise of trust - ing May glo - ri - fy each hour: }
2. { Our com - mon days are ho - ly, And years an East - er - tide, }
   { For those who with the Ris-en One In Ris - en Life a - bide; }

REFRAIN

Then let his true love fold thee, Keep si - lence at his word;

Be still, and he shall mould thee; Oh, rest thee in the Lord!

TUNE—*Mendelssohn.* p. 6.

60 *Easter Festival.*

1 Lo! the Day of days is here,
Earth puts on her robe of cheer;
Day of hope and prophecy,
Feast of Immortality!
Fields are smiling in the sun,
Loosened streamlets seaward run,
Tender blade and leaf appear,
'Tis the springtide of the year!

REFRAIN.

Day of hope and prophecy.
Feast of Immortality!

2 Lo! the Day of days is here,
Hearts awake, and sing with cheer!

He who robes his earth anew
Careth for his children too;
They who look to him in faith,
Triumph over fear and death;
Speaks the angel by the door,
"They are risen" evermore.—REF.

3 Lo! the Day of days is here.
Music thrills the atmosphere;
Join, ye people all, and sing
Love, and praise, and thanksgiving!
Rocky steep or flowery mead,
One the Shepherd that doth lead,
One the hope within us born,
One the joy of Easter morn.—REF.

F. L. HOSMER.

61 Morn of Glory. 7.

Easter Hymn.—LYRA DAVIDICA.

1. All the air with joy is rife,
2. Morn of glo - ry— no al - loy
3. Let no earth - ly dis - cord glide

} Al - le - lu - ia!

Springing life from death is born;
Can thy match-less splen - dor dim;
Thro' the grand up - swell - ing lay:

} Al - le - lu - ia!

Plas - tic na - ture feels the strife,
Sing, O heart, thy song of joy—
Sing, O hearts, what - e'er be - tide,

} Al - le - lu - ia!

'Tis the res - ur - rec - tion morn.
Sing thy great tri - um - phal hymn,
For the Lord is ris'n to - day.

} Al - le - lu - ia!

62 Alleluia. 7. 6. D.

Tr. by J. M. Neale.

1. Al-le - lu - ia! Al-le - lu - ia! Al-le - lu - ia! The day of res - ur-
2. Al-le - lu - ia! Al-le - lu - ia! Al-le - lu - ia! Our hearts be pure from
3. Al-le - lu - ia! Al-le - lu - ia! Al-le - lu - ia! Now let the heav'ns be

rec - tion! Earth, tell it out a - broad! The pass - o - ver of glad-ness,
er - ror, That we may see a - right The Lord in rays e - ter - nal
joy - ful! Let earth her song be - gin! Let the round world keep tri - umph,

The pass - o - ver of God! From death to life e - ter - nal,
Of res - ur - rec - tion light; And, list - 'ning to his ac - cents,
And all that is there - in! In - vis - i - ble and vis - i - ble,

From earth un - to the sky. Our Christ has brought us o - ver.
May hear, so calm and plain, His own "All Hail!" and, hear - ing.
Their notes let all things blend, For Christ the Lord hath ris - en.

With hymns of vic - to - ry. Al-le - lu - ia! Al-le - lu - ia! Al-le - lu - ia!
May raise the vic-tor-strain. Al-le - lu - ia! Al-le - lu - ia! Al-le - lu - ia!
Our joy that hath no end. Al-le - lu - ia! Al-le - lu - ia! Al-le - lu - ia!

63　Abide in Me. L. M.

Zephyr.　WM. B. BRADBURY.

1. Be-side the dead I knelt for pray'r, And felt a pres-ence as I prayed:
Lo! it was Je-sus standing there: He smiled, and said: "Be not a-fraid."

Used by arr. with The Bizlow & Main Co., owners of copyright.

2 "Lord, thou hast conquered death, we know,
Restore again to life," I said,
"This one who died an hour ago."
He smiled, and said: "She is not dead."

3 "Asleep then, as thyself didst say,
But thou canst lift the lids that keep
Her prisoned eyes from ours away."
He smiled, and said: "She does not sleep."

4 "Nay then, though haply she do wake,
And look upon some fairer dawn,
Restore her to our hearts that ache."
He smiled, and said: "She is not gone."

5 "Alas! too well we know our loss,
Nor hope again our joy to touch
Until the stream of death we cross."
He smiled, and said: "There is no death."

6 "But our beloved seem so far,
The while we yearn to feel them near,
Albeit with thee we trust they are."
He smiled, and said: "And I am here."

7 "Dear Lord, how shall we know that they
Still walk unseen with us and thee,
Nor sleep, nor wander far away?"
He smiled, and said: "Abide in me."

W. W. R., in *Christian Union.*

TUNE *Bernard.* p. 26.

64　Easter Morn.

1 On eyes that watch thro' sorrow's night,
On aching hearts and worn,
Rise thou with healing in thy light,
O happy Easter morn!

2 The dead earth wakes beneath thy rays,
The tender grasses spring;
The woods put on their robes of praise,
And flowers are blossoming.

3 O shine within the spirit's skies,
Till, in thy kindling glow,
From out the buried memories
Immortal hopes shall grow:

4 Till from the seed oft sown in grief,
And wet with bitter tears,
Our faith shall bind the harvest sheaf
Of the eternal years.

F. L. HOSMER.

65   There is No Death.   P. M.

MARTHA B. ENSIGN.
PLUMA M. BROWN.

1. Ah, no: There is no death! The flow'rs we loved and cherished
2. We do not walk a - lone! Low foot-falls vi - brate on the
3. We make no plaint or moan For those life's cur - rent drift - ed

in the spring Will wa - ken to e - ter - nal blos - som - ing,
voice-less air, And forms un - seen at - tend us ev - 'ry - where:
from our side; We know some flow - ing stream or ebb - ing tide

Touched by In - fi - nite breath,— Touched by In - fi - nite breath.
Our loved ones have not gone,— Our loved ones have not gone.
Will bear us to our own,— Will bear us to our own.

Tune.—Bernard. p. 26.

66   My Dead.

1 I cannot think of them as dead
Who walk with me no more;
Along the path of life I tread
They have but gone before.

2 The Father's house is mansioned fair,
Beyond my vision dim;
All souls are his, and here or there
Are living unto him.

3 And still their silent ministry
Within my heart hath place,

As when on earth they walked with me
And met me face to face.

4 Their lives are made forever mine;
What they to me have been
Hath left henceforth its seal and sign
Engraven deep within.

5 Mine are they by an ownership
Nor time nor death can free:
For God hath given to Love to keep
Its own eternally.

F. L. HOSMER.

67 Our Heaven. H. M.

ENGLISH.

1. Bound in the gold-en span Of love's e-ter-nal years. Un-trod by mor-tal man, Our heav'n-ly home ap-pears: Its glo-ries shine with beams so bright, No out-ward eyes can bear the sight.

2 Here Christ the Savior reigns,
  And all his image bear;
No griefs, nor woes, nor pains
  Molest the dwellers here.
It is the home of pure delight,
No outward eyes can bear the sight.

3 Upon these shining plains.
  And in these peaceful vales.
Eternal sunshine reigns,
  And endless morn prevails.
O blessed home of love and light!
No outward eyes can bear the sight.

68 The Risen Christ. C. M.

Beatitudo. J. B. DYKES.

Where life is wa-king all around, Where love's sweet voi-ces sing. The first bright blos-som may be found Of an e-ter-nal spring.

69 **Hymn of Heaven.** 10.   *Savannah*—I. PLEYEL.

1. Be-hold my coun-try! Hast thou ev-er trod A world so glo-rious? Lo! the smile of God Beams in the sea-sons, builds the match-less dome: Art, wis-dom, beau-ty, here have made their home.

2 Wouldst know its name, this country? 'Tis the one
That through all regions and all works doth run:
Not time nor space may grasp it in their span;
'Tis inmost presence-world of God with man.

3 'Tis in us, o'er us, near us, high above;
Bounded by wisdom, organized by love;
Framed for all uses, free to all mankind
Their life in faith and charity who find.

T. L. HARRIS.

TUNE—*The Risen Christ.*

2 The shade and gloom of life are fled
This resurrection day,
Henceforth in Christ are no more dead,
The grave hath no more prey.

3 In Christ we live, in Christ we sleep,
In Christ we wake and rise,
And the sad tears death makes us weep.
He wipes from all our eyes.

4 Then wake, glad heart! awake! awake!
And seek thy risen Lord.
Joy in his resurrection take,
And comfort in his word:

5 And let thy life, through all its ways,
One long thanksgiving be,
Its theme of joy, its song of praise—
Christ lives, he lives for me.

JOHN S. B. MONSELL.

70　The Realm of Gladness.　P. M.

Scotch.

"To be spiritually minded is life and peace."

1. There is a realm of glad-ness Where sor-row is not known,

Nor dark-ling shades of sad-ness, For Truth reigns there a-lone.

For Truth reigns there a-lone. With joys in end-less store;

In the glo-ries of this king-dom, I'll rest for-ev-er-more.

2　'Tis the realm of mind immortal,
　　The realm of life and peace;
And safe within its portal,
　　Unrest and longing cease.
Unrest and longing cease,
　　For heaven spreads wide and free;
Oh, the glories of this kingdom
　　Are open now to me.

3　Close lies this region glorious,
　　Within, around, above.
And spirit sings victorious
　　Of all-redeeming love.
Of all-redeeming love,
　　The Father's love so free;
And the glory of his presence
　　Transfigures life for me.

GERALDINE D. ROBINSON.

71 Thy Rest. 10. 6.

Arr. fr. MENDELSSOHN.

1. I heard one ask, "Where is a land of rest? For I am wea - ry, and my heart is faint: Is it in some fair val - ley of the West, Or clois-ter old and quaint?"

2 And then the answer came: "It lieth here—
Thy feet do now invade its sacred bound,
And songs celestial swell beside thine ear
   That may not catch their sound."

3 "'Come unto me and rest,'—thus One did speak
To those of old whose hearts seemed faint like thine;
Lo! still he calleth unto all who seek
   That land of peace divine.

4 "Pour out the incense of thy loving thought,
Where the world's half-forgotten wanderers stray;
And every deed by hand and spirit wrought,
   Shall point the heavenly way.

5 "Unto the Father, he who made us all,
Ope in the silence deep thy longing breast;
Take the sure bounties from his hands that fall,
   And thou shalt find thy rest."

AMELIA Y. COLE.

72   The Heavenly Land.   L. M.

Ware.—Geo. Kingsley.

1. There is a land mine eye hath seen In vi-sions of en - rap-tured thought,

So bright that all which spreads between Is with its radiant glo - ries fraught.

2 A land upon whose blissful shore
There rests no shadow, falls no stain:
There those who meet shall part no more,
And those long parted meet again.

3 Its skies are not like earthly skies,
With varying hues of shade and light;
It hath no need of suns to rise
To dissipate the gloom of night.

4 There sweeps no desolating wind
Across that calm, serene abode;
The wanderer there a home may find
Within the paradise of God.
         G. ROBINS.

73   Looking Into Heaven.

1 This common earth, by mortals trod,
Is hallowed by the present God;
And lo! great heaven is all unfurled
In light and beauty o'er the world.

2 Look up, O man! behold the same
Celestial throngs of old who came,
For thee descend the spirit host;
Thine all the tongues of Pentecost.

3 Let worldlings toil for golden ore;
Do thou the angel heaven explore;

Thy heart shall then seraphic sing,
And dwell for aye with morn and spring.

4 While others see but chance and change,
Thy soul through heavenly worlds shall range,
And there discern, with spirit sense,
The heart of God's great providence.

5 The quiet chamber of thy rest
Shall beam with many an angel guest;
And nature lay her tribute sweet
Of health and beauty at thy feet.
         T. L. HARRIS.

74   Our Home.

1 There is a river pure and bright,
Whose streams make glad the heavenly plains;
Where in eternity of light,
The city of our God remains.

2 Built by the word of his command,
With his unclouded presence blest,
Firm as his throne the bulwarks stand;
There is our home, our hope, our rest.
         J. MONTGOMERY.

75 The Glory of Heaven. 8. 7. D.

Austria.—F. J. HAYDN.

1. { Glo-rious things of thee are spo-ken, Zi-on, cit-y of our God: / He, whose word can-not be bro-ken, Formed thee for his own a-bode: }

On the Rock of A-ges found-ed, What can shake thy sure re-pose?

With sal-va-tion's walls sur-round-ed, Thou mayst smile at all thy foes.

2 See the streams of living waters,
  Springing from eternal love,
Well supply thy sons and daughters,
  And all fear of want remove:
Who can faint while such a river
  Ever flows their thirst to assuage—
Grace which, like the Lord, the Giver,
  Never fails from age to age?

3 Round each habitation hovering,
  See the cloud and fire appear,
For a glory and a covering,
  Showing that the Lord is near:
Thus deriving from their banner
  Light by night and shade by day,
Safe they feed upon the manna
  Which he gives them when they
    pray.

J. NEWTON.

4 There, like streams that feed the gar-
    den,
  Pleasures without end shall flow,
For the Lord, your faith rewarding,
  All his bounty shall bestow.
Still in undisturbed possession,
  Peace and righteousness shall reign:
Never shall you feel oppression,
  Hear the voice of war again.

5 Ye, no more your suns descending,
  Waning moons no more shall see:
But, your griefs forever ending,
  Find eternal noon in me:
God shall rise, and, shining o'er you,
  Change to day the gloom of night;
He, the Lord, shall be your glory,
  God your everlasting light.

WM. COWPER.

76　The Beautiful Open Secret. P. M.

LUCY LARCOM.
PLUMA M. BROWN.

1. Oh, heav'n has come down to meet us; It hangs in our at-mos-phere:
2. We should walk there with one an-oth - er, Nor, halt-ing dis-heart-ened, wait
3. For the cool, sweet riv - er of E - den Flows fresh thro' our dust-y streets:

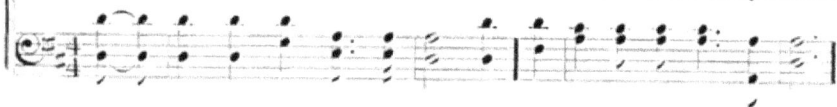

Its beau-ti - ful o - pen se - cret, Is whispered in ev-'ry ear;
To en - ter a dreamed-of cit - y By a far - off shad-owy gate:
We may feel its spray on our fore-heads, A-mid weari-some noon-tide heats:

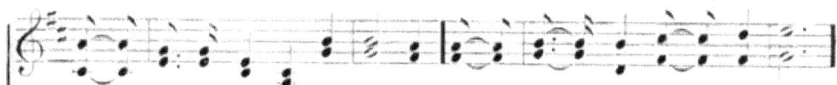

And ev'rywhere, here and al-ways, If we would but o - pen our eyes.
Dull earth would be dull no long - er, The clod would sparkle a gem:
We may share the joy of God's an-gels On the errands that he has giv'n:

We should find thro' fa-mil - iar foot-paths, Our way in - to par - a - dise.
And our hands at their commonest la - bor, Would be building Je-ru - sa - lem
We may live in a world trans - fig-ured, And sweet with the air of heav'n

The Beautiful Open Secret—Concluded.

REFRAIN.

We know   that the realm   of our long - - ing
Oh, yes, we know   that the realm of our long - - ing

Is   here   in the   world   where we   dwell.
Is   here   in the world   where we   dwell.

77 Heaven Within Us. P. M.

LUCY LARCOM.
PLUMA M. BROWN.

1. They whose hearts are whole and strong, Loving ho-li- ness,   Liv-ing clean from
2. On - ly the a - noint-ed eye Sees in common things,—Gleam of wave, and

UNISON.

soil of wrong, Wearing Truth's white dress—They un-to   no   far - off height
tint of sky,—Heav'nly blos - som-ings. To the hearts where light has birth,

Wea-ri - ly need climb; Heav'n to them is close in sight From these shores of time.
Nothing can be drear: Budding thro' the bloom of earth, Heav'n is always here.

78   Come Up Hither.   7.

Horton.—X. Schnyder.

1. "Come up hith-er! come a-way:" Thus the Truth-taught children sing;

Here is cloud-less, end-less day: Here is ev-er-last-ing spring.

2 Come up hither; come and dwell
  With the living hosts above;
Come, and let your bosom swell
  With their burning songs of love.

3 Come up hither; come and share
  In the sacred joys that rise,
Like an ocean, everywhere
  Through the myriads of the skies.

4 Come up hither; come and shine
  In the robes of spotless white;
Palms, and harps, and crowns are thine;
  Hither, hither wing your flight.

5 Come up hither; hither speed;
  Rest is found in heaven alone;
Here is all the wealth you need;
  Come and make this wealth your own.

                    E. H. Nevin.

79   *Eden.*

1 All before us lies the way,—
  Give the past unto the wind!
All before us is the day,
  Night and darkness are behind.

2 Eden with its angels bold,
  Love and flowers and coolest sea,
Is not ancient story told,
  But a glowing prophecy.

3 In the spirit's perfect air,
  In the passions tame and kind,
Innocence from selfish care.
  The real Eden we shall find.

4 When the soul to sin hath died,
  True and beautiful and sound,
Then all earth is sanctified,
  Upsprings Paradise around.

                    Eliza T. Clapp.

83 My Country. 7. 6. D.   *Ewing.*—A. EWING.

1. For thee, O dear, dear coun - try! Mine eyes their vig - ils keep;
For ver - y love, be - hold - ing Thy hap - py name, they weep;—
O one, O on - ly man - sion!—O par - a - dise of joy!
Where tears are ev - er ban - ished, And bliss hath no al - loy.

2 Thy ageless walls are bonded
With amethyst unpriced;
The saints build up its fabric,
The corner-stone is Christ!
Upon the Rock of Ages
They raise thy holy tower;
Thine is the victor's laurel,
And thine the golden dower.

3 They stand, those halls of Zion,
All-jubilant with song;
And bright with many an angel,
With many a martyr-throng;

The Prince is ever in them,
The light is aye serene,
The pastures of the blessèd
Are decked in glorious sheen.

4 There is the throne of David;
And there, from toil released,
The shout of them that triumph,
The song of them that feast;
And they who with their Leader,
Have conquered in the fight,
Forever and forever
Are clad in robes of white!

Tr. by J. M. NEALE.

84 Infinite Nearness. P. M.

A. BEIRLY.

1. In - fi - nite Near-ness! thee I see re - vealed In song of bird, the
2. Mys-ter - y shrouds thee, but to - day I saw Thee mirrored in a
3. In - fi - nite Near-ness! tell me not of God Who dwells a-far, a-

flow - er at my door,...... The hap-py laugh-ter of a lit - tle child,
glance of moth-er - love;..... A bit - ter word, unsaid, bro't God-born strength
part, in oth-er spheres: My Fa-ther's here, he shares my common life.

The star at night, the peb - ble on the shore, Each un - to each al -
A - kin to that for which the mar - tyrs strove, And grow-ing from a
In - spires my du - ties, and al - lays my fears; And when night falls, like

lied and all to thee. Thou ten - der, lov - ing, grand re - al - i - ty,
small un - self - ish deed, Came that rare peace for which the an - gels plead;
tir - ed child I creep In - to his arms, who lov - eth all, to sleep.

Infinite Nearness—Concluded.

Who art so near, so near! Who art so near!
So near thou art, so near! Thou art so near!
He is so near, so dear! He is so dear!

85 What Is God? C. M.

Springtide.—J. BARNBY.

God is the good-ness of the good, The glo - ry of the great:

God is the beau - ty of the soul, And its en - tire es - tate.

2 God is the justice of the just.
 The wisdom of the wise,
 The knowledge of the knowing one,
 The life that never dies.

3 God is the power of the strong,
 The courage of the brave,
 The victory of the conqueror,
 The freedom of the slave.

4 God is the love of loving ones,
 The crown of every goal,
 The virtue of the pure in heart,
 The wholeness of the whole.

5 God is the light that ever shines,
 The majesty of might,
 The meekness of humility,
 The righteousness of right.

6 God is the splendor of the stars.
 The music of the spheres.
 The breath of flowers, the glow of suns,
 The endlessness of years.

7 God is the ocean, limitless.
 That doth all springs supply·
 God is the ·'I am that I am,''
 The Self of every ''I.''

HANNAH MORE KOHAUS.

56

86 Thoughts of God. L. M. 6 l.

St. Catherine.—J. G. Walton.

1. I saw the beauty of the world Before me like a flag unfurled, The splendor of the morning sky, And all the stars in company: I thought, How beautiful it is!— My soul said, "There is more than this."

2 Sometimes I have an awful thought,
That bids me do the thing I ought;
It comes like wind, it burns like flame;
How shall I give that thought a name?
It draws me like a loving kiss—
My soul says, "There is more than this."

3 Yea, there is One I cannot see,
Or hear, but he is Lord to me;
And in the heavens and earth and skies,
The good which lives till evil dies,
The love which I cannot withstand.
God writes his name with his own hand.
W. B. RANDS.

87 The Glory of God.

1 Thy glory, Lord, the heavens declare;
The firmament displays thy skill;
The changing clouds, the viewless air,
Tempest and calm, thy word fulfill;
Day unto day doth utter speech,
And night to night thy knowledge teach.

2 While these transporting visions shine
Along the path of Providence,
Glory eternal, joy divine,
Thy word reveals, transcending sense;
My soul thy goodness joys to see,
Thy love to man, thy love to me.
J. MONTGOMERY.

88 The Lord, Seen in His Works.

1 Thou art, O Lord! the life and light
Of this celestial world we see;
Its angel-songs of truth and right
Are but responses unto thee.
Through every soul thy glories shine,
And all things pure and true are thine.

2 Sun of the soul! Thy beauteous rays
Gild all the purple clouds of even;
Through visions of thy love we gaze
Into the golden deeps of heaven.
Through earth and heaven thy mercies shine,
And all things pure and true are thine.

89   Omnipresence.   L. M. 6 l.

PLUMA M. BROWN.

1. Lo! when the morning's ear-ly light Comes softly o'er the eastern sea.

And the gray phantoms of the night Be-fore its roseate beau-ties flee:

Great Fa-ther! thro' that glowing sky, More fair than morn, thou passeth by.

2 And when the daylight splendor fades,
  By gathering darkness overborne;
Thou walk'st amid the evening shades,
  As thro' the glorious fields of morn;
Thy brooding love fills all the air
And day and night proclaim thy care.

3 So near forever, O my God!
  Our inmost thoughts before thee lie;
Well may life's every path be trod,
  With faith that feels thee ever nigh;
For still the darkest path may be
The one that leadeth unto thee!

AMELIA Y. COLE.

90   The Glories of Nature.

1 Thou art, O God! the life and light
Of all this wondrous world we see:
Its glow by day, its smile by night,
  Are but reflections caught from thee;
Where'er we turn, thy glories shine.
And all things fair and bright are thine.

2 When day, with farewell beam, delays
  Among the opening clouds of even,
And we can almost think we gaze
  Through opening vistas into heaven,
Those hues that mark the sun's decline,
So soft, so radiant, Lord, are thine.

3 When night, with wings of starry gloom,
  O'er-shadows all the earth and skies—
Like some dark beauteous bird whose plume
  Is sparkling with unnumbered eyes.—
That sacred gloom, those fires divine.
So grand, so countless. Lord, are thine.

4 When youthful spring around us breathes,
  Thy spirit warms her fragrant sigh;
And every flower that summer wreathes
  Is born beneath thy kindling eye:
Where'er we turn. thy glories shine.
And all things fair and bright are thine.

T. MOORE.

91   **The Universal Soul.**   8. 7. D.

L. H. H.
Arr. fr. HIMMEL.

1. Stron-ger than the Al - pine tor-rents That be - yond the mountains roll:
2. In the warm-ing rains of spring-time: In the sum-mers's sun - ny glow:
3. We can see his bright re - flec-tion With our spir - it - see - ing eyes,

Soft - er than the flush of dawn - ing, Is the U - ni - ver - sal Soul.
In the zeph - yrs of the au - tumn; In the blust'ring win - ter's snow:
In the low - liest crea-ture, earth - ly, In the vi - sions of the skies.

In the storm-cloud that is hov - 'ring O'er the bos - om of the deep;
In the dis - tant plan-ets roll - ing: In our own con - tent - ed sod:
All cre - a - tion lies with - in him, He with - in it hides his face:

In the ra-ging storms, that, an - gry, O'er the foam-ing wa - ters sweep:
In the star - ry sky of ev - 'ning, Can we trace the soul of God.
We must pierce the veil of mat - ter, If we see his smil-ing grace.

92 His Holy Place. C. M. D.

W. C. GANNETT.
PLUMA M. BROWN.

1. The Lord is in his ho - ly place, In all things near and far:
2. He hides him - self with - in the love Of those whom we love best;

She - ki - nah of the snow-flake, he, And glo - ry of the star:
The smiles and tones that make our homes Are shrines by him pos-sessed;

The se - cret of the A - pril-land, That stirs the field to flow'rs,
He tents with - in the lone - ly heart, And shep - herds ev - 'ry thought;

Whose lit - tle tab - er - na - cles rise To hold him thro' the hours.
We find him, not by seek - ing long— We lose him not, un - sought.

Omnipresence.

93 The Source of Blessing. C. M.

Newbold. —GEO. KINGSLEY.

1. Je - ho-vah, God, thy gracious pow'r On ev-'ry hand we see; Oh, may the

bless-ings of each hour Lead all our thoughts to thee, Lead all our thoughts to thee.

2 If on the wings of morn we speed
  To earth's remotest bound,
Thy hand will there our footsteps lead,
  Thy love our path surround.

3 Thy power is in the ocean deeps,
  And reaches to the skies;
Thine eye of mercy never sleeps,
  Thy goodness never dies.

4 From morn till noon—till latest eve,
  Thy hand, O God! we see;
And all the blessings we receive,
  Proceed alone from thee.
                                        J. THOMSON.

94   Inner Life of Nature.

1 With inner sight our hearts behold
  The souls of all the flowers,
Attired in robes of liquid gold,
  In summer's radiant bowers.

2 The viewless thoughts of God are born
  Within the morning ray;
And fairer lives our world adorn
  Than outward eyes survey.

3 All lovely things from Love receive
  The grace wherein they stand;
To hearts, in purity that live,
  Earth is a spirit-land.

4 The shadow to the eye appears,—
  The substance to the soul;
And girdled with celestial spheres
  Life's burning axles roll.
                                        T. L. HARRIS.

95   Omnipresent Life.

1 There seems a voice in every gale,
  A tongue in every flower,
Which tells, O Lord! the wondrous tale
  Of thy almighty power.

2 Shall I be mute, great God! alone
  Midst nature's loud acclaim?
Shall not my heart, with answering tone,
  Breathe forth thy holy name?

3 All nature's debt is small to mine;
  Nature shall cease to be;
Thou gavest—proof of Love divine—
  Immortal life to me.
                                        A. OPIE.

96 The Never-Failing Presence. C. M.

Hummel.—H. C. Zeuner.

1. There is an Eye that nev - er sleeps Be-neath the wing of night;

There is an Ear that nev - er shuts When sink the beams of light.

2 There is an Arm that never tires
  When human strength gives way;
  There is a Love that never fails
  When earthly loves decay.

3 That Eye unseen o'erwatcheth all;
  That Arm upholds the sky;
  That Ear doth hear the sparrow's call;
  That Love is ever nigh.
                        J. C. WALLACE.

4 Oh, sweeter than aught else besides,
  The tender mystery
  That like a veil of shadow hides
  The Light I may not see!

5 And dearer than all things I know
  Is childlike faith to me.
  That makes the darkest way I go
  An open path to thee.
                        F. L. HOSMER.

97 So Far, So Near.

1 O thou, in all thy might so far,
  In all thy love so near,—
  Beyond the range of sun and star,
  And yet beside us here:—

2 What heart can comprehend thy name,
  Or, searching, find thee out?
  Who art within, a quickening Flame,
  A Presence round about!

3 Yet though I know thee but in part,
  I ask not, Lord, for more:
  Enough for me to know thou art,
  To love thee and adore!

98 The Divine Man.

1 O Christ, our Lord! in all mankind
  Thy wondrous work we see:
  Thou art in every heart enshrined,
  And nature worships thee.

2 Within thy thoughts eternal years
  The universes roll;
  Thou art the Sovereign of the spheres,
  The life of every soul.

3 Thou art, O Lord! our sure defense,
  In every age the same:—
  We feel thy Love's omnipotence.
  And bless thy holy name.

99 The Inmost. P. M.

RICHARD REALF.
PLUMA M. BROWN.

1. Fair are the flow'rs and the children, But their sub-tle sug-ges-tion is
2. Nev-er a dai-sy that grows, But a mys-ter-y guid-eth the
3. Back of the can-vas that throbs, The paint-er is hint-ed and
4. Great are the sym-bols of be-ing, But that which is sym-boled is
5. Space is as noth-ing to spir-it, The deed is out-done by the

fair-er: Rare is the rose-burst of dawn. But the se-cret that
grow-ing. Nev-er a riv-er that flows, But a maj-es-ty
hid-den: In-to the stat-ue that breathes, The soul of the
great-er: Vast the cre-ate and be-held, But vast-er the
do-ing: The heart of the woo-er is warm. But warm-er the

clasps it is rar-er: Sweet the ex-ult-ance of song,
scep-tres the flow-ing: Nev-er a Shakespeare that soared.
sculp-tor is bid-den; Un-der the joy that is felt.
in-ward cre-a-tor; Back of the sound broods the si-lence
heart of the woo-ing; And up from the pits where these shiv-er,

But the strain that pre-cedes it is sweet-er; And nev-er was
But a strong-er than he did en-fold him, Nor ev-er a
Lie the in-fi-nite is-sues of feel-ing: Crown-ing the
Back of the gift stands the giv-ing: Back of the
And up from the heights where those shine, Twin voi-ces and

The Inmost—Concluded.

po - em   yet   writ,   But the mean-ing   out - mas-tered   the   me-tre.
prophet   fore - tells,   But a   might - i - er   seer hath fore - told him.
glo - ry   re - vealed   Is the   glo - ry   that crowns the   re - veal-ing
hand that re - ceives Thrill the   sen - si - tive nerves of   re - ceiv-ing.
shad-ows swim star-ward, And the   es - sence of   life   is   di - vine.

100 Thought Omnipotence. 7.

Nuremberg.—J. R. AHLE.

1. Hast thou e'er, with quickened sense, Felt a thought's om-nip - o - tence?

Hast thou found the pow'rs that bind   Spir - its   to   Om - ni - scient Mind?

2 Spoken thoughts of Deity
Are the worlds of life we see;
Heaven is but a lasting thought:
Man a spirit-word outwrought.

3 All the worlds shall pass away,
But the Lord's creative ray
Lengthens out the starry chain,
To return to him again.

4 Wouldst thou find the master key
Of creation's harmony?
'Tis the thought of God inspires;
Offer him thy pure desires.

5 All thy soul from self unchain,
If thou wouldst his wisdom gain:
Love, the bosom shall unbar
To the thoughts of God that are.
T. L. HARRIS

101   Consider the Lilies. 7. 6. D.

W. C. GANNETT.
Arr. fr. HANDEL.

1. He hides with-in the lil - y   A strong and ten - der care,
2. We lin - ger at the vig - il   With him who bent the knee
3. O toil - er of the lil - y,   Thy touch is in the man!
4. Shy yearn - ings of the sav - age,   Un - fold - ing thought by thought,

That wins the earth-born at - oms To glo - ry of the air,   To glo-ry
To watch the old-time lil - ies In dis - tant Gal - i - lee,   In dis-tant
No leaf that dawns to pet - al But hints the an - gel - plan,   But hints the
To ho - ly lives are lift - ed, To vi - sions fair are wrought,   To vi-sions

of the air; He weaves the shining garments Un - ceas-ing - ly and still.
Gal - i - lee: And still the wor-ship deep - ens And quick-ens in - to new,
an - gel - plan: The flow'r-ho - ri - zons o - pen, The blos-som vast-er shows.
fair are wrought; The ra - ces rise and clus - ter. And e - vils fade and fall.

A - long the qui - et wa - ters, In nich - es of the hill,
As, bright-'ning down the a - ges, God's se - cret thrill-eth through,
We hear thy wide world's ech - o, "See how the lil - y grows!"
Till cha - os blooms to beau - ty, Thy pur - pose crown-ing all,

Consider the Lilies—Concluded.

A - long the qui - et wa - ters, In nich - es of the hill.
As, bright-'ning down the a - ges, God's se - cret thrill-eth through.
We hear thy wide world's ech - o, "See how the lil - y grows!"
Till cha - os blooms to beau - ty, Thy pur - pose crown-ing all.

102 Fiat. P. M.

PLUMA M. BROWN.

1. Swing to the right and the left. Gates of sor-row and sin.

Let the glo - ry of Love and her Peace. O-ver earth's children reign!

Copyright, 1896, by Pluma M. Brown.

2 Down with the walls that have barred
   Thought in its heavenward flight;
For the trump of victorious Truth
   Strikes its key-note of might.

3 Fetters and bonds fall away,
   Doubts roll back like a scroll.
And the white light of freedom speeds up
   High in the heaven of soul.

GERALDINE D. ROBINSON.

103 God In All. L. M.

Arr. fr. BELLINI.

1. God of the earth, the sky, the sea! Ma-ker of all a-bove, be-low!

Cre - a - tion lives and moves in thee, Thy pres-ent life through all doth flow.

2 Thy love is in the sunshine's glow,
Thy life is in the quickening air;
When lightnings flash and storm-winds
blow,
There is thy power; thy law is there.

3 We feel thy calm at evening's hour,
Thy grandeur in the march of night;
And, when the morning breaks in power,
We hear thy word, "Let there be light!"

4 But higher far, and far more clear,
Thee in man's spirit we behold,
Thine image and thyself are there,—
The Indwelling God, proclaimed of old.
S. LONGFELLOW.

104 With God Everywhere.

1 My Lord, how full of sweet content
I pass my years of banishment!
Where'er I dwell, I dwell with thee,
In heaven, in earth, or on the sea.

2 To me remains nor place nor time;
My country is in every clime;
I can be calm and free from care
On any shore, since God is there.

3 While place we seek, or place we shun,
The soul finds happiness in none;
But with a God to guide our way,
'Tis equal joy to go or stay.

4 Could I be cast where thou art not,
That were indeed a dreadful lot;
But regions none remote I call,
Secure of finding God in all.
Madame GUYON.

105 The Creed of Life.

1 Canons and rubrics own I none,
Save one upon the granite writ:
"I, Lord of Lords, have fashioned it,
And graved it with my rains and sun."

2 One creed low whispered everywhere
I take into my soul like fire;
Till flashing through me with desire,
The world is molten in my prayer.

3 "It is my beating heart." I turn,
I face the stream, I brave the hills,
With the same word the bird's breast
fills,
With the same God the bushes burn.
J. TUNIS.

106 Out of the Dark. L. M.

Germany.—Arr. fr. Beethoven.

1. Out of the dark the cir-cling sphere Is rounding on-ward to the light;

We see not yet the full day here, But we do see the pal - ing night:

2 And Hope, that lights her fadeless fires,
And Faith, that shines, a heavenly will,
And Love, that courage re-inspires,—
These stars have been above us still.

3 O sentinels! whose tread we heard
Through long hours when we could not see.
Pause now; exchange with cheer the word,—
The unchanging watchword. Liberty!

4 Look backward, how much has been won!
Look round, how much is yet to win:
The watches of the night are done;
The watches of the day begin.

5 O thou, whose mighty patience holds
The night and day alike in view.
Thy will our dearest hope enfolds:
Oh, keep us steadfast, patient, true!
S. Longfellow.

107 The Chant Sublime.

1 I heard the bells on Christmas Day,
Their old familiar carols play.
And wild and sweet the words repeat
Of peace on earth, good-will to men!

2 And thought how, as the day had come.
The belfries of all Christendom

Had rolled along the unbroken song
Of peace on earth, good-will to men!

3 Till, ringing, singing on its way,
The world revolved from night to day.
A voice, a chime, a chant sublime
Of peace on earth, good-will to men!
H. W. Longfellow.

108 Old and New.

1 Through the harsh noises of our day
A low, sweet prelude finds its way:
Through clouds of doubt and creeds of fear
A light is breaking, calm and clear.

2 Henceforth my heart shall sigh no more
For olden time and holier shore:
God's love and blessing, then and there.
Are now, and here, and everywhere.
J. G. Whittier.

109 Freedom.

1 How happy is he, born or taught,
Who serveth not another's will;
Whose armor is his honest thought.
And simple truth his highest skill.

2 That man is free from servile bands.
Of hopes to rise, or fears to fall;
Lord of himself, though not of lands;
And having nothing, yet hath all.
Wenton.

110　The Liberty Angel. 9. 8.

T. L. HARRIS.
PLUMA M. BROWN.

1. The An-gel of free-dom is call-ing, The mu-sic is borne from the sky,
2. There is not a bos-om but pin-eth To burst from all slav-ish con-trol:
3. The stars in their glo-ry are sing-ing—"The race of op-pres-sion is run!"

The chains of the bondsmen are fall-ing, The Ju-bi-lee morning is nigh.
To bask in the brightness that shin-eth To-day from the in-fi-nite soul.
And slaves in-to he-roes are springing, For love binds the na-tions in one.

Now chant ye the might-y e-van-gel, And hast-en the Spir-it to free;
Make way for the life-bringing An-gel, And hast-en the Spir-it to free;
Christ comes in the Lib-er-ty-an-gel: He hastens the Spir-it to free,

For lib-er-ty's beau-ti-ful An-gel Hath come from the Fa-ther to thee.
For lib-er-ty's ho-ly e-van-gel Hath come from the Fa-ther to thee.
And speaks thro' the ho-ly e-van-gel That comes from the Fa-ther to thee.

The Liberty Angel—Concluded.

REFRAIN.

Now chant ye the might-y e - van - gel. And hast-en the Spir-it to free;

For lib-er-ty's beau-ti-ful An - gel Hath come from the Fa-ther to thee.

111 My Birthright. P. M.

EMMA (CURTIS) HOPKINS.
PLUMA M. BROWN.

1. I will be light and free. E'en tho' my seem-ing way Be

darker than night's gloom. For freedom is my birth-right. Joy is mine by right.

And gloom-y fears but her-alds be Of my own soul's de - light.

112   Liberty. L. M. 6 l.

PLUMA M. BROWN.

1. Thro' mid-night a - ges dark and lone, Op - pres-sion triumphed o'er the free:
2. Robed in the sa - ble veil of fear, The mourners haste at ear - ly day;
3. O Christ, our Sav - ior! thou who art The Lord and Ru - ler of the free,

They set the watch, they rolled the stone Up - on the grave of lib - er - ty:
But an - gels from a bright-er sphere, Disperse their gloom-y cares a - way;
Re - veal to ev - 'ry hu - man heart The free-dom that is found in thee:

When lo! the an-gels burst the gloom, And Free - dom ri - ses from the tomb.
"Re - joice! O earth, re-joice!" they cry, For Free - dom lives, no more to die.
So shall the world's last ty - rant fall, And Love and Light be all in all.

When lo!   And Freedom

113   *The Golden Age.*

1 Our weary years of wandering o'er,
We greet with joy this radiant shore—
The promised land of liberty—
The dawn of freedom's morn we see:
O promised land, we enter in,
With "peace on earth, good-will to men!"

2 The "Golden Age" now comes again,
And breaketh every bond and chain;
While every race, and sect, and clime,
Shall equal share in this glad time.
The spirits true in every age
Have won for us this heritage.

3 O golden dawn, O promised day,
When error's lost in truth's clear ray;
When all shall know that God is love,
His kingdom here, around, above,
The world one equal brotherhood,
And evil overcome with good.

ELIZABETH B. HARBERT.

114 Life. P. M.

GERALDINE D. ROBINSON.
PLUMA M. BROWN.

1. In firm faith a - bid - ing, The hand of love guid-ing, My bark is now
2. All doubts are thrown o - ver; No dark shadows hov-er: For Christ the true
3. With him I am sail - ing Thro' calm that's un-fail-ing, In faith that's a -

rid - ing The waves of Life's sea. Heav'n's breezes are thrill-ing Its
lov - er Reigns now in my heart: No storm can o'er - take me,— To
vail - ing To bring what is mine: As on - ward I'm mov-ing To

tho't-sails, and fill-ing With ea - ger and will-ing De - light to be free.
Truth he did wake me: He'll nev - er for-sake me. Nor from me de- part.
full - ness of lov - ing: To full - ness of prov-ing That Life is di - vine.

Tune—Southport. p. 95.

115   Life in Christ.

1 Life is a strain of sacred love
  The inmost spirit sings;
Then rises to the spheres above,
  While heaven with gladness rings.

2 Life is a hymn of holy thought,
  From God's paternal mind;

A soul into his image wrought
And in his truth enshrined.

3 Life is, to be a beauteous part
  Of nature's perfect whole:
To dwell in fellowship of heart
  With the Creative Soul.

116   Awakening.   11. 10.   *Come, Ye Disconsolate.* —S. WEBBE.

1. Life is a wak-'ning in-to spheres e-lys-ian: A spir-it-sun-rise, full of light and love: The mind's en-throne-ment and the heart's fru-i-tion: The vict'ry-march thro' angel-heav'ns a-bove.

2 Life is the inward spirit's resurrection
    From the sepulchral tenement of fear:
The joy, the peace, the beautiful perfection
    Of souls in whom God's attributes appear

3 Life is an anthem of accordant voices,
    Chanted throughout eternity's domain;
The psalm wherein the universe rejoices,
    While sun to sun repeats the long refrain.

4 Life is the calm, sweet rapture of the spirit,
    Whose form and faculties in God began;
Who doth the universal heaven inherit,
    In perfect harmony with God and man.

T. L. HARRIS.

117 I Shall Live Alway. 11.

Frederick.—Geo. Kingsley.

1. Oh, I shall live al-way: e - ter - ni-ty's mine, A life grand and
glo-rious flows from the Di - vine. Time fades from my sight as my
thoughts turn to thee. All pow'r-ful Cre - a - tor which mak - eth me free.

2 Who would not live alway in union with God,
Which makes e'en of earth a most blissful abode?
Oh, perfect the life in communion with thee.
All-powerful Creator, which maketh me free.

3 Yes, I shall live alway the Christ-life divine,
A life pure and holy, mysterious, sublime:
A life filled with love which shall center in thee.
All-powerful Creator, which maketh me free.

Tune—Beatitudo, p. 42.

118   A Word of Life.

1 Life springs on every field and hill,
Life sings in every tree;
Life broodeth o'er the waters still,
And stirs the mighty sea.

2 Life calls us to the perfect way,
And wins in every strife,
While nature's changes all display
The upward push of Life.

3 Life gives, from cares of mortal mind
A sure and sweet release:
And turns the thoughts of humankind
To ways of health and peace.

4 Life soothes the weary, heals the faint,
And rules where sin is rife.
Come! lay aside our human plaint,
And rest in endless Life.

HELEN M. FLETCHER.

119 **Let there be Light.** 10.   *Faroon.*—J. BARNBY.

1. Forth from the Mas - ter - mind went out the thought, "Let there be

light to show the work I've wrought." And, lo! ef - ful - gent

radiance quickly spread To glow a-round, while mist and dark - ness fled.

2 Let there be light, bid error cease to sway,
Nor shut from thee the perfect thought away.
Held in the Infinite, revealed to thee,
Reflect on all the truth that maketh free.

3 Let there be light to man, dwelling within,
Lifting thee up from sickness, death, and sin;
Bringing thee near the Father's perfect love
Whose Spirit gives us being from above.

4 Then shall the darkness born of mortal mind,
And all the shadows its beliefs may find,
Flee from the Spirit's touch, and disappear,
Giving us harmony instead of fear.

C. H. H.

120 Walk in the Light. C. M.   *Eckhardtsheim.—H. C. ZEUNER.*

1. Walk in the light! so shalt thou know That fel - low - ship of love.

His Spir - it on - ly can be - stow Who reigns in light a - bove.

2 Walk in the light! and thou shalt find
Thy heart made truly his.
Who dwells in cloudless light enshrined,
In whom no darkness is.

3 Walk in the light! and thou shalt own
Thy darkness passed away,
Because that light hath on thee shone
In which is perfect day.

4 Walk in the light! and e'en the tomb
No fearful shade shall wear;
Glory shall chase away its gloom.
For Christ hath conquered there.

5 Walk in the light! thy path shall be
Peaceful, serene, and bright:
For God, by grace, shall dwell in thee.
And God himself is light.

BERNARD BARTON.

TUNE—*Faroon.*

121   *The Everlasting Yea.*

1 Soul, struggle on! Within the darkest night
Still broods the majesty of deathless Right.
If to its promptings clear thou still art true.
The larger, sweeter lights will flash to view.

2 The stars will shine, and the blue pomp of day,
And to thine ear the Everlasting Yea
Will breathe its music and its lofty song:
And we shall know that Beauty still is strong;

3 That there is heart and life, the good, the fair,
That God is smiling in the sunny air,
And Wisdom shaping to remotest star,
And Love is yearning where the lowest are.

S. P. PUTNAM.

      Light.

122   O Love Divine.   L. M.   *Hursley.* W. H. Monk.

1. O Love Di-vine, whose constant beam Shines on the eyes that will not see.

And waits to bless us, while we dream Thou leav'st us when we turn from thee!

2 All souls that struggle and aspire,
   All hearts of prayer, by thee are lit;
And, dim or clear, thy tongues of fire
   On dusky tribes and centuries sit.

3 Nor bounds, nor clime, nor creed thou
     know'st;
   Wide as our need thy favors fall;
The white wings of the Holy Ghost
   Stoop, unseen, o'er the heads of all.

4 Shine on us with the light which glowed
   Upon the trance-bound shepherd's
     way,
Who saw the darkness overflowed
   And drowned by everlasting day.
             J. G. Whittier.

123   *The Presence.*

1 Mysterious Presence, Source of all,—
   The world without, the soul within,
Fountain of Life, oh, hear our call,
   And pour thy living waters in!

2 Thou breathest in the rushing wind,
   Thy Spirit stirs in leaf and flower;
Nor wilt thou from the willing mind
   Withhold thy light and love and power.

3 Thy hand unseen to accents clear
   Awoke the psalmist's trembling lyre,
And touched the lips of holy seer
   With flame from thine own altar-fire.

4 That touch divine still, Lord, impart,
   Still give the prophet's burning word;
And vocal in each waiting heart
   Let living psalms of praise be heard.
             S. C. Beach.

124   *Sun of Our Life.*

1 Sun of our life! thy quickening ray
Sheds on our path the glow of day;
Star of our hope! thy softened light
Cheers the long watches of the night.

2 Lord of all life! below, above,
Whose light is truth, whose warmth is
     love,
Before thy ever-blazing throne
We ask no lustre of our own.

3 Grant us thy truth to make us free,
And kindling hearts that burn for thee,
Till all thy loving altars claim
One holy light, one heavenly flame.
             O. W. Holmes.

125 One by One. 8. 7. D. *Autumn.* - F. H. BARTHELEMON.

1. One by one earth's wrongs are smitten, One by one its er-rors fall;

FINE.

One by one are carved and writ-ten Truth's great triumphs o - ver all.

D.S.—One by one God's fin - ger tra - ces Moon and stars up - on the night.

D. S. 𝄋:

One by one earth's dreary pla - ces Glow with green, and gush with light:

2 One by one are rent and riven
  All the links of falsehood's gyves;
One by one the cords of heaven
  Gently, strongly, clasp our lives.

One by one earth's bitter weanings
  Leave us nearer to the skies;
One by one life's higher meanings
  Burst like sunlight on our eyes.
                    RICHARD REALF.

TUNE—*Horsley.*

126   *I Love Thee, Lord.*

1 I love, I love thee, Lord most high!
    Because thou first hast lovéd me;
  I seek no other liberty
    Than that of being bound to thee.

2 May memory no thought suggest
    But shall to thy pure glory tend.
  My understanding find no rest
    Except in thee, its only end.

3 All mine is thine; say but the word,
    Whate'er thou willest shall be done;
  I know thy love, all-gracious Lord!
    I know it seeks my good alone.

4 Apart from thee all things are naught;
    Then grant, O my supremest Bliss,
  Grant me to love thee as I ought;
    Thou givest all in giving this.
                    F. XAVIER.

127   God is Wisdom, God is Love.   8. 7.   *Stockwell.*—D. E. JONES.

1. God is Love; his mer-cy bright-ens All the path in which we rove:

Bliss he wakes and woe he light-ens: God is wis-dom, God is love.

2 Time and change are busy ever;
   Earth decays, and ages move;
But his mercy waneth never;
   God is wisdom, God is love.

3 E'en the hour that darkest seemeth
   Will his changeless goodness prove;
From the mist his brightness streameth,
   God is wisdom, God is love.

4 He all earthly care unbindeth,
   Rest he sendeth from above.
Everywhere the glory shineth,
   God is wisdom, God is love.
              J. BOWRING.

128   *The Love of God.*

1 There's a wideness in God's mercy.
   Like the wideness of the sea:
There's a kindness in his justice
   Which is more than liberty.

2 For the love of God is broader
   Than the measure of man's mind;
And the heart of the Eternal
   Is most wonderfully kind.

3 If our love were but more simple.
   We should take him at his word,
And our lives would be all sunshine
   In the sweetness of our Lord.
              F. W. FABER.

129   *Freedom of God's Love.*

1 Know, the love of God is boundless.
   Giving takes not from his store:
Do not fear to use his blessings.
   He will only have the more.

2 Largely draw; his love is deeper.
   Fuller than the trackless main:
Stoop and lift.—his gifts outnumber
   Sands on shore or desert plain.

3 Ask his favor, it is freer
   Than the blossoms of the field:
Use his bounties, far exceeding
   Countless buds the forests yield.

God is Good.

1 God is good, the sky is saying;
   God is great. the hills declare;
God is love, the flowers are telling;
   God is round us everywhere.

130 God's Love. P. M.

Wm. F. Sherwin.

1. Grand-er than o-cean's sto-ry, Or songs of for-est trees—
2. Dear-er than an-y lov-ings The tru-est friends be-stow;
3. Rich-er than all earth's treas-ures, The wealth my soul re-ceives:

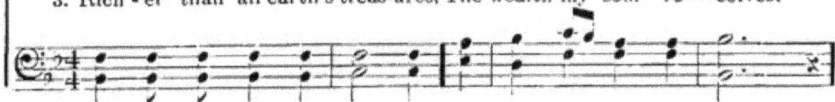

Pur-er than breath of morn-ing, Or ev-'ning's gen-tle breeze—
Stronger than all the yearn-ings A moth-er's heart can know:
Brighter than roy-al jew-els, The crown that Je-sus gives:

Clear-er than mountain ech-oes Ring out from peaks a-bove—
Deep-er than earth's foun-da-tions, And far a-bove all thought:
Won-drous the lov-ing-kind-ness, And grace be-yond de-gree!

Rolls on the glo-rious an-them Of God's e-ter-nal love.
Broad-er than heav'n's high arch-es The love that Christ has brought.
I would be ev-er sing-ing The love of Christ to me.

Used by per. of Mr-. Wm. F. Sherwin.

131 Immortal Love. C. M.

Manoah Arr. fr. Haydn.

1. Im - mor - tal Love, for-ev - er full, For -ev - er flow - ing free,

For - ev - er shared, for- ev - er whole, A nev - er - ebb - ing sea.

2 Our outward lips confess the name
All other names above;
Love only knoweth whence it came,
And comprehendeth love.

3 Blow, winds of God, awake and blow
The mists of earth away!
Shine out, O Light Divine, and show
How wide and far we stray!

4 Hush every lip, close every book,
The strife of tongues forbear;
Why forward reach, or backward look,
For love that clasps like air?

5 O Love! O Life! Our faith and sight
Thy presence maketh one:
As through transfigured clouds of white
We trace the noonday sun.

6 The letter fails, the systems fall,
And every symbol wanes;—
The Spirit over-brooding all,
Eternal Love, remains.

J. G. Whittier.

132 Love of God.

1 Thou Grace Divine, encircling all,
A shoreless, soundless sea,
Wherein thou hidest all thine own,
O Love of God most free!

2 When over dizzy heights we go,
One soft hand blinds our eyes,
The other leads us safe and slow,—
O Love of God most wise!

3 And though we turn us from thy face,
And wander wide and long,
Thou hold'st us still in thine embrace,
O Love of God most strong!

4 The saddened heart, the restless soul,
The toil-worn frame and mind,
Alike confess thy sweet control,
O Love of God most kind!

5 And filled and quickened by thy breath,
Our souls are strong and free
To rise from sense of sin and death,
O Love of God, to thee!

Eliza Scudder.

133 I Look to Thee. H. M.

Zebulon.—L. MASON.

1. I look to thee in need, And nev-er look in vain:

I feel thy touch, O Love, And all is well a-gain:

The thought of thee is might-ier far Than sin, and pain, and sor-row are.

2 Discouraged in my work.
  Disheartened by its load.
Its failures or its fears.
  I sink beside the road;—
But let me only think of thee.
And then new heart springs up in me.

3 Thy calmness bends above,
  My restlessness to still;
Around me flows thy life
  To nerve my faltering will;
Thy presence fills my solitude;
Thy providence turns all to good.

4 Embosomed in thy love,
  Held in thy law, I stand;
Thy hand in all behold.
  And all things in thy hand;

Thou leadest me by unsought ways.
And turn'st my mourning into praise.
Arr. fr. S. LONGFELLOW.

134   *Peace, be Still!*

1 God's perfect law of love
    Destroys each doubt and fear;
  But when we look away,
    Forget his presence near.
We cannot hear his "Peace, be still!"
We cannot know our Father's will.

2 God's love! no tongue can tell
    What blessings sweetly fall,
  When humble spirits wait
    Obedient to his call.
'Tis then we learn the "Peace, be still,"
And see the goodness of God's will.
H. UMBACH.

135 God is Love. L.M.6l.

PLUMA M. BROWN.

1. From all who dwell in heav'n a-bove We hear the anthem, "God is Love!"
2. Oh, while this glorious faith we own, Be love in all our acts made known:
3. Teach us, O Lord, like thee, to give To all that love wherein we live:

While thro' the souls of all be - low, His ten-der mer-cies ev - er flow,—
Then blind - ed eyes shall ope to see God is not wrath, but char - i - ty.—
Till earth be - low to heav'n a - bove, Re - peats the an-them, "God is Love!"

While thro' the souls of all be - low, His ten der mer-cies ev - er flow.
Then blind-ed eyes shall ope to see God is not wrath, but char - i - ty.
Till earth be - low to heav'n a - bove, Re-peats the an-them, "God is Love!"

Copyright, 1896, by Pluma M. Brown.

136 Thee Will I Love.

1 Thee will I love, my strength, my tower;
Thee will I love, my joy, my crown;
Thee will I love with all my power,
In all my works, and thee alone:
Thee will I love till sacred fire
Fill my whole soul with pure desire.

2 I thank thee, uncreated Sun,
That thy bright beams on me have shined;
I thank thee who hast overthrown
My foes, and healed my wounded mind;
I thank thee whose enlivening voice
Bids my free heart in thee rejoice.

JOHANN SCHEFFLER.

137   The Father's Voice. 7. 6 l.   Arr. fr. KÜCKEN.

1. O'er the bil-lowy waves of fear, Hark! the Fa-ther's voice I hear:
"Child of my most ten-der care, Fear no foe, no earth-ly snare:
I am all in all to thee, And my love has made thee free."

2 O'er the sobbing sea of woe
Comes the voice so sweet and low:
"All is joy, and rest, and peace;
Let thy weary yearnings cease;
Dry thine eyes, thou art not sad.
For my love hath made thee glad."

3 In the grass, the flower, the tree,
Speaks the Father's voice to me:
"I am thine eternal health,
I am thine eternal wealth;
Thou art rich, for thou art mine,
And the whole of heaven is thine."
ANNIE F. CLOSE.

138   *God is Love.*
1 Earth, with her ten thousand flowers,
Air, with all its beams and showers,
Ocean's infinite expanse,
Heaven's resplendent countenance,—
All around, below, above,
Hath this record, "God is Love."

2 All the tender hopes that start
From the fountain of the heart;
All the quiet bliss that lies
In our human sympathies;—
These are voices from above,
Sweetly whispering, "God is Love."
T. R. TAYLOR.

139   *God's Household.*
1 Father, now our prayer is said,
Lay thy hand upon our head;
Pleasures pass from day to day,
But we know that love will stay.
While we sleep it will be near:
We shall wake and find it here.

2 Love is old, and Love is new:
Love outlasteth firm and true:
And the Lord who made it thus,
Did it in his love for us,
We shall feel it in the air,
When we say our morning prayer.
W. B. RANDS.

140   God is Good.   L. M.

Migdol—L. Mason.

1. Yes, God is good: in earth and sky, From ocean depths and spreading wood,

Ten thousand voices seem to cry, "God made us all, and God is good!"

2 The sun that keeps his trackless way,
  And downward pours his golden flood,
Night's sparkling hosts all seem to say,
  In accents clear, that "God is good."

3 The merry birds prolong the strain,
  Their song with every spring renewed;
And balmy air, and falling rain,
  Each softly whisper, "God is good."

4 Yes, "God is good," all nature says,
  By God's own hand with speech en-
    dued;
And man, in louder notes of praise,
  Should sing for joy that "God is
    good."

                E. L. Follen, alt.

141   *Power Divine.*

1 A Love that casteth out all fear;
A Love that causeth ne'er a tear;
A Love, that makes me wholly free;
This is the Love that keepeth me.

2 Free from all sin, and free from pain,
From every ill of mortal brain;
Oh, that the world could only see,
This mighty Love to make it free.

3 This heavenly truth, that all is good,
Gives health, and strength, and daily
    food,
And good, and only good we see,
In every creature, bond and free.

                W. M. Conner.

142   *Never-Ceasing Love.*

1 Great Source of being and of love!
Thou waterest all the worlds above;
And all the joys which we may know,
From thine exhaustless fountain flow.

2 A sacred spring, at thy command,
From Zion's mount, in Canaan's land,
Beside thy temple cleaves the ground,
And pours its limpid stream around.

3 Close by its banks, in order fair,
The blooming trees of life appear;
Their blossoms fragrant odors give,
And on their fruit the nations live.

4 Flow, wondrous stream, with glory
    crowned,
Flow on to earth's remotest bound;
And bear us, on thy gentle wave,
To him who all thy virtues gave.

                P. Doddridge.

143 Love Divine. C. M. D.

HANNAH MORE KOHAUS.
German Melody.

1. O Love di - vine! where'er I am, Thou dost a - bide with me;
2. O Love di - vine! whate'er be - fall, If good or ill my lot:
3. Se - cure - ly may I trust in thee, Thou Love di - vine so sure:

What - ev - er path in life I take, I still re - main in thee:
What - ev - er I may bring to pass, O Love! thou changest not:
Un - moved as the e - ter - nal hills, Thou dost for aye en - dure:

For thou art here and ev - 'ry-where, Thou fill - est ev - 'ry spot:
Thou art the same, un - va - ry - ing, Thro'-out e - ter - ni - ty:
O Love di - vine! I would be filled With substance like to thee.

O ev - er - pres - ent Love di - vine, O Love! thou mov - est not.
All-stead-fast, changeless, help-ful, good, O Love! art thou to me.
That thou and I for - ev - er - more May in - ter - wo - ven be.

144   The Song and the Star.   C. M. D.

PLUMA M. BROWN.

1. The song the her-ald an-gels sang, O'er Bethlehem's star-lit plain.

Still ech-oes in the heart of man, A gladsome, sweet re-frain. A

glad-some, sweet refrain, Peace, peace on earth, good-will to men. Our Fa-ther

reigns supreme, And love fills all the u-ni-verse, E-vil is but a dream.

Copyright, 1891, by Pluma M. Brown.

2 Thro' all these eighteen hundred years,
  This song of peace and love,
Has breathed its balm of blessing,
||:And hovered like a dove, :||
Above the restless pulse of man,
  Bidding his passions cease,
Till war and strife are ended,
  And nations dwell in peace.

3 Through all the ages yet to come,
  'Twill whisper sweet and low,
If man but love his brother man,
||:'Tis heaven begun below:||
And so with song and radiance,
  The way will grow more bright,
Till the star that shines o'er Bethlehem,
  Fills all the world with light.

JENNIE WAYNE.

145   In Quiet Hours. L. M.   *Warner. — Arr. by Geo. Kingsley.*

1. In qui - et hours the tran-quil soul Re-flects the beau-ty of the sky;

No pas-sions rise or bil-lows roll, And on - ly God and heav'n are nigh.

2 The tides of being ebb and flow.
Creating peace without alloy:
A sacred happiness we know,
Too high for mirth. too deep for joy.

3 Like birds that slumber on the sea.
Unconscious where the current runs.
We rest on God's infinity
Of bliss. that circles stars and suns.

4 His perfect peace has swept from sight
The narrow bounds of time and space.
And looking up with still delight
We catch the glory of his face.
              AUGUSTA LARNED.

146   *O'er Seas of God.*

1 The winds that o'er my ocean run
Reach through all worlds beyond the sun:
Through life and love, through fate. through time,
Grand breaths of God they sweep sublime.

2 A thread of law runs thro' my prayer
Stronger than iron cables are:
And love and longing towards her goal
Are pilots sweet to guide the soul.

3 O thou God's mariner, heart of mine!
Spread canvas to the airs divine!

Spread sail! and let thy fortune be
Forgotten in thy destiny.

4 The wind ahead? The wind is free!
Forevermore it favoreth me:
To shores of God still blowing fair.
O'er seas of God my bark doth bear.

5 For life must live. and soul must sail.
And unseen over seen prevail:
And all God's argosies come to shore,
Let ocean smile. or rage. or roar.
              D. A. WASSON.

147   *The Retreat.*

1 Now. hushing every adverse sound,
Songs of defence my soul surround.
As if all saints encamped about
One trusting heart pursued by doubt.

2 And oh. how solemn. yet how sweet.
Their one assured. persuasive strain!
"The Lord of Hosts is thy retreat.
Still in his hands thy times remain."

3 O tender word! O truth divine!
Lord. I am altogether thine:
I have bowed down. I need not flee:
Peace, peace is mine in trusting thee.
              ANNA L. WARING.

148 Waiting. L. M. D.

JOHN BURROUGHS.
PLUMA M. BROWN.

1. Se - rene, I fold my hands and wait, Nor care for wind, or tide, or sea:
2. A - sleep, a-wake, by night or day, The friends I seek are seek - ing me;
3. The wa-ters know their own, and draw The brook that springs in yonder height;

I rave no more 'gainst time or fate, For lo! my own shall come to me.
No wind can drive my bark a - stray, Nor change the tide of des - ti - ny.
So flows the good, with e-qual law, Un - to the soul of pure de-light.

I stay my haste, I make de - lays, For what a-vails this ea - ger pace?
What mat - ter if I stand a - lone? I wait with joy the com-ing years;
The stars come night-ly to the sky, The ti - dal wave un - to the sea;

I stand a - mid e - ter - nal ways, And what is mine shall know my face;
My heart shall reap where it has sown, And gar - ner up its fruit of tears;
Nor time, nor space, nor deep, nor high, Can keep my own a - way from me;

Waiting—Concluded.

I stand a-mid e-ter-nal ways, And what is mine shall know my face.
My heart shall reap where it has sown, And gar-ner up its fruit of tears.
Nor time, nor space, nor deep, nor high, Can keep my own a-way from me.

149 Asleep in Jesus. L. M.

Rest.—WM. B. BRADBURY.

1. "A-sleep in Je-sus!" Sweeter far Than light of sun, or moon, or star,

Is that true rest which fol-lows pray'r,—The sleep of childhood ev-'ry-where!

Used by arr. with The Biglow and Main Co., owners of copyright.

2 "Asleep in Jesus!" Every night
Our world of beauty wheels from sight;
And trustful beings, robed in white,
Enter this realm of pure delight.

3 "Asleep in Jesus!" Earth-worn guest,
Wouldst thou attain this perfect rest?
Break faith with man-made laws of pain,
And be a child in trust again.

4 "Asleep in Jesus!" Angels bring
The hallowed draught from hidden
        spring;
And heaven, to crown this tho't of rest,
Reveals the jewels on her breast!

5 Awake in Jesus! Ye who sleep
In sensuous nature's slumber deep,
Christ came your mortal dream to break;
Arouse! and his dominion take!

6 Awake in Jesus all shall be
When Truth's strong angel sets us free,
And from the troubled dream of sense
We wake to spirit consciousness.

7 "Asleep in Jesus!" Matchless rest!
The first is dream, the last is best,
From which we wake no more to sleep,
But dwell with Christ in heaven's deep.

IONE G. DANIELS.

150 Secret of a Happy Day. 7.

Seymour.—Arr. fr. Weber.

1. Just to trust him, this is all! Then the day will sure-ly be
Peaceful, what-so-e'er be-fall, Bright and bless-ed, calm and free.

2 Just to take thy orders straight
  From the Master's own command!
Blessed day! when thus you wait
  Always at your Sovereign's hand.

3 He who formed thee for his praise
  Will not miss the gracious aim;
So to-day and all thy days
  Shall be moulded for the same.

4 Just to listen, and to stay,
  Where you cannot miss his voice;
This is all! and thus to-day,
  In communing, you rejoice.

5 This is all! and yet the way
  Marked by him who loves thee best!
Secret of a happy day,
  Secret of his promised rest.
                FRANCES R. HAVERGAL.

151   The Gracious Call.
1 Come! said Jesus' sacred voice,
Come! and make the Truth your choice;
It will guide you to your home;
Weary pilgrim, hither come!

2 Thou who, houseless, sole, forlorn,
Long hast borne the proud world's scorn,
Long hast roamed the barren waste,
Weary pilgrim, hither haste!

3 Ye who, tossed on beds of pain,
Seek for ease, but seek in vain;
Ye, by fiercer anguish torn,
In remorse for guilt who mourn;

4 Hither come! in Truth is found
Balm that flows for every wound,
Peace that ever shall endure,
Rest eternal, sacred, sure.
                ANNA L. BARBAULD.

152   Loving and Loved.
1 Loved with everlasting love,
  Led by grace that love to know!
Spirit breathing from above,
  Thou hast taught me it is so.

2 Oh, this full and perfect peace!
  Oh, this transport all divine!
In a love which cannot cease,
  I am his and he is mine.

3 Things that once caused wild alarms
  Cannot now disturb my rest,
Closed in everlasting arms,
  Pillowed on his loving breast.

4 Oh, to lie forever here,
  Care, and doubt, and self resign;
While he whispers in my ear,
  I am his and he is mine.

153 *Perfect Harmony of Life.*

5 His forever, only his!
  Who the Lord and me can part?
  Ah! with what a rest of bliss
  Christ can fill the loving heart!

6 Heaven and earth may fade and flee,
  First-born light in gloom decline;
  But while God and I shall be,
  I am his and he is mine.

1 If the heart is stayed on thee,
  Perfect freedom it shall see;
  No more worry in the race,
  No more jealousy of place.

2 No more anxious thought for health,
  No more undue wish for wealth;
  But that harmony of life
  That dispels all care and strife.

J. J. WELLS.

154 My Peace. 6. D.

Arr. fr. WEBER.

1. "My peace I leave with thee;" Thus soft-ly speaks the Son To ev-'ry troub-led heart—To ev-'ry sorrowing one; "Not as the cold world gives, Give I this gift divine; Come. rest within my love, And know this peace of mine."

2 I come, O Christ, to thee.
  The Life, the Truth, the Way;
Thy yoke of service true
  Upon my heart I lay,
Teach thou my willing soul
  The truth of Love supreme,
Till all unrest and care
  Fade like a fleeting dream.

3 No more shall doubt or fear
  Disturb my tranquil breast;
For thou, O Christ, art here,
  And in the truth I rest.
Peace! peace! sweet peace of Christ!
  O peace divinely free!
Enfold, pervade me now,
  And through eternity.

GERALDINE D. ROBINSON.

155 At Even-Tide. C. M. 6 l.

Arr. fr. *Paradise.* —J. BARNBY.

1. O Shad-ow in a sul-try land! We gath-er to thy breast,

Whose love, en-fold-ing us like night, Brings qui-e-tude and rest:

Glimpse of a fair-er life to be. In fore-taste here pos-sessed.

2 From all our wanderings we come,
From drifting to and fro,
From tossing on life's restless deep,
Amid its ebb and flow;
The grander sweep of tides serene
Our spirits yearn to know.

3 That which the garish day has lost,
The twilight vigil brings;—
The breezes from celestial hills,
The draughts from deeper springs,
The sense of an immortal trust,
The touch of angel wings.

C. M. PACKARD.

156 Led.

1 Sweet is the solace of thy love,
My Heavenly Friend, to me,
While through the hidden way of faith
I journey home to thee,
Learning by quiet thankfulness
As a dear child to be.

2 Oft in a dark and lonely place
I hush my hastened breath,
To hear the comfortable words
Thy loving Spirit saith;
And feel my safety in thy hand
From every kind of death.

3 When I seem feeble as a child,
And flesh and heart give way,
Then on thine everlasting strength
With passive trust I stay,—
And the rough wind becomes a song,
The darkness shines like day!

4 Deep unto deep may call, but I
With peaceful heart will say,
Thy loving-kindness hath a charge
No waves can wrest away:
Then let the storm that speeds me home
Deal with me as it may!

ANNA L. WARING.

157 All is Well. P. M.

E. PAXTON HOOD.
PLUMA M. BROWN.

1. I hear a sweet voice ring - ing clear, All is well!
2. Clouds can - not long ob - scure my sight: All is well!
3. In morn - ing hours, se - rene and bright, All is well!

It is my Fa - ther's voice I hear; All is well! Wher-
I know there is a land of light; All is well! From
In ev - 'ning hours or dark-'ning night, All is well! My

e'er I walk that voice is heard; It is my God, my Fa - ther's word,
strength to strength, from day to day, I tread a-long the world's high-way;
peace, because I trust in thee, Is deep as is the sound-less sea:

"Fear not, but trust: I am the Lord:" All is well!
Or oft - en stop to sing or say, All is well!
Joy rich - er, full - er, can - not be— All is well!

Tune—*Paradise*.

"Give me the rest that springs from love,
Abiding, pure, and deep:
The love that trusts so perfectly
That it can fall asleep
Beneath the shadow of thy throne,
Or where the tempests sweep."

158   My Psalm.   c. m.

Hermon.—L. Mason.

1. No longer for-ward or be - hind I look, in hope or fear:

But, grateful, take the good I find, God's blessing now and here.

2 I plough no more a desert land,
    To harvest weed and tare;
The manna dropping from God's hand
Rebukes my painful care.

3 I break my pilgrim staff,—I lay
    Aside the toiling oar;
The angel sought so far away
I welcome at my door.

4 And all the jarring notes of life
    Seem blending in a psalm,
And all the angles of its strife
Slow rounding into calm.

5 And so the shadows fall apart,
    And so the west winds play;
And all the windows of my heart
I open to the day.

J. G. Whittier.

159   Be Still.

1 Be still in God! who rests on him
    Enduring peace shall know,
And with a spirit fresh and free,
Through life shall cheerly go.

2 Be still in faith! forbear to seek
    Where seeking naught avails;
Unfold thy soul to that pure light
From heaven, which never fails.

Tr. fr. Julius Sturm.

160   The Will of God.

1 I worship thee, dear Will of God!
    And all thy ways adore;
And every day I live I seem
To love thee more and more.

2 When obstacles and trials seem
    Like prison-walls to be,
I do the little I can do,
And leave the rest to thee.

3 I have no cares, O blessed Will!
    For all my cares are thine;
I live in triumph, Lord! for thou
Hast made thy triumphs mine.

4 I know not what it is to doubt;
    My heart is ever gay;
I run no risk, for, come what will,
Thou always hast thy way.

F. W. Faber.

161 Thy Name. C. M.

Southport. — GEO. KINGSLEY.

1. Thy name is now a ho-ly spell Which holds me as thine own:
And bless-ed dreams of light and love Now bear me to thy throne.

2 My spirit calmly rests in thee.
  Safe hid from praise or blame:
What else have I on earth to keep.
  Except thy sacred name?

3 For now, just now. unchanging love
  Thou dost reveal to me;
A love which thrills my inmost heart.
  And tells me I am free.

4 Thou art that friend who promises
  Forever to remain:
To make me satisfied in thee.
  And ask no other gain.

5 And thus thy name, thy blessed name.
  Is manifest to me
Thro' Christ. the Truth. forever here.
  The Truth which makes me free.

6 Without. beyond. no more I seek
  To find my heavenly home;
Thy spirit softly speaks to me.
  Oh. now thy peace has come.
          FRANC W. LORD.

162 I Rest in Peace.

1 In perfect confidence I rest.
  And earthly scenes remove.
While gently. thro' my quiet breast.
  I feel the peace of love.

2 What strange delight. to sense un-
    known.
  Through all my being flows:
O truth divine, thou art my own.
  While heavenly worlds unclose.

3 Thou art my everlasting light:
  The clouds of sense remove, —
Triumphant faith dispels the night. —
  And crowns me with its love.

163 Christ Revealed Within.

1 Sweet is the hour when Christ unvails
  His image in the breast;
A boundless spirit-peace prevails.
  And in his love we rest.

2 The world without may nail our hands
  Upon the martyr tree;
But. in the heart Messiah stands.
  To set the spirit free.

3 In all we think and do and see.
  A present Lord we find.
While still we pray that all may be
  The temples of his mind.

164 Perfect Peace and Rest. 6. 5.

J. BARNBY.

1. { Like a riv-er glo-rious Is God's per-fect peace.
   { Per-fect—yet it flow-eth Full-er ev-'ry day:

O-ver all vic-to-rious In its bright in-crease.)
Per-fect—yet it grow-eth Deep-er all the way.)

2 Hidden in the hollow
   Of his blessed hand,
 Never foe can follow,
   Never traitor stand.
 Not a surge of worry,
   Not a shade of care.
 Not a blast of hurry
   Touch the spirit there.

3 We may trust him solely
   All for us to do;
 They who trust him wholly,
   Find him wholly true.
 Stayed upon Jehovah,
   Hearts are fully blest.
 Finding, as he promised,
   Perfect peace and rest.

FRANCES R. HAVERGAL.

165 Peace of Christ. 6. 4.

New Haven.—T. HASTINGS.

1. Peace, peace I leave with you, My peace I give to you. Trust to my care! Thus the Re-

deemer said, And bowed his sacred head, Lone in the garden shade, Wrestling in prayer.

166 Sabbath Rest. P. M.

J. G. WHITTIER.
St. John.—PLUMA M. BROWN.

1 O Sab-bath rest by Gal-i-lee! O calm of hills a-bove,
2. Drop thy still dews of qui-et-ness, Till all our striv-ings cease:
3. Breathe thro' the heats of our de-sire Thy cool-ness and thy balm:

Where Je-sus knelt to share with thee The si-lence of e-
Take from our souls the strain and stress, And let our or-dered
Let sense be dumb, let flesh re-tire, Speak thro' the earth-quake,

ter-ni-ty In-ter-pret-ed by love.
lives con-fess The beau-ty of thy peace.
wind, and fire, O still, small voice of calm!

TUNE—*New Haven.*

2 Peace, peace, I leave with you,
My peace I give to you,
Perfect and pure;
Not as the world doth give.
Words that the soul deceive;
Ye who in me believe
Shall rest secure.

3 Peace, peace, I leave with you.
My peace I give to you,
No foes invade;
All power is given to me.
I will your refuge be.
Now and eternally;
Be not dismayed!

T. HASTINGS.

167 Perfect Peace. P. M.

Kevin.—A. SULLIVAN.

"Thou wilt keep him in perfect peace whose mind is stayed on thee."

1. Per-fect peace the Fa-ther gives To the trust-ing spir-it:
Who in him a-bides and lives, Shall his love in-her-it.

REFRAIN.

Per-fect peace, O per-fect peace, Be my por-tion ev-er,
While my trust-ing spir-it rests Stayed up-on the Fa-ther.

2 He will keep in perfect peace,
  All who trust him wholly,
  Be they in the court of kings,
  Or among the lowly.— REF.

3 Let me know that perfect peace
  Passing understanding,
  Bidding all my sorrows cease,
  All my fears commanding.— REF

4 Father, keep my mind on thee,
  Be thy peace mine ever—
  Let thy love abide in me
  Ever and forever.— REF.

D. B. PAGE.

168 The Spirit of Peace. P. M.

GERTRUDE L. CAMPBELL.
PLUMA M. BROWN.

1. O   Peace, thy touch is like moonlight! Soft as plumage of an - gel wings,
2. En-wrapt in thy soft, white man - tle, I   feel   no chast'ning rod:
3. O   Peace, be - yond un-der-stand-ing! Thou fill - est the far and near,

Thou hast touched my in - most be - ing, And my heart with - in me sings.
But the rest and   trust that "clos-es Round the soul that dwells in God."
In   word-less, "soundless re-veal-ing" That "the Spir-it of Peace is here."

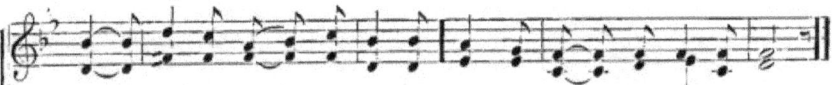

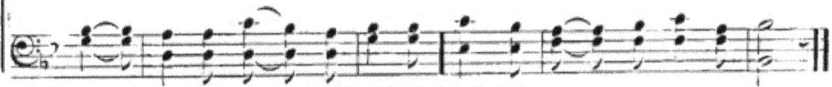

Thou hast touched my in - most be-ing, And my heart with-in me sings.
But the rest and trust that "closes Round the soul that dwells in God."
In   word-less, "soundless re-veal-ing" That "the Spir-it of Peace is here."

Oh, the peace at the heart of nature!
Oh, the light that is not of day!
Why seek it afar forever,
When it cannot be lifted away.

W. C. GANNETT.

169   The Calm of the Soul.   11. 10.

Mrs. H. B. Stowe.
Arr. fr. Nessler.

1. When winds are rag - ing o'er the up - per   o - cean, And bil - lows wild con -
2. So   to the heart that knows thee, Love E-ter - nal, There is   a   tem - ple

tend with an - gry   roar, 'Tis said, far down be-neath the wild com-mo - tion,
sa - cred ev - er - more, And all the   ba - bel of life's an - gry voi - ces

That peaceful still-ness reign-eth, ev - er-more, Far, far   be - neath, the
Dies, in hushed still-ness, at   its peace-ful door, Far, far   a - way, the

noise of tem-pests di - eth, And   sil-ver waves chime ev - er peace-ful - ly,
roar of pas - sion di - eth, And lov-ing tho'ts rise calm and peace-ful - ly:

And   no rude storm, how fierce so-e'er it   fli - eth, Dis - turbs the Sab - bath
And   no rude storm, how fierce so-e'er it   fli - eth, Dis - turbs the soul   that

The Calm of the Soul—Concluded.

of that deep - er sea; And no rude storm, how fierce so - e'er it
dwells, O Lord, in thee; And no rude storm, how fierce so - e'er it

fli - eth. Dis - turbs the Sab - bath of that deep - er sea.
fli - eth, Dis - turbs the soul that dwells, O Lord, in thee.

170 The Ocean of Thy Peace. L. M.

Ernan.—L. Mason.

1. In - to the o - cean of thy peace, Al-might-y One, my tho'ts would flow;

Bid their un-rest - ful murmuring cease, And thy great calmness let me know.

2 The world is bright and glad in thee!
No hopeless gloom her face enshrouds;
Joy lights her mountains, thrills her sea,
And weaves gay tints thro' all her
clouds.

3 O God, how beautiful is life,
Since thou its soul and sweetness art!
How dies its childish fret and strife
On thy all-harmonizing Heart!

4 Leaving behind me dust and clay,
From selfish hindrances set free,
I find at last my broadening way
Unto my ocean-rest in thee.

5 One soul with thee forevermore,
Borne high beyond the gulfs of death,—
A joy that ripples on thy shore,—
With Life's vast hymn I blend my
breath.

Lucy Larcom.

171 The Pure in Heart. L. M. D.

ELLA DARE.
PLUMA M. BROWN.

1. The pure in heart, the pure in tho't, Shall learn the law the Mas-ter taught,
2. The pure in heart, the pure in word, Make mu-sic, sweet-est ev - er heard,

Shall turn from ill and earth-ly strife, And seek the sum - mits high in life.
And wake the tones of gra-cious good, The tones of peace and broth-er - hood!

The pure in heart, the pure in deed, Shall sow each hour some fruit-ful seed.
The pure in heart, the pure in pray'r, Shall feel God's pres-ence ev - 'ry - where;

Which, fall-ing here and falling there, Shall plant for harvests rich and rare.
Shall see his work on ev - 'ry side, And know that life is glo - ri - fied.

Copyright, 1891, by Pluma M. Brown.

172   *Victors.*

1 They are the victors, they alone,
Who roll away love's burial stone,
And, from the cross where self expires,
Unfold the life that heaven inspires.
Deny thyself if thou wouldst gain
The upper world where angels reign;
They walk alone with Christ above,
Who conquer self by perfect love.

2 They live to God, who live to win
The erring hearts from strife and sin;
Whose words and works of love express
The Savior's loving tenderness.
Deny thyself if thou wouldst gain
The upper world where angels reign;
They walk alone with Christ above,
Who conquer self by perfect love.

T. L. HARRIS.

173 Heavenly Helper. P. M.

A. SULLIVAN.

1. Un - to thee, a - bid-ing ev - er, Look I in my need, Strength of ev - 'ry

REFRAIN.

good en-deav-or, Ho - ly thought and deed! Heav'nly Help-er, ev - er pres-ent,

Thou, O Christ, art mine in-deed.

3 Origin and end of being.
  All things in and through.—
  Light thou art of all my seeing.
  Power to will and do.—REF.

2 Thou dost guide the stars of heaven,
  Heal the broken heart.
  Bring in turn the morn and even.—
  Law and Love thou art.—REF.

4 Through my life, whate'er betide me,
  Thou my trust shalt be:
  Whom have I on earth beside thee,
  Whom in heaven but thee?—REF.

F. L. HOSMER.

174 *Light O'er Us.*

1 Light o'er us divinely gleaming—
  Rests our troubled sea.
  'Tis the love of Christ that's beaming
  Peace down over me.

REFRAIN.—
  Light of Love that drops no shading.
  Light of day, unchanging—free.

2 Light of all my years of gladness.
  Now to thee I flee—
  Strength in Christ. I know no sadness.
  For thou art in me.—REF.

3 Light of life, my health bestowing.
  I lift eyes to thee;
  From thy love forever flowing
  Joy now comes to me.—REF

175 *Fear Not.*

1 Listen! for the Lord hath spoken!
  "Fear thou not," saith he:
  "When thou passest thro' the waters,
  I will be with thee.

REFRAIN.—
  Thou art mine, oh, therefore fear not!
  Thou art precious unto me.

2 Fear not, for I have redeemed thee;
  All my sheep I know:
  When thou passest thro' the rivers,
  They shall not o'erflow.—REF.

3 Fear not! by thy name I called thee,—
  Mine thy heart hath learned:
  When thou walkest thro' the fire,
  Thou shalt not be burned."—REF.

FRANCES R. HAVERGAL.

176   The Thought of God.   C. M.   *Coventry.—English.*

1. One thought I have, my am - ple creed, So deep it is and broad, And e - qual to my ev - 'ry need.—It is the thought of God.

2 Each morn unfolds some fresh sur-
   prise,
I feast at Life's full board,
And rising in my inner skies
   Shines forth the thought of God.

3 At night my gladness is my prayer;
   I drop my daily load,
And every care is pillowed there
   Upon the thought of God.

4 I ask not far before to see,
   But take in trust my road;
Life, health and immortality
   Are in my thought of God.

5 Be still the light upon my way,
   My pilgrim staff and rod,
My rest by night, my strength by day,
   Oh, blessed thought of God.
                 F. L. HOSMER.

177   *Divine Help.*

1 O Name, all other names above,
   What art thou not to me,
Now I have learned to trust thy love,
   And cast my care on thee!

2 What is our being but a cry,
   A restless longing still,
Which thou alone canst satisfy,
   Alone thy fullness fill!

3 And sweet it is to tread the ground
   O'er which all faith hath trod;
But sweeter far, when thou art found,
   The soul's own sense of God!

4 The thought of thee all sorrow calms,
   Our anxious burdens fall;
His crosses turn to triumph-palms
   Who finds in God his all!
                 F. L. HOSMER.

178   *All Good.*

1 O Lord! I would delight in thee,
   And on thy care depend;
To thee in every trouble flee,
   My best, my only Friend!

2 When all of earthly streams are dried
   Thy fullness is the same;
May I with this be satisfied,
   And glory in thy name.

3 No good in creatures can be found
   But may be found in thee;
I must have all things, and abound,
   While God is God to me.

4 O Lord! I cast my care on thee;
   I triumph and adore;
Henceforth my great concern shall be
   To love and praise thee more.
                 J. RYLAND.

179 A Present Help. c. m.

Holy Cross.—Arr. fr. MENDELSSOHN.

1. We may not climb the heav'n-ly steeps To bring the Lord Christ down;

In vain we search the low-est deeps, For him no depths can drown.

2 But warm, sweet, tender, even yet
   A present help is he:
And faith has now its Olivet.
   And love its Galilee.

3 The healing of the seamless dress
   Is by our beds of pain;
We touch him in life's throng and press,
   And we are whole again.

4 O Lord and Master of us all.
   Whate'er our name or sign.
We own thy sway, we hear thy call.
   We test our lives by thine!

J. G. WHITTIER.

180 *The Hands of Christ.*
Hands—strong, efficient thoughts.

1 The hands of Christ are soft, white
      hands
   That like cool lilies lie
Upon my fevered, throbbing brow.
   And soothe, and satisfy.

2 The hands of Christ are clean, pure
      hands,
   And on my parched lips
The love-dew, caught in his sweet palms.
   In constant mercy drips.

3 The hands of Christ are kind, true
      hands
   Wherein I trusting lay
My own weak hands, glad to be led
   By one who knows the way.

4 The hands of Christ are kingly hands
   Wherewith he giveth free.
To him who loveth, largesses
   Of Love's eternity.

5 The hands of Christ are mighty hands
   That builded and uphold
The universe—he openeth them
   And centuries are unrolled.

6 The hands of Christ are gentle hands:
   Ah, with what tender grace
He lifts me up that I may catch
   The lovelight in his face.

7 Strong pledge of peace, abiding life:
   Love's, Mercy's, Wisdom's plan.
The loving hands of Christ out-stretched
   To rescue every man!

INGRAM CROCKETT.

Refuge.

181 Safe to the Land. 8. 4.

H. ALFORD.
PLUMA M. BROWN.

1. My bark is waft - ed to the strand By breath di - vine,
2. He holds me when the bil - lows smite; I shall not fall:

And on the helm there rests a hand Oth - er than mine.
If sharp, 'tis short; if long, 'tis light; He tem - pers all.

How can I fear the storm to sail, With him on board?
Safe to the land! safe to the land! The end is this:

A - bove the ra - ging of the gale I hear my Lord.
And then with him go hand in hand Far in - to bliss.

185 The Light, our Refuge. 8. 7. D.   Arr. fr. Mozart.

1. Oh, the Light! Im-mor-tal radiance, Flung a-cross life's storm-y wave:

Burdened souls will feel thy cadence, Hearts distressed thy love will save.
D.S.—Grandest hope of man has nev-er Compassed all thy truth un-told.

Oh, the Light! Di-vine for-ev-er, Bless-ings rich thy ways un-fold:

2 Oh, the Light! Thy brightness beam-
ing,
Rescues man from every fear;
Gone the shadows and the seeming;
Light of day comes full and clear.

Oh, the Light! Supreme, eternal,
Waking human hearts to see
Thine own goodness reigns supernal:
Changeless bonds link them to thee.
CLARA E. CHOATE.

Tune—Ellerton.

2 It lies about me like the warm embrace
Of mother-tenderness and mother-care,
Still touching life with sweet, benignant
grace,
And filling it with gifts divinely
fair.

3 So I, who can but understand in part
The love that keeps, whatever may
befall,
Will nestle closer to the tender heart
Of God,—that heart which is the
heart of all.
HELEN CHAUNCEY.

186   Security   P. M.

GERALDINE D. ROBINSON.
PLUMA M. BROWN

1. As soft-ly rests the nest-ed bird 'mid shelt'ring leaves, Dwells
2. Tho' darts of mal-ice fall a-bout me thick and fast, And
3. Se-cure I stand up-on th' e-ter-nal, change-less Rock, Whose

ev-er-more this tho't within my peace-ful breast: Tho' earth may shiv-er
er-ror's host be marshalled close be-side my way: The poi-soned arrows
cleft shall cra-dle me to sweet, re-pose-ful sleep. No un-at-tained de-

as the tem-pest mad-ly raves: Al-though the sea may
of false words fly harm-less past: Nor doubts nor ter-rors
sire my soul se-rene can mock, For faith the "Se-cret

roar and lash her an-gry waves: God is my ref-uge and my rest.
o'er my heart their snares may cast: God is my strong de-fense and stay.
Place" of treasure doth un-lock,—Je-ho-vah's store-house vast and deep.

187 All Through the Night. P. M.

Words adapted.
Arr. fr. Welsh Air.

DUET.

1. Child, fear not if sad thy dream-ing   All thro' the night,
2. An - gels watch-ing ev - er round thee   All thro' the night,

Tho' o'er-cast, bright stars are gleam-ing   All thro' the night.
In   thy slum-bers close sur-round thee   All thro' the night.

Joy will come as comes the morn-ing, Life with sun - ny hope a - dorn-ing,
Thot's of love, of fears dis-arm thee, No fore - bod - ings can a-larm thee.

On - ly dreams are dark with warn-ing   All thro' the night.
They will let no per - il harm thee   All thro' the night.

188 God Thy Defense. 7. 6. D.

C. WESLEY.
Amsterdam. J. NARES.

1. { See the Lord, thy Keep-er, stand! Om-nip-o-tent-ly near; }
{ Lo! he holds thee by the hand, And ban-ish-es thy fear: }

2. { God shall bless thy go-ing out, Shall bless thy com-ing in, }
{ Kind-ly com-pass thee a-bout And save thee from all sin. }

Shad-ows from the heat thy head, Guards from all im-pend-ing harms.
He is still thy sure de-fence: Thou his con-stant care shalt prove:

Round thee and be-neath are spread The ev-er-last-ing arms.
Kept by watch-ful Prov-i-dence And ev-er-wak-ing Love.

189 Jehovah Lives. H. M.

Haddam.—Arr. by L. MASON.

1. { The Lord Je-ho-vah lives, And blessed be my Rock! }
{ Tho' earth her bo-som heaves, [Omit. . . . .] And mountains feel the shock,

Tho' o-ceans rage and tor-rents roar, He is the same for-ev-er-more.

190 Come Unto Me. 11. 10. English.

1. "Come un-to me when shadows darkly gather, When the sad heart seems wea - ry and dis - tressed; Seek-ing for com - fort from your heav'nly Fa-ther, Come un - to me and I will give you rest."

2 "Large are the mansions in thy Father's dwelling,
   Glad are the homes that sorrows never dim;
   Sweet are the harps in holy music swelling,
   Soft are the tones that raise the heavenly hymn.

3 "There, like an Eden blossoming in gladness,
   Bloom the fair flowers the earth too rudely pressed,
   Come unto me, all ye who droop in sadness,
   Come unto me, and I will give you rest."

CATHRINE H. WATERMAN.

TUNE—*Haddam.*

2 The Lord Jehovah lives
    To hear and answer prayer;
  Whoe'er in him believes
    And trusts his guardian care,
A Father's tender love shall know,
Whence living streams of comfort flow.

T. HASTINGS.

191 *Protection.—Ps. 121.*
  1 Upward I lift mine eyes,
    From God is all my aid;
  The God who built the skies,
    And earth and nature made:
God is the tower | His grace is nigh
To which I fly; | In every hour.

2 My feet shall never slide,
    Nor fall in fatal snares,
  Since God, my guard and guide,
    Defends me from my fears:
Those wakeful eyes | Shall Israel keep
That never sleep, | When dangers rise

3 No burning heats by day,
    Nor blasts of evening air,
  Shall take my health away,
    If God be with me there:
Thou art my sun, | To guard my head
And thou my shade. | By night or noon.

I. WATTS.

192   God Thy Salvation.   7. 6. D.   *Gladness.*—J. BARNBY.

1. God is my strong sal-va-tion: What foe have I to fear? In darkness and temp-
In dark - ness
ta - tion, My light, my help, is near: Tho' hosts encamp a - round me, Firm
in the fight I stand: What terror can confound me, With God at my right hand?

2 Place on the Lord reliance;
　My soul, with courage wait;
His truth be thine alliance.
　Thou art not desolate;
His might thy heart shall strengthen,
　His love thy joy increase;
Mercy thy days shall lengthen;
　The Lord will give thee peace.
　　　　　　　　J. MONTGOMERY.

193   *I will Fear No Change.*

1 In heavenly love abiding,
　No change my heart shall fear;
And safe is such confiding.
　For nothing changes here.
The storm may roar without me,
　My heart may low be laid,
But God is round about me,
　And can I be dismayed?

2 Wherever he may guide me,
　No want shall turn me back;
My Shepherd is beside me,
　And nothing can I lack.
His wisdom ever waketh,
　His sight is never dim,
He knows the way he taketh,
　And I will walk with him.
　　　　　　　　ANNA L. WARING.

194   *Lo! I am with You Always.*

1 Lo! I am with you always.
　What then is there to fear?
Can any ill befall thee.
　With God, thy keeper, near?
Of all earth's mortal seeming,
　Then stand no more in awe,
For on the heights 'tis written
　That Good alone is Law.
　　　　　　　　HANNAH MORE KOHAUS.

195 A Sure Defense. P. M.

JULIE M. KENNEALLY.
Carmen Cœli.—J. BARNBY.

1. O thou! who art the same thro' endless a - ges, A sure defense that knows not
2. A-bove earth's tumult comes a voice entreating, A voice most sweet and tender,
3. Our darkness is dispelled, our burdens lightened; Gone are our old beliefs, our
4. Within Love, in-fi - nite, for aye a - bid-ing, Safe from all harm, no foe can
5. We fear no foe; our guide is with us, lead-ing; Truth is our weapon, battling

change nor time, What tho' the war with self most fiercely wa - ges;
soft and low; "Come un - to me, all ye who peace are seek-ing;"
weight of woe; The bless-ed truth has all our pathway brightened,
reach us there; In shad-ow of the Rock se-cure - ly hid - ing,
care and sin; Love is our safe-guard, com-fort-ing and heal - ing,

REFRAIN.

Thou dost en - dure, e - ter-nal, true, sub - lime.)
To him we turn our foot-steps, fal - t'ring, slow. |
And guides our foot-steps wheresoe'er we go. } A sure de-fense, knowing
Sur-round-ed on all sides by ten - d'rest care. |
And ours the vic-t'ry, we must ev - er win.)

no change or time, Thou dost en - dure, e - ter-nal, ev - er true, sub - lime.

196   Every Good Gift.   7. D.

Martyn.—S. B. MARSH.

FINE.

1. (Fa-ther, thy pa - ter - nal care   Has my guardian been, my   guide!
  (Ev - 'ry hallowed wish and prayer Has thy hand of   love   sup - plied:
D.C.—Ev - 'ry hope thine off-spring is,   Beam-ing from fu - tu - ri - ty.

D. C.

Thine is   ev-'ry thought of   bliss   Left by hours and days gone   by:

2 Every sun of splendid ray;
   Every moon that shines serene;
   Every morn that welcomes day;
   Every evening's twilight scene;

Every hour which wisdom brings;
   Every incense at thy shrine;
   These, and all life's holiest things,
   And its fairest,—all are thine.

J. BOWRING.

197   The Goodness of God.   S. M.

Dennis.—L. MASON.

1. How   gen - tle   God's com-mands, How   kind   his   pre - cepts are!

Come, cast your bur-dens   on   the   Lord, And trust his   con-stant care.

198 God is My Refuge. P. M.

T. HASTINGS.

1. O thou in whom I live, and move, And have e-ter-nal be-ing,—
I to thy mount of per-fect love In con-fi-dence am flee-ing;
In thee my faith is quite at rest, I lean up-on a Fa-ther's breast.

2 The verdant earth, the air that blows,
  The simplest little flower,
The mighty sea that ebbs and flows,
  Alike proclaim thy power;
I am secure, I fear no harm,
For safe I rest within thine arm.

3 Each step I take, each breath I draw,
  Each smile of joy that lights me,
Proclaim aloud thy perfect law,—
  No evil can affright me.
In thee I am, and live, and move,
And nothing fear, for thou art Love.

Mrs. Hirschheimer.

TUNE—Dennis.

2 Beneath his powerful sway
  His saints securely dwell;
That hand which bears all nature up
Will guide his children well.

3 His goodness stands approved,
  Unchanged from day to day;
I'll drop my burden at his feet,
And bear a song away.

P. Doddridge.

199 My Friend.

1 Truth whispers in my breast
  Sweet words of holy cheer,
How they who seek in God their rest
Shall ever find him near;—

2 How God hath built, in love,
  A city fair and new,
Where eye and heart shall see and
    prove
What faith has counted true.

3 My heart for gladness springs;
  It cannot more be sad;
For very joy it smiles and sings,—
Sees naught but sunshine glad.

4 The sun that lights mine eyes
  Is Christ, the Lord I love;
I sing for joy of that which lies
Stored up for me above.

200   Ninety-First Psalm.   8. 7.   Vesper.—Arr. fr. FLOTOW.

1. Call Je-ho-vah thy sal-va-tion. Rest beneath th' Al-mighty's shade;

In his se-cret hab-it-a-tion Dwell, nor ev-er be dis-mayed;

2 There no tumult can alarm thee,
   Thou shalt dread no hidden snare;
Guile nor violence can harm thee,
   In eternal safeguard there.

3 From the sword, at noon-day wasting,
   From the noisome pestilence
In the depth of midnight blasting,
   God shall be thy sure defence:

4 He shall charge his angel legions
   Watch and ward o'er thee to keep,
Tho' thou walk thro' hostile regions,
   Tho' in desert wilds thou sleep.

5 Fear not thou the deadly quiver
   When a thousand feel the blow;
Mercy shall thy soul deliver
   Tho' ten thousand be laid low.

6 Since, with pure and warm affection
   Thou on God hast set thy love,
With the wings of his protection
   He will shield thee, from above.
          J. MONTGOMERY.

201   *Yes, for Me.*

1 Yes, for me, for me he careth,
   With a Father's tender care:
Yes, with me, with me he beareth
   Every burden, every fear.

2 Yes, in me abroad he sheddeth
   Joys unearthly, love and light;
And, to cover me, he spreadeth
   His protecting wing of might.

3 Yes, o'er me, o'er me he watcheth,
   Ceaseless watcheth, night and day;
Yes, e'en me, e'en me, he snatcheth
   From the perils of the way.

4 Yes, in me, in me he dwelleth,
   I in him, and he in me;
And my longing soul he filleth,
   Here, and through eternity.
          H. BONAR.

202 Our Help. C. M. *Romberg.—T. Hastings.*

1. O God! our help in a - ges past, Our hope for years to come,

Our shel - ter from the storm - y blast, And our e - ter - nal home,—

2 Before the hills in order stood.
Or earth received her frame.
From everlasting thou art God.
To endless years the same.

3 Under the shadow of thy throne
Thy children dwell secure;
Sufficient is thine arm alone,
And their defence is sure.

4 O God! our help in ages past,
Our hope for years to come,
Be thou our guard while life shall last,
And our eternal home.
I. Watts.

203 *The Covenant.*

1 My God! the covenant of thy love
Abides forever sure,
And in its matchless grace I feel
My happiness secure.

2 I welcome all thy sovereign will.
For all that will is love;
And when I know not what thou dost.
I wait the light above.
P. Doddridge.

204 *The Name of Christ.*

1 How sweet the name of Jesus sounds
In a believer's ear;

It soothes his sorrows, heals his wounds,
And drives away his fear.

2 It makes the wounded spirit whole,
And calms the troubled breast;
'Tis manna to the hungry soul,
And to the weary, rest.

3 Jesus! my Shepherd, Husband, Friend,
My Prophet. Priest, and King,
My Lord. my Life, my Way, my End!
Accept the praise I bring.
J. Newton.

205 *Martyr-Faith.*

1 Glory to God! whose witness-train,
Those heroes bold in faith,
Could smile on poverty and pain.
And triumph ev'n o'er death.

2 God whom we serve. our God, will save,
Will damp the scorching flame.
Will build an ark. will smooth the wave.
For all who love his name.

3 Because thine arm supports us still
With its eternal strength,
We shall o'ercome the mightiest ill,
And conquerors prove at length.
Tr. fr. Zinzendorf.

206　Cast Thy Burden on the Lord.　7.

Last Hope.--Arr. fr. GOTTSCHALK.

1. Cast thy bur-den on the Lord, On-ly lean up-on his word;

Thou wilt soon have cause to bless His e-ter-nal faith-ful-ness.

Used by arr. with Oliver Ditson Co., owners of copyright.

2 He sustains thee by his hand,
He enables thee to stand;
He hath promised to fulfill
All the pleasure of his will.

3 Jesus! Guardian of thy flock,
Be thyself our constant Rock;
Make us, by thy powerful hand,
Strong as Sion's mountain stand.
R. HILL.

207　Daily Food.

1 Day by day the manna fell:
Oh, to learn this lesson well!
Still by constant mercy fed,
Give me, Lord, my daily bread.

2 "Day by day" the promise reads,
Daily strength for daily needs;
Cast foreboding fears away,
Take the manna of to-day.

3 Lord, my times are in thy hand;
All my sanguine hopes have planned,
To thy wisdom I resign,
And would make thy purpose mine.

4 Thou my daily task shalt give:
Day by day to thee I live;

So shall added years fulfill.
Not mine own—my Father's will.

5 Fond ambition, whisper not;
Happy is my humble lot.
Anxious, busy cares, away!
I'm provided for to-day.

6 Oh, to live exempt from care
By the energy of prayer;
Strong in faith, with mind subdued,
Yet elate with gratitude!
J. CONDER.

208　"As Thy Days."

1 Wait, my soul, upon the Lord,
To his gracious promise flee.
Laying hold upon his word,
"As thy days thy strength shall be."

2 If the sorrows of thy case
Seem peculiar still to thee.
God has promised needful grace,
"As thy days thy strength shall be."

3 Rock of Ages, I'm secure,
With thy promise full and free.
Ever faithful, ever sure
"As thy days thy strength shall be."
W. F. LLOYD.

209 Trust in Divine Love. L. M.

Via Bona—J. B. Dykes.

1. We ask not what our life shall be When be-ing wins an am - ple field:

The glo - ries of fu - tu - ri - ty, O Lord! are in thy love concealed.

2 So, day by day, the manna fell,
So, night by night, the guiding flame,
And, from the rock, the cooling well,
To ancient Israel duly came.

3 With constant strength for constant
needs,
Thou still descendest, Lord! and we
Plant from thy hand the fruitful seeds,
That shall become our future's tree.

210 *All's Well.*
1 O wealth of life beyond all bound!
Eternity each moment given!
What plummet may the present sound?
Who promises a *future* heaven?
Or glad, or grieved, oppressed, relieved,
In blackest night, or brightest day,
Still pours the flood of golden good,
And more than heartfull fills me aye.

2 "All mine is thine," the sky-soul saith:
"The wealth I am, must thou become:
Richer and richer, breath by breath,—
Immortal gain, immortal room!"
And since all his mine also is,
Life's gift outruns my fancies far,
And drowns the dream in larger stream,
As morning drinks the morning-star.
D. A. WASSON.

211 *Our Supply.*
1 Peace, troubled soul, thou needst not
fear;
Thy great provider still is near;
Who fed thee last, will feed thee still:
Be calm, and sink into his will.

2 Without reserve give Christ your
heart;
Let him his righteousness impart;
Then all things else he'll freely give;
With him you all things shall receive.
SPENCE'S COLL.

TUNE—*Last Hope.*
212 *Daily Mercies.*
1 Tender mercies, on my way
Falling softly like the dew,
Sent me freshly every day,
I will bless the Lord for you.

2 Though I have not all I would,
Though to greater bliss I go,
Every present gift of good
To Eternal Love I owe.

3 Source of all that comforts me,
Well of joy for which I long,
Let the song I sing to thee
Be an everlasting song!
ANNA L. WARING.

213   Twenty-Third Psalm. s. m.   *Aileen.* —J. BARNBY.

1. The Lord my Shep-herd is. I shall be well sup - plied;

Since he is mine and I am his, What can I want be - side?

2 He leads me to the place
Where heavenly pasture grows,
Where living waters gently pass,
And full salvation flows.

3 If e'er I go astray,
He doth my soul reclaim,
And guides me in his own right way.
For his most holy name.

4 While he affords his aid
I cannot yield to fear;
Tho' I should walk thro' death's dark
shade,
My Shepherd's with me there.

5 Amid surrounding foes
He doth my table spread;
My cup with blessings overflows,
And joy exalts my head.

6 The bounties of his love
Shall crown my endless days;

Nor from his house will I remove,
Nor cease to speak his praise.
I. WATTS.

214   *Delight in God.*

1 Lord, I delight in thee,
And on thy care depend;
To thee in every trouble flee,
My best, my only Friend.

2 When nature's streams are dried,
Thy fullness is the same;
With this will I be satisfied,
And glory in thy name.

3 Who made my heaven secure,
Will here all good provide;
While Christ is rich, can I be poor?
What can I want beside?

4 I cast my care on thee!
I triumph and adore;
Henceforth my greatest joy shall be
To love and please thee more.
J. RYLAND.

215 God's Mercies. C. M.

Elizabethtown.—GEO. KINGSLEY.

1. Faith - ful, O Lord, thy mer - cies are, A rock that can not move: A thou-sand prom - is - es de - clare Thy con - stan - cy of love.

2 Thy goodness and thy truth to me.
To every soul abound;
A vast unfathomable sea
Where all our thoughts are drowned.

3 Its streams the whole creation reach,
So plenteous is the store:
Enough for all, enough for each,
Enough forevermore.

4 Throughout the universe it reigns.
Unalterably sure;
And while the truth of God remains.
His goodness must endure.
C. WESLEY.

216 The One Thing Needful.

1 Compared with Christ, in all beside
No comeliness I see;
The one thing needful, dearest Lord!
Is to be one with thee.

2 Less than thyself will not suffice
My comfort to restore:
More than thyself I cannot crave.
And thou canst give no more.

3 Whate'er consists not with thy love.
Oh, teach me to resign:
I'm rich to all th' intents of bliss.
For thou, O God, art mine.
A. M. TOPLADY.

217 Twenty-third Psalm.

1 The Lord's my Shepherd. I'll not want:
He makes me down to lie
In pastures green; he leadeth me
The quiet waters by.

2 My table he has furnished
In presence of my foes;
My head he dost with oil anoint,
And my cup overflows.

3 Goodness and mercy. all my life,
Shall surely follow me;
And in God's house forevermore
My dwelling-place shall be.
F. ROUS.

218 They shall Neither Hunger or Thirst.

1 Christ comes to men of loving will
To make them all his own:
He guides them to his holy hill.
And feeds them from his throne.

2 They hunger not for earthly bread;
With thirst they faint no more;
But from the Word their hearts are fed,
While they by love adore.

3 "He is the Way. the Truth. the Life."
They cry with one accord.
"He saves the world from sin and strife:
Hosanna to the Lord!"

219　Confidence in God. 7. 6. D.

Magister.—J. B. DYKES.

1. In ho-ly con-tem-pla-tion, We sweetly now pur-sue The theme of God's sal-va-tion, And find it ev-er new: Set free from pres-ent sor-row, We cheer-ful-ly can say. Let the unknown to-mor-row Bring with it what it may.

2 It can bring with it nothing
　But he will bear us through;
Who gives the lilies clothing.
　Will clothe his people too:
Beneath the spreading heavens
　No creature but is fed;
And he who feeds the ravens
　Will give his children bread.

3 Though vine nor fig-tree neither
　Their wonted fruit should bear.
Though all the fields should wither.
　Nor flocks nor herds be there;
Yet God the same abiding,
　His praise shall tune my voice:
For while in him confiding.
　I cannot but rejoice.

WM. COWPER.

220　He Knoweth.

1 Unto our heavenly Father
　We will not fear to pray
For little needs and longings
　That fill our every day;
And when we dare not whisper
　A want that lieth dim,
We say "Our Father knoweth,"
　And leave it all to him.

2 For his great love hath compassed
　Our nature and our needs:
We know not; but he knoweth,
　And he will bless indeed.
Therefore, O heavenly Father,
　Give what is best to me;
And take the wants unanswered
　As offerings made to thee.

221 I Know Not What Awaits Me. 7. 6 D. *St. Hilda — E. Husband.*

1. I know not what a - waits me, But this I feel to - day, Tho' kin and
friends forsake me, I can-not go a - stray. A voice from out the si - lence Is
calling, "Follow me, Remember all my counsels, And truth shall make you free."

2 I know not what awaits me,
    And yet I do not fear;
There comes a loving whisper,
    "Lo! I am always near;
Make truth your constant counsel,
    Your strong, unerring friend;
It never will forsake thee,
    But all your conflicts end."

3 I'm trusting and believing
    The majesty of love;
I hearken to its pleading,
    And thus am lured above;
Above all anxious striving,
    And lust for pomp or place;
The world has naught to give me,
    'Tis Christ gives truth and grace.

4 I care not what awaits me;
    With love and truth as guide,
There is a light to cheer me
    Wherever I abide.
I care not what awaits me.

I'm rich in knowing thee;
With love there is no fearing,
    "The truth has me free."
M. B. Benedict.

222 *Never Separated from Christ.*

1 I know no life divided,
    O Lord of life, from thee;
In thee is life provided
    For all mankind and me:
I know no death, O Jesus,
    Because I live in thee;
Thy death it is which frees us
    From death eternally.

2 I fear no tribulation,
    Since, whatsoe'er it be,
It makes no separation
    Between my Lord and me.
If thou, my God and Teacher,
    I know to be my own,
Though poor, I yet am richer
    Than monarch on his throne.
C. J. P. Spitta.

Supply.

223 The Unfailing One. P. M.

FRANCES R. HAVERGAL.
PLUMA M. BROWN.

1. He who hath made thee whole Will heal thee day by day:
2. He who hath made thee nigh Will draw thee near-er still:
3. He who hath won thy heart Will keep it true and free:
4. Then trust him for to-day As thine un-fail-ing Friend.

He who hath spo-ken to thy soul Hath man-y things to say.
He who hath giv'n the first sup-ply Will sat-is-fy and fill.
He who hath shown thee what thou art Will show him-self to thee.
And let him lead thee all the way, Who lov-eth to the end.

He who hath gen-tly taught, Yet more will make thee know;
He who hath giv'n thee grace, Yet more and more will send;
He who hath bid thee live, And made thy life his own,
And let the mor-row rest In his be-lov-ed hand:

He who so won-drous-ly hath wrought, Yet great-er things will show.)
He who hath set thee in the race Will speed thee to the end. } He
Life more a-bund-ant-ly will give, And keep it his a-lone.)
His good is bet-ter than our best, As we shall un-der-stand,—If

The Unfailing One—Concluded.

lov - eth al - ways, fail - eth nev - er; So rest on him, to-day, for - ev - er!
trust-ing him who fail - eth nev-er, We rest on him, to-day, for - ev - er!

224 Truth's Pinions. P. M.

HANNAH MORE KOHAUS.
Arr. fr. A. S. SULLIVAN.

1. Truth hov - ers o'er us, ev - er - more glo - rious; Spread-ing its
2. With it sur - round - ed, faith - ful - ly ground - ed, Fast to the
3. Lift - ing our long - ing where "right" is throng-ing, Ev - er a -
4. Reach-ing the ha - ven un - to all giv - en, Bless we the

white wings to bear us a - bove; Up to the free - dom, wait - ing to
Rock— the Christ of the soul— Er - ror ways leav - ing, un - to truth
loit on Truth's pin-ions we soar; Flee-ing the low - ly, see - ing the
Truth which has led us on high; Trusting its pow - er, hour on

wel - come, All to its shel - ter—the bos - om of Love.
cleav-ing, Swift - ly we fly to be con - scious - ly whole.
ho - ly, Dark - ness and death we par - take of no more.
hour, Un - to the realm of the High - est we fly.

225 Truth. P. M.

E. H. Hastings.
Pluma M. Brown.

1. Truth needs no cham-pi - on; In ev - er - last - ing
2. An ev - er - flow - ing stream, So vast, re - sist - less,
3. In per - fect har - mo - ny, Forth from the might - y
4. Ef - ful - gent, glo - rious Truth! So full of life and

soul its strength a - bides, From na - ture's heart its might - y
sure, no pow'r di - vides The per - fect tho't from him, the
Source its con - cepts flow, Re - flect - ing wis - dom, high - est
light to us be - low, En - ter our minds and cast all

pul - ses leap. In na-ture's veins its strength un - dy - ing tides.
In - fi - nite,Whose boundless love our whole ex - ist - ence guides.
truth di - vine; It - self a law be - yond all o - ver-flow.
er - ror out, Lift-ing us up from fear, God's love to know.

Copyright, 1896, by Pluma M. Brown.

Tune—Pleyel.

226   Heirship.

1 Heir of all the ages, I.—
Heir of all that they have wrought.
All their store of emprise high,
All their wealth of precious thought!

2 Every golden deed of theirs
Sheds its lustre on my way;
All their labors, all their prayers
Sanctify this present day.

3 Heir of all that they have earned
By their passion and their tears;
Heir of all that they have learned
Through the weary, toiling years·

4 Aspirations pure and high;
Strength to do and to endure;—
Heir of all the ages, I.—
Lo, I am no longer poor!

Julia C. R. Dorr.

227 Life of Ages. 7.   Pleyel's Hymn.—I. PLEYEL.

1. Life of a - ges, rich - ly poured. Love of God, unspent and free.

Flow - ing in the proph - et's word. And the peo - ple's lib - er - ty!

2 Never was to chosen race
    That unstinted tide confined:
  Thine is every time and place.
    Fountain sweet of heart and mind!

3 Breathing in the thinker's creed.
    Pulsing in the hero's blood,
  Nerving simplest thought and deed,
    Freshening time with truth and good.

4 Consecrating art and song,
    Holy book and pilgrim track,
  Hurling floods of tyrant wrong
    From the sacred limits back,—

5 Life of ages. richly poured,
    Love of God, unspent and free.
  Flow still in the prophet's word.
    And the people's liberty!
                          S. JOHNSON.

228   Evolution.
1 Life of ages, richly poured.
    Soul of worlds, unspent and free.
  Nature's uncreated Word.
    Atom and Infinity!

2 Secret of the morning stars.
    Motion of the oldest hours.
  Pledge through elemental wars
    Of the coming spirit's powers!

3 Rolling planet. flaming sun.
    Stand in nobler Man complete:
  Prescient laws thine errands run.
    Frame a shrine for Godhead meet.

4 Homeward led, his wondering eye
    Upward yearned. in joy or awe.
  For the love that waited nigh.
    Guidance of thy guardian Law

5 In the touch of earth it thrilled!
    Down from mystic skies it burned
  Right obeyed and passion stilled.
    Its eternal gladness earned!

6 Still the immortal flame upspeeds,
    Kindling worlds to pure desire:
  Where the unerring Spirit leads.
    Ages wonder and aspire.
                          S. JOHNSON.

229   Silent Thought.   L. M.

Duke Street.—J. HATTON.

1. How lim - it - less the power with- in The clear,sweet,deep,and si - lent tho't;

Re- sist-less in its on-ward rush, Life's deathless deeds by it are wrought.

2 It speaks in every living soul,
    Is heard by every listening ear:
  Persistent, secret, patient, low,
    Pleading for right, that all may hear.

3 It moves prophetic lips to speak,
    Inspires the preacher's words and
      tones:
  It points the poet's magic pen,
    Builds up or overthrows earth's thrones.

4 It guides our commerce, builds our
      ships,
    Rules all the world from pole to pole;
  Omniscient, omnipresent, and
    Omnipotent in its control.

5 'Tis Spirit force in mortal guise,
    Within a seeming human frame:
  'Tis God's own presence ruling there,
    We greet it in his holy name.
                    MRS. C. B. SAWYER.

230   Wisdom Divine.

1 Wisdom divine! who tells the price
  Of Wisdom's costly merchandise?
  Wisdom to silver we prefer,
  And gold is dross compared to her.

2 Her hands are filled with length of
      days,

True riches, and immortal praise;
  Her ways are ways of pleasantness,
  And all her flowery paths are peace.

3 Happy the man who wisdom gains;
  Thrice happy who his guest retains:
  He owns, and shall forever own,   [one.
  Wisdom, and Christ, and heaven—the
                    C. WESLEY.

231   Living Will.

1 O Living Will that shalt endure
  When all that seems shall suffer shock,
  Rise in the spiritual rock,
    Flow through our deeds, and make
      them pure!

2 Let knowledge grow from more to
      more,
  But more of reverence in us dwell,
  Till mind and soul, according well,
    Make music vaster than before!
                    A. TENNYSON.

L. M. 6 l.

So to the calmly gathered thought
The innermost of truth is taught:
The mystery, dimly understood,
That love of God is love of Good,
That to be saved is only this,
Salvation from our selfishness.

232 The Word. 7. D.

PLUMA M. BROWN.

1. An - gel, tell us of the Word: Came it forth from God or man?
2. An - gel, is the Word a - lone Loved be-neath these out-ward skies?
3. An - gel, tell us of the Word, Thou its in - ner heart dost see?

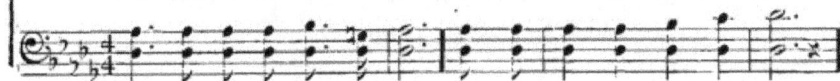

"Christian, it was with the Lord, Ere the earth or skies be - gan."
"Christian, round Im - man-uel's throne Seraphs in its truth are wise."
"Christian, it makes known the Lord In Di - vine Hu - man - i - ty.

An - gel, do its glor - ies shine In the worlds of space a - far?
An - gel, tell us, will its page In the fu - ture ere be furled?
Christian, 'tis a lamp of gold, Held in God the Sav- ior's hand,

"Christian, lo! its truths di -vine, Speed in light from star to star."
"Christian, lo! from age to age, 'Twill with noon-day fill the world."
Shin-ing o'er his earth-ly fold, Guid-ing to his in-most land."

233 Glory of the Word. C. M.

Warwick.—S. Stanley.

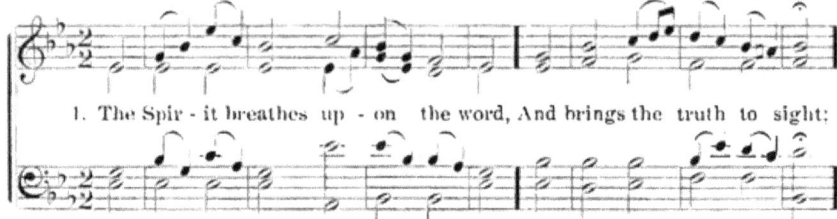

1. The Spir - it breathes up - on the word, And brings the truth to sight;

Pre-cepts and prom-is - es af - ford A sanc - ti - fy - ing light.

2 A glory gilds the sacred page,
　Majestic, like the sun;
　It gives a light to every age—
　It gives, but borrows none.

3 The hand that gave it still supplies
　The gracious light and heat;
　His truths upon the nations rise—
　They rise, but never set.

4 Let everlasting thanks be thine
　For such a bright display
As makes a world of darkness shine
　With beams of heavenly day.
Wm. Cowper.

234   Power of the Word.

1 Where'er the sacred Word unfolds
　Its page by day or night,
　An angel stands, and for us holds
　The lamp of God's own light.

2 There, while we read, our bosoms yearn
　For heavens of Love divine;
　And "thoughts that breathe, and words
　　　that burn,"
　Within us make their shrine.

3 Our faith, that was a barren tree,
　Now blooms like Aaron's rod:
　With it we smite the stormy sea,
　And journey safe with God.

235   The Law of God.

1 Oh, how I love thy holy law!
　'Tis daily my delight;
　And thence my meditations draw
　Divine advice by night.

2 How doth thy word my heart engage!
　How well employ my tongue!
　And in my tiresome pilgrimage
　Yields me a heavenly song.

3 Am I a stranger or at home,
　'Tis my perpetual feast;
　Not honey dropping from the comb
　So much allures the taste.

4 No treasures so enrich the mind,
　Nor shall thy word be sold
For loads of silver well refined,
　Nor heaps of choicest gold.
I. Watts.

236 The Gospel Feast. C. M.

Laight Street. — T. HASTINGS.

1. Let ev-'ry mor-tal ear at-tend, And ev - 'ry heart re-joice: The trumpet
of the gos-pel sounds With an in - vit-ing voice, With an in - vit-ing voice.

2 Ho! all ye hungry, starving souls,
That feed upon the wind:
And vainly strive with earthly toys
To fill an empty mind;

3 Eternal Wisdom hath prepared
A soul-reviving feast.
And bids your longing appetites
The rich provision taste.

4 Ho! ye that pant for living streams,
And pine away and die,
Here you may quench your raging thirst
With springs that never dry.

5 Rivers of love and mercy here
In a rich ocean join;
Salvation in abundance flows.
Like floods of milk and wine.

6 The happy gates of gospel grace
Stand open night and day:
Lord, we are come to seek supplies,
And drive our wants away.

I. WATTS.

237   The Word My Choice.

1 Lord. I have made thy word my choice.
My lasting heritage;

There shall my noblest powers rejoice.
My warmest thoughts engage.

2 I'll read the histories of thy love,
And keep thy laws in sight. .
While through the promises I rove
With ever fresh delight.

3 'Tis a broad land of wealth unknown,
Where springs of life arise;
Seeds of immortal bliss are sown.
And hidden glory lies.

I. WATTS.

238   Delight in the Word.

1 Father of mercies! in thy word
What endless glory shines!
Forever be thy name adored
For these celestial lines.

2 Here the Redeemer's welcome voice
Spreads heavenly peace around.
And life and everlasting joys
Attend the blissful sound.

3 Oh, may these heavenly pages be
My ever dear delight,
And still new beauties may I see,
And still increasing light.

ANNE STEELE.

239   Truth Words.   P. M.

IONE G. DANIELS,
PLUMA M. BROWN.

1. Sing the glo - ri - ous words of Truth O - ver a - gain to me,
2. Sing the words of e - ter - nal Life, Je - sus, the Christ, hath giv'n,
3. Words of Christ are the vi - tal pow'rs Mov-ing the world to - day:
4. Word and Spir - it u - nit - ed lead In - to the heav'n - ly mind;

Let the light of e - ter - nal youth Breathe in their ec - sta - cy.
Bring - ing har - mo - ny out of strife, Wed-ding the earth to heav'n.
Spo-ken, they fall in heal - ing show'rs O - ver earth's rug-ged way.
He who hun-gers shall sure - ly feed, He who search-es, find.

Words of health and beau - ty, Mak - ing joy of du - ty,—
While our lips are sing - ing, Words of Life are wing - ing,—
Words of love and heal - ing, Je - sus Christ re - veal - ing,—
Words of strength and pow - er, Meet for ev - 'ry hour.—

Glo - ri - ous words, beau - ti - ful words, Won - der-ful words of Truth!
Glo - ri - ous words, beau - ti - ful words, Won - der-ful words of Life!
Glo - ri - ous words, beau - ti - ful words, Won - der-ful words of Life!
Beau - ti - ful words, heav - en - ly words, Won - der-ful words of Life!

243 Out of the Silence. 8. 7. 6 l. English.

1. I am list-'ning, low - ly list-'ning For the still, small voice so dear:
I am list-'ning, low - ly list-'ning, That my heart and soul may hear
All the truth God is re-veal-ing To his chil-dren far and near.

2 Day by day I'm learning something
Of the purer, better way;
Day by day I grow in knowledge
Of the life, the truth, the way—
How to love, and help God's children
Realize that brighter day.

3 When the light of truth is shining
Through my mind and soul so clear;
When my intuition guides me,
And I know that God is here.—
Then no more can sorrow touch me;
Then is banished all my fear.
A. E. DENNING.

244 Prayer for Divine Knowledge.
(To be sung to first and last lines of music.)
Jesus Christ, thou only Savior!
Make us know thy Word aright:
All our inward strivings favor,
While we seek the better light.

2 To us give the priceless treasure
In its truth divine that lies:
Finding there thy holy pleasure;
Serving thee with angels wise.

3 Ope to us those burning pages
Which thy wondrous love record;
Show the providence of ages,
That mankind shall own thee Lord.

4 While the outer vail is riven,
Wrapt in wonder, may we see
Every truth of earth and heaven
Praising and adoring thee:

5 Till the spirit, through the letter,
Shines upon us like the sun,
Guiding us to know thee better;
And eternal life is won.
T. L. HARRIS.

245 The Living Word. P. M.

LILY A. LONG.
PLUMA M. BROWN.

1. Shin-ing tho'ts that ev - er hu-man speech have starred, Make the sa - cred
2. Down to ev - 'ry na - tion from the faith - ful past Comes the trust of
3. Ev - 'ry life lived no - bly, e - ven tho' un-known, Add - eth to the

scrip-tures that the a - ges guard; Be it word of proph - et,
add - ing new truth to the last, That the fu - ture's fee grow
scrip-ture gra - ven not on stone. Be it word or ac - tion,

be it song of bard, Ev - 'ry truth is Ho - ly Writ.
vast - er and more vast; Ev - 'ry truth is Ho - ly Writ.
be it tho't a - lone, Ev - 'ry truth is Ho - ly Writ.

REFRAIN.

Quick - ly dies the day, na - tions fade a - way. But the truth, made

man - i - fest, shall live for aye! With the light of Si - nai

The Living Word—Concluded.

each new morn is lit, Ev - 'ry truth is Ho - ly Writ.

246 The Inmost Word. L. M. 6 l.

Brownell.—Arr. fr. Haydn.

1. With-in the sa - cred scriptures shine The gra-ces of the Man Di - vine:

Whate'er the out - ward sense may be, The in-most word is De - i - ty:

So in the flow'r his Spir-it lives, And form and fragrance both he gives.

2 All is divine; with holy awe
We read that pure and perfect law;
Through its effulgent vails are given
The inmost truths of every heaven;
By it the heavenly sphere descends;
In it the heart with Jesus blends.

3 Like Jacob's ladder, we behold.
Upon its rounds of shining gold,
The guardian angels come and go.

Inspired with love for man below:
We clasp it. and, like Aaron's rod,
It blossoms from the life of God.

4 Book of the fathers! in its page
We find the ancient, golden age;
Once more we hear the songs they sung,
And speak the loved ancestral tongue,
Enjoy their states of peaceful mind,
And rest in Paradise enshrined.

T. L. Harris.

247   The Glory of the Gospel.   L. M.

All Saints. —WM. KNAPP.

1. Up - on the Gospel's sa - cred page The gathered beams of a - ges shine;

And, as it hast-ens, ev-'ry age But makes its brightness more di-vine.

2 On mightier wing. in loftier flight.
From year to year does knowledge
     soar;
And. as it soars, the Gospel light
Becomes effulgent more and more.

3 More glorious still, as centuries roll.
Now regions blest. new powers un-
     furled.
Expanding with the expanding soul.
Its radiance shall o'erflow the world.—

4 Flow to restore, but not destroy:
As when the cloudless lamp of day
Pours out its floods of light and joy.
And sweeps the lingering mist away.
              J. Bowring.

248   The Everlasting Word.

1 The starry firmament on high.
And all the glories of the sky,
Yet shine not to thy praise, O Lord.
So brightly as thy written word.

2 Almighty Lord. the sun shall fail,
The moon forget her nightly tale.
And deepest silence hush on high
The radiant chorus of the sky;

3 But, fixed for everlasting years,
Unmoved amid the wreck of spheres.
Thy word shall shine in cloudless day.
When heaven and earth have passed
     away.
              R. GRANT.

TUNE —*Ardita.* p. 157.

249   The Divine Love.

1 The brightness of thy glory,
    O Lord! is love alone;
The pure and sacred story
    Into our hearts hath grown.
Thro' all thy word's evangels,
    As in the heaven above.
More sweet than tongues of angels.
    We hear thy speech of love.

2 As, in the deeps of ocean.
    The stars reflected shine.
Our souls, in their devotion.
    Reflect thy love divine.
Thro' all thy word's evangels,
    As in the heaven above.
More sweet than tongues of angels,
    We hear thy speech of love.
              T. L. HARRIS.

250   The Will of God.   P. M.

MARIANNE FARNINGHAM.
PLUMA M. BROWN.

1. Thy will is to bring the sum - mer......... In - to the
2. Thy will is to make men ho - ly With the gift of
3. Thy will is to make men hap - py Thro' the loss of a
4. Thy will is to make men wealth - y With rich - es— a

hearts of men— The sing-ing of birds in morn - ing hours,
Christ to all— To ban - ish sin from the weep - ing earth,
load of care— To make the lives of the chil - dren glad,
store un - told— With love and gen - tle - ness, joy and peace,

The noon-tide glo - ry of myr - i - ad flow'rs, The heal - ing
And fill the cit - ies with sweet, true mirth, And make Love
To ban - ish ev - 'ry thought that's sad, To lift Hope's
And a plen-teous har - vest that shall not cease, Of the true heart's

beams, and the rip-pling streams And the E - den life a - gain.
king, till the world shall ring In joy - ous fes - ti - val.
light thro' the dark-est night, And to bring joy ev - 'ry-where.
good, and the dai - ly food Of love that is more than gold.

251 Thy Will be Done. P. M.

M. L. W. TOWLE.
PLUMA M. BROWN.

1. Why beg and plead for that which
2. Know you it is his will that
3. Know that to find the good with-

you will find, The ev - er - pres - ent good of heart and mind?
you shall stand Where naught but good re-sponds to your com-mand.
in your breast, A rec - og - nized and ev - er - pres-ent guest,

The king-dom is with-in you sweet and kind, Just as God wills;
And where you find on earth your "Beu-lah Land." Just now and here:
Is to be-come for aye su-preme-ly blest, Just as God wills;

The kingdom is with-in you sweet and kind, Just as God wills.
And where you find on earth your "Beu-lah Land." Just now and here.
Is to be-come for aye su-preme-ly blest, Just as God wills.

252   Thine Eyes shall See.   P. M.

Is. 33: 17.

Arr. fr. J. Barnby.

1. Thine eyes shall see! Yes, thine, who, blind ere - while,

Now trem - bling tow'rds the new - found light dost flee;

Leave doubting. and look up with trustful smile—Thine eyes—thine eyes shall see!

2 Thine eyes shall see! Not in some dream Elysian.
   Not in thy fancy, glowing though it be:
Not e'en in faith, but in unveiléd vision.
   Thine eyes—thine eyes shall see!

3 Thine eyes shall see! Not on thyself depend
   God's promises, the faithful, firm. and free:
Ere they shall fail, earth, heaven itself, must end:
   Thine eyes—thine eyes shall see!

4 Thine eyes shall see! Not in a swift glance cast.
   Gleaning one ray to brighten memory.
But while a glad eternity shall last,
   Thine eyes—thine eyes shall see!

FRANCES R. HAVERGAL.

If we will strive to be pure and true.
   To each of us there will come an hour
When the tree of life will burst into flower,
   And rain at our feet a glorious shower
Of something grander than ever we knew.

253 Faithful Promises. 6. 5. 0.

FRANCES R. HAVERGAL.
A. SULLIVAN.

1. Standing at the por-tal   Of the op'ning year.   Words of comfort meet us,
2. I, the Lord, am with thee, Be thou not a - fraid!   I will help and strengthen,
3. For the year be-fore us   Oh, what rich supplies!   For the poor and needy
4. He will nev - er fail us,   He will not for-sake: His e - ter-nal cov'nant

Hushing ev - 'ry   fear;   Spo-ken thro' the si-lence   By our Father's voice.
Be thou not dis - mayed!   Yea, I will up-hold thee With my own right hand:
Living streams shall rise;   For the sad and sin - ful   Shall his grace abound;
He will nev - er   break.   Rest-ing on his prom-ise, What have we to fear?

Ten-der, strong, and faithful, Making us re - joice.
Thou art called and chosen In my sight to stand.   } Onward then, and fear not,
For the faint and fee - ble Perfect strength be found. }
God   is all-suf - fi - cient For the coming year.

Ped.

Faithful Promises—Concluded.

Children of the day! For his word shall never, Never pass a - way.

254 All. P. M.

FRANCES R. HAVERGAL.
PLUMA M. BROWN.

1. God's re - it - er - a - ted "All!" O won - drous word
2. On - ly all his word be - lieve, All peace and joy
3. "All I have is thine," saith he. "All things are yours."
4. He shall all your need sup - ply. And he will make
5. All his work he shall ful - fill, All the good pleas-

of peace and pow'r! Touch - ing with its tune - ful fall
your heart shall fill, All things asked ye shall re - ceive;
he saith a - gain: All the prom - is - es for thee
all grace a - bound: Al - ways all - suf - fi - cien - cy
ure of his will. Keep - ing thee in all thy ways,

The ris - ing of each hid - den hour, All the day.
This is thy Fa - ther's word and will, For to - day.
Are sealed with Je - sus Christ's A - men. For to - day.
In him for all things shall be found. For to - day.
And with thee al - ways "all the days," And to - day.

255   Be Still.   P. M.

Mrs. S. M. I. Henry.
Pluma M. Brown.

1. Be still! just now be still! Some-thing thy soul hath nev-er heard,
2. Be still! just now be still! There comes a presence ver-y mild and sweet.

Some-thing unknown to an-y song of bird, Some-thing un-known to
White are the san-dals on his noise-less feet: It is the com-fort-

wind, or wave, or star. A mes-sage from the fa-ther-land a - far.
er, whom Je - sus sent To teach thee all the words he ut-tered meant:

That with sweet joy the homesick soul shall thrill. Com-eth to thee if
The waiting, will-ing spir-it he doth [Omit. . . . .

thou canst but be still.
. . . .] fill: If thou would hear his message, soul, be still!

256 God's Promises. H. M.   *Lischer.—F. Schneider.*

1. { The prom-is - es I sing. Which sov-'reign love hath spoke: }
{ Nor will th'e-ter-nal King His words of grace re-voke: } They

stand se - cure and stead-fast still: Not Zi - on's hill a-

bides so sure, Not Zi - on's hill a - bides so sure.

Not Zi - on's hill a - bides so sure.

2 The mountains melt away
  When once the Judge appears,
And sun and moon decay,
  That measure mortal years;
But still the same, | The promise shines
In radiant lines | Thro' all the flame.

3 Their harmony shall sound
  Through my attentive ears.
When thunders cleave the ground
  And dissipate the spheres;
Midst all the shock | I stand serene.
Of that dread scene. | Thy word my rock.
  P. DODDRIDGE.

257   *Promise of Harvest.*
1 Mark the soft-falling snow,
  And the descending rain!

To heaven, from whence it fell.
  It turns not back again:
But waters earth through every pore.
And calls forth all her secret store.

2 Arrayed in beauteous green
  The hills and valleys shine.
And man and beast are fed
  By Providence divine.
The harvest bows its golden ears.
The copious seed of future years.

3 "So," saith the God of Grace.
  "My gospel shall descend.
Almighty to effect
  The purpose I intend;
Millions of souls shall feel its power.
And bear it down to millions more."

258　A Song of To-day. P. M.

"All things are yours."—1 Cor. 3. 21.

MARY A. LATHBURY.
W. F. SHERWIN.

1. Sing pæ - ans o - ver the past! We bur - y the dead years
2. And hail, all hail to the new! The fu - ture lies like a
3. All things, all things are yours! The spoil of na-tions, the
4. A - rise and con-quer the land! Not one shall fail in the
5. The Lord shall sev - er the sea! And o - pen a way in the

ten - der - ly, To find them a - gain in e - ter - ni - ty, All
world new - born. All steeped in sun-shine and mists of morn. And
arts sub - lime That arch the a - ges from eld - est time, The
march of life; Not one shall fall in the hour of strife Who
wil - der - ness, To faith that fol - lows—to feet that press On

safe in its cir - cle vast. Sing pæ - ans o - ver the past!
arched with a cloud - less blue. All hail, all hail to the new!
Word that for aye en-dures.—All things, all things are yours!
trusts in the Lord's right hand. A - rise and con-quer the land!
in - to the great To - Be! The Lord shall sev - er the sea!

Used by arr. with J. H. Vincent, owner of copyright.

TUNE - *Emanuel.* p. 151.

259　*The Fullness of God.*

1 The fullness of his blessing now
Encompasseth our way;
The fullness of his promises
Crowns every brightening day.

2 The fullness of his glory bright
Is beaming from above.
While more and more we realize
The fullness of his love.

FRANCES R. HAVERGAL.

His word of promise is my food,
His Spirit is my guide;
Thus daily is my strength renewed.
And all my wants supplied.

260   Know Well, My Soul.   P. M.

J. G. WHITTIER.
PLUMA M. BROWN.

1. Know well, my soul, God's hand con-trols What-e'er thou fearest:
2. In life, in death, in dark and light, All are in God's care:
3. That cloud it - self which now be - fore thee Lies dark in view,
4. Lean-ing on him, make with rev-'rent meek-ness His own thy will;

Round him in calm-est mu - sic rolls What-e'er thou hearest:
Sound the black a - byss, pierce the deep of night, And he is there!
Shall with beams of light from the in - ner glo - ry Be strick-en thro';
And with strength from him shall thy ut - ter weakness Life's task ful - fill;

What to thee is shad-ow, to him is day, And the end he know-eth.
All which is real now re - main - eth, And fad - eth nev - er;
And like mead - ow mist thro' autumn's dawn, Up - roll - ing thin,
Then of what is to be, of what is done, Why que-riest thou?—

And not on a blind and aim-less way The Spir - it go - eth.
The hand which upholds it now, sus-tain-eth The soul for - ev - er.
Its thick - est folds when a - bout thee drawn, Let sun-light in.
The past and the time to be are one. And both are now.

261   My Appeal.   C. M.

Kenneth — Arr. fr. Beethoven.

1. Come, list - en to the words of Christ, Whose truth is peace and health:

Un - fold thy heart to things di - vine, Whose gifts are great - est wealth.

2 Bow down thine ear to love's sweet
    strain,
Sung through the life of him
Whose glory shines in lifting up
From sickness, weakness, sin.

3 No thought he gave to human kind
But thrills the world to-day;
Love's law the heavens must emulate,
Love's law man must obey.

4 For thee his blessings freely wait,
His faith, his truth, his might;
So lay aside earth's doubts and fears,
Receive his wondrous light.

5 No measure unto thee is given:
Seek, though thy strength is tried;
Make Christ thine own, thyself a Christ, —
Thou shalt be satisfied.

            CLARA E. CHOATE.

262   God Is My Strength.

1 I view the length of shining road,
Through heaven's Beulah land;
God is my strength, he holds me in
The hollow of his hand.

2 I hear his word, so small and still:
"Arise, and come to me,
For I have heard thee, and I will
Sustain and comfort thee.

3 "Thy Truth I am, thy Power, thy Might,
Thy Lord, thy God, thy All;
A Cloud, a Flame, by day, by night,
Thy Staff, — thou canst not fall."

            MRS. HIRSCHEIMER.

263   My Easy Yoke.

1 "My yoke upon thy neck I lay,
Its easy weight now bear,
And follow me; I am the Way,
If thou my peace wouldst share.

2 "Learn thou of me, for I am meek,
And I will give thee rest;
I am the Strength that thou didst seek;
Lean thou upon my breast.

3 "Wait on the Lord, thy strength renew;
Mount as on eagles' wing,
Till heaven's glories thou dost view,
Its wondrous anthems sing."

            MRS. HIRSCHEIMER.

264 Strength in Truth. C. M. *Emanuel.—S. Webbe.*

1. Far more than thou canst do for Truth Can she on thee con-fer,

If thou, O heart, but give thy youth And man-hood un - to her.

2 For she can make thee inly bright,
 Thy self-love purge away,
And lead thee in the path whose light
 Shines to the perfect day.

3 Who follow her, though men deride,
 In her strength shall be strong;
Shall see their shame become their pride,
 And share her triumph song!
  F. L. HOSMER.

265 Freedom of Thought.

1 God works for all. Ye cannot hem
 The hope of being free,
With parallels of latitude,
 With mountain range or sea.

2 Put golden padlocks on Truth's lips,
 Be callous as ye will,
From soul to soul o'er all the world,
 Leaps one electric thrill.
  J. R. LOWELL.

266 The Law of Love.

1 Make channels for the streams of love,
 Where they may broadly run;
And love has overflowing streams
 To fill them every one.

2 But if at any time we cease
 Such channels to provide,
The very founts of love for us
 Will soon be parched and dried.

3 For we must share, if we would keep
 That blessing from above;
Ceasing to give, we cease to have:—
 Such is the law of love.
  R. C. TRENCH.

267 Loyalty.

1 When courage fails, and faith burns low,
 And men are timid grown,
Hold fast thy loyalty and know
 That Truth still moveth on.

2 For unseen messengers she hath
 To work her will and ways,
And even human scorn and wrath
 God turneth to her praise.

3 She can both meek and lordly be,
 In heavenly might secure;
With her is pledge of victory,
 And patience to endure.

4 The race is not unto the swift,
 The battle to the strong,
When dawn her judgment-days that sift
 The claims of right and wrong.
  F. L. HOSMER.

268 Looking unto Jesus. 6. 5. D.

FRANCES R. HAVERGAL.
J. C. D. PARKER.

1. Look-ing un - to Je - sus! Bat - tle-shout of faith, Shield o'er all the
2. Look a - way to Je - sus, Look a - way from all: Then we need not
3. Look-ing un - to Je - sus, Wond'ringly we trace Heights of pow'r and

ar - mor, Free from scar or scathe. Stand-ard of sal -
stum - ble, Then we need not fall: From each snare that
glo - ry, Depths of love and grace. Vis - tas far un -

va - tion, In our hearts un - furled. Let its el - e -
lur - eth. Foe or phan - tom grim, Safe - ty this en -
fold - ing Ev - er stretch be - fore, As we gaze be -

REFRAIN.

va - tion O-ver-come the world!
sur - eth: Look a - way to him. } Lord, on thee de - pend - ing,
hold - ing Ev-er more and more. }

Now, con-tin-ual - ly, Heart and mind as-cend-ing, Let us dwell with thee.

269 Forward into Light. 6. 5. D.

H. ALFORD.
H. SMART.

1. Far o'er yon ho - ri - zon Rise the cit - y tow'rs Where our God a - bid - eth:
2. In - to God's high temple On-ward as we press, Beauty spreads a-round us,
3. Naught that cit-y need-eth Of these aisles of stone: Where the Godhead dwelleth,
4. To th' e-ter - nal Fa-ther Loud-est anthems raise: To the Son and Spir - it

That fair home is ours: Flash the streets with jas - per, Shine the gates with gold:
Born of ho - li - ness: Arch, and vault, and carv-ing, Lights of va - ried tone:
Tem - ple there is none: All the saints that ev - er In these courts have stood,
Ech - o songs of praise: To the Lord of Glo - ry Bless-ed Three in One.

Flows the gladd'ning river Shedding joys un - told: Thither, onward, thith-er.
Softened words and ho-ly, Prayer and praise a-lone: Ev-'ry thought up-rais-ing
Are but babes, and feeding On the children's food. On thro' sign and to - ken,
Be by men and an - gels End-less hon-or done. Weak are earthly prais-es,

In the Spir-it's might: Pilgrims to your coun - try, Forward in - to Light!
To our cit - y bright, Where the tribes as-sem-ble Round the throne of Light!
Stars a-midst the night; Forward thro' the dark-ness, Forward in - to Light!
Dull the songs of night: Forward in - to tri - umph, Forward in - to Light!

270 Everywhere and Evermore.   P. M.

EMMA E. MAREAN.
PLUMA M. BROWN.

1. O-ver all the prai-ries, rich with grow-ing corn. O-ver sand-y
2. Love, that holds the planets con-stant on their way, Guides the swal-low's
3. Fear and doubting van-ish, all the way seems plain; Hid-den mean-ings

marsh-es waste and bare,   O-ver wind-blown mountains, where the
flight to sun-ny skies,   Leads the na-tions up-ward to the
flash up-on our sight;   Tri-als turn to bless-ing, peace blooms

streams are born, Rule e-ter-nal right and lov-ing care.
per-fect day, Yet re-veals it-self in ba-by eyes.
out of pain, Love is one with u-ni-ver-sal Right.

REFRAIN. ALTO.   SOPRANO.

Ev-er, ever shall the right prevail! Nev-er, nev-er shall the promise fail:

Writ in wondrous letters on the sea and shore: Lo! the Truth shall reign forevermore.

271 The Coming of the Healer. C. M. D.

Spohr.—Arr. fr. Spohr.

1. O Ten-der One, O Might-y One, Who nev-er sent a-way

The sin-ner or the suf-fer-er, Thou art the same to-day!

FINE.

D. S.-To heal the mul-ti-tudes that come, Yea, "who-so-ev-er will!"

The same in love, the same in pow'r, And thou art wait-ing still,

D. S.

2 We know thee, blessed Savior, who
  "Hast filled us with good things;"
Thou has arisen on our land,
  With healing in thy wings;
Thou hast arisen on our hearts,
  With light and life divine;
Now bid us be thy messengers,
  Bid us "arise and shine!"

3 Oh, let thy Spirit fire our zeal,
  That we may now "send out,"
And tell that thou art come "in all
  The country round about—"
That thou art waiting now to heal,
  That thou art strong to save,
That thou hast spoilt the spoiler, Death,
  And triumphed o'er the grave.
                    FRANCES R. HAVERGAL.

272 The Voice of Jesus.

1 I heard the voice of Jesus say,—
  "Come unto me and rest;
Lay down, thou weary one, lay down
  Thy head upon my breast!"

I came to Jesus as I was,
  Weary, and worn, and sad;
I found in him a resting-place,
  And he hath made me glad.

2 I heard the voice of Jesus say,—
  "Behold, I freely give
The living water; thirsty one,
  Stoop down, and drink, and live!"
I came to Jesus, and I drank
  Of that life-giving stream;
My thirst was quenched, my soul revived,
  And now I live in him.

3 I heard the voice of Jesus say,—
  "I am this dark world's light:
Look unto me, thy morn shall rise,
  And all thy day be bright!"
I looked to Jesus, and I found
  In him my Star, my Sun;
And in that light of life I'll walk,
  Till all my journey's done.
                    H. BONAR

273 Leave the Shadow. 8. 7. 4.

Zion. —T. Hastings.

1. Leave be-hind earth's emp-ty pleas-ure, Fleet-ing hope and changeful love;
Leave its soon cor-rod-ing treas-ure: There are bet-ter things a-bove.

CHORUS.

Leave the dark-ness—Leave the shad-ow land be-hind:
En-ter in the Realms of glo-ry,— wel-come find.

2 Leave, oh, leave thy fond aspirings,
Bid the restless heart be still;
Cease, oh, cease thy vain desirings.
Only seek thy Father's will.—Cho.

3 Leave behind thy faithless sorrow.
And thine every anxious care;
Only he who knows the morrow
Can for thee its burden bear.—Cho.

274 Denial of Self.

1 Well for him who all things losing.
E'en himself doth count as naught.
Still the one thing needful choosing.
That with all true bliss is fraught!

Chorus.—‖: Well for him who
Walketh not in shadows vain.:‖

2 Well for him who nothing knoweth
But his God, whose boundless love
Makes the heart wherein it gloweth
Calm and pure as saints above!—Cho.

275 The Message.

1 Waiting. listening for the summons
To the task I am to do!
Watching for the first faint signal
To the path I must pursue.

Chorus.—‖: Hark, the message!
Listen to the still, sweet voice!:‖

2 Hark! the silent message cometh!
Listen to the still, sweet voice!
"Write of love. peace, faith and patience.
Bid all timid hearts rejoice. — Cho.

3 "Love that passeth understanding.
Pure, unchanging, free to all.
Love divine, and never failing—
Let it every heart enthrall.—Cho.

4 "Touch each spirit by its magic.
Let the answering key-notes thrill;
Banishing all fear and discord.—
Harmony controlling will."—Cho.

Mrs. C. B. Sawyer.

276 The Service that Gaineth All. 7. 6. D.

J. G. WHITTIER.
Ardita.—English.

1. Who counts his broth-er's wel - fare As sa - cred as his own,
2. No prayer for light or guid - ance Is lost up - on mine ear:

And loves, for-gives, and pit - ies, He serv - eth me a - lone.
The child's cry in the dark - ness Shall not the Fa - ther hear?

I note each gra-cious pur - pose, Each kind - ly word and deed;
My love all love ex - ceed - ing The heart must needs re - call;

Are ye not all my chil - dren? Shall not the Fa - ther heed?
Its self - sur - ren-d'ring free - dom, Its loss that gain - eth all.

277 *The Toilers.*

1 Ye constant, tireless toilers
   In every work of life,
With brain or hand unceasing,
   In peacefulness or strife;
With millions or with pennies,
   In high estate or low,
Know, loving eyes watch o'er you
   And see the way you go.

2 That piercing vision seeth
   Deep into every soul;
The unseen motive readeth
   Which secret thoughts control;
Be patient, O ye toilers!
   Look up, be not cast down;
Your loving Father weareth
   No fearful, angry frown.

C. B. SAWYER.

278 Coming. P. M.

EMMA E. MAREAN.
PLUMA M. BROWN.

1. There's a Hope that is fair-er than day, And it brightens the earth and the
2. There's a Faith that is tru-er than sight, And it leads us thro' pathways un-
3. There's a Love that is deeper than all, And it puls - es in life ev-'ry-

sky: We may scat - ter our seed by the way, For the har - vest will
known: Not a spar - row can fall in the night, Not a soul can be
where: Neith-er fail - ure nor loss can be-fall When we rest in the

come by and by. For we trust in the Lord,— For we trust in the Lord,—
lost from its own. For we trust in the Lord,— For we trust in the Lord,—
In - fi-nite care. For we live in the Lord.— For we live in the Lord,—

For we trust in the Lord, And his king-dom will come by and by.
For we trust in the Lord, And his king-dom will come by and by.
For we live in the Lord, And his king-dom will come by and by.

279 Battle-Hymn. P. M.   JULIA WARD HOWE.

1. Mine eyes have seen the glo - ry of the com - ing of the Lord: He is
2. He has sounded forth the trumpet that shall nev - er call re-treat; He is
3. In the beauty of the lil - ies, Christ was born a-cross the sea, With a

trampling out the vin-tage where the grapes of wrath are stored: He hath
sift - ing out the hearts of men be - fore his judgment-seat; Oh, be
glo - ry in his bos - om that trans-fig - ures you and me; As he

loosed the fateful lightning of his terrible, swift sword! His truth is marching on.
swift, my soul, to answer him! be ju - bi-lant, my feet! Our God is marching on.
lived to make men ho-ly, let us live to make men free, While God is marching on.

REFRAIN.

Glo - ry! glo-ry! Hal - le - lu - jah! Glo - ry! glo-ry! Hal-le - lu - jah!

Glo - ry! glo-ry! Hal - le - lu - jah! His truth is marching on.

280   **True Christianity.**   L. M. D.

C. L. HARRIS.
PLUMA M. BROWN.

DUET.

1. In vain the name of Christ we bear   Un-less the heart of Christ we   share;
2. In vain the name of Christ we bear   Un-less the cross of Christ we   share;

FINE.

Thro' faith and char-i - ty a - lone,   Is Christ received, and felt, and   known.
The path that leads us   to the   skies Demands love's perfect sac-ri - fice.

D.S.—Not words alone, but deeds shall prove The living faith that works by   love.
D.S.—That love that bids the dying   live, And whispers on the cross, "for - give."

D. S.

In vain the name of Christ we bear   Un-less the cross of Christ we share;
In vain the name of Christ we bear   Un-less the cross of Christ we share;

281   *Our Prayer.*

1 Be this our prayer; to love the good;
  To do the right; to seek the true;
  To keep eternally in view
The truth of human brotherhood;
To tread the paths the good have trod,
  In every age since time began;
  Our creed, the brotherhood of man,
Our faith, the Fatherhood of God.

282   *Christ Service.*

1 One cup of healing oil and wine.
One offering laid on mercy's shrine.
Is thrice more grateful. Lord, to thee,
Than lifted eye or bended knee.
In true and inward faith we trace
The source of every outward grace;
Within the loving heart it plays,
A living fount of joy and praise.

W. H. DRUMMOND

283 Climbing to Rest. L. M.
Wimborne.—Arr. ft. WHITAKER.

1. Still must I climb if I would rest; The bird soars upward to his nest: The young leaf on the tree-top high, Cra-dles it-self with-in the sky.

2 The streams that seem to hasten down.
Return in clouds, the hills to crown;
The plant arises from her root,
To rock aloft her flowers and fruit.

3 I cannot in the valley stay:
The great horizons stretch away!
The very cliffs that wall me round
Are ladders unto higher ground.

4 To work—to rest—for each a time;
I toil, but I must also climb:
No soul can ever be at ease
Shut in by earthly boundaries.

5 I am not glad till I have known
Life that can lift me from mine own:
A loftier level must be won,
A mightier strength to lean upon.

6 And heaven draws near as I ascend;
The breeze invites. the stars befriend:
All things are beckoning toward the Best;
I climb to thee, my God, for rest!
LUCY LARCOM.

284 In Lonely Vigil.
1 O thou in lonely vigil led
To follow Truth's new risen star

Ere yet her morning skies are red.
And vale and upland shadowed are,—

2 Gird up thy loins and take thy road.
Obedient to the vision be:
Trust not in numbers. God is God.
And one with him, majority!

3 Soon pass the judgments of the hour.
Forgotten are the scorn and blame:
The Word moves on. a gladdening power.
And safe enshrines the prophet's fame.

4 Now. as of old. in lowly plight
The Christ of larger faith is born:
The watching shepherds come by night,
And then—the kings of earth at morn!
F. L. HOSMER.

285 Thy Life-Work.
1 Be true to thy Redeeming Friend.
His voice to thine shall music lend:
His heart through thine shall say. "Be still!"
To every wave of human will.

2 Sweet mercy's pulse in thine shall beat,
And holy ends direct thy feet:
Till angels own thy work divine,
And see thy Savior's life in thine.

286 Our Watchword. 6. 5. D.

H. ALFORD.
St. Alban.—Arr. fr. HAYDN.

1. Forward! be our watchword, Steps and voices joined; Seek the things before us.
2. Forward! flock of Je - sus, Salt of all the earth, Till each yearning purpose
3. Glo - ries up - on glo - ries Hath our God prepared, By the souls that love him
4. Far o'er yon ho - ri - zon Rise the cit - y tow'rs, Where our God a - bid - eth:

Not a look be - hind: Burns the fier - y pil - lar At our ar - my's head:
Spring to glorious birth: Sick, they ask for heal - ing: Blind, they grope for day:
One day to be shared: Eye hath not be - held them, Ear hath nev - er heard:
That fair home is ours: Flash the streets with jas - per, Shine the gates with gold:

Who shall dream of shrinking, By our Captain led? Forward, out of er - ror.
Pour up - on the na - tions Wisdom's lov - ing ray. Forward, out of er - ror.
Nor of these hath uttered Thought or speech a word: Forward, marching east - ward
Flows the glad'ning river Shedding joys un - told: Thither, on - ward thith - er,

Leave behind the night: Forward thro' the dark - ness, For - ward in - to light!
Leave behind the night: Forward thro' the dark - ness, For - ward in - to light!
Where the heav'n is bright, Till the veil be lift - ed, Till our faith be sight!
In the Spir - it's might: Pilgrims to your coun - try. For - ward in - to light!

287 Onward. 6. 5. D.

SABINE BARING-GOULD.
A. SULLIVAN.

1. Onward, Christian soldiers! Marching as to war, With the cross of Je - sus
2. Like a might-y ar-my Moves the Church of God: Brothers, we are treading
3. Onward, then, ye peo-ple! Join our happy throng; Blend with ours your voices

Go - ing on be - fore. Christ, the roy - al Mas-ter, Leads a-gainst the foe:
Where the saints have trod: We are not di - vid - ed, All one bod - y we:
In the tri-umph-song: Glo - ry, laud, and hon - or Un-to Christ, the King:

REFRAIN.

For-ward in - to bat - tle. See, his ban-ners go! ⎤
One in hope and doc-trine, One in char - i - ty. ⎬ Onward, Christian soldiers!
This thro' countless a - ges Men and angels sing. ⎦

Marching as to war. With the cross of Je - sus Go - ing on be-fore.

288 **We March to Victory.** P. M.

G. MOULTRIE.
J. BARNBY.

We march, we march to vic - to - ry, With the cross of the Lord be - fore us,

With his lov - ing eye look - ing down from on high, And his

FINE.

ho - ly arm spread o'er us. His ho - ly arm spread o'er us.
His arm spread o'er us.

1. We come in the might of the Lord of light, With ar-mor bright, to meet him:
2. Our sword is the Spir - it of God on high; Our hel-met, his sal - va - tion:

And we put to flight the ar - mies of night, That the
Our ban - ner the cross of Cal - va - ry: Our

WORK.

165

We March to Victory—Concluded.

D. C.

sons of the day may greet him, The sons of the day may greet him.
watchword, the In - car - na - tion, Our watchword, the In - car - na - tion.

289 Holy Habits. 7. 5.

St. Piran.—E. J. Hopkins.

1. Slow - ly fash-ioned, link by link, Slow - ly wax - ing strong.

Till the spir - it nev - er shrink, Save from touch of wrong.

2 Holy habits are thy wealth,—
  Golden, pleasant chains.
Passing earth's prime blessing—health—
  Endless, priceless gains.

3 Holy habits give thee place
  With the noblest, best.—
All most Godlike of thy race.
  And with seraphs blest.

4 Holy habits are thy joy,—
  Wisdom's pleasant ways.
Yielding good without alloy,
  Lengthening, too, thy days.

5 Seek them, Christian, night and morn;
  Seek them noon and even:
Seek them till thy soul be born
  Without stains—in heaven.

T. Davis.

290   Unfurl the Standard.   C. M. D.

Ellacombe —St. Gall's Coll.

1. Un-furl the Chris-tian Standard now! Lift man-ful-ly on high,

And ral-ly where its shin-ing folds Wave out a-gainst the sky!

D.S.—Un-furl the Chris-tian Standard high, And fol-low with a cheer!

A-way with weak half-heart-ed-ness, With faith-less-ness and fear!

2 In God's own name we set it up,
   This banner brave and bright,
Uplifted for the cause of Christ,
   The cause of truth and right;
The cause that none can overthrow,
   The cause that must prevail,
Because the promise of the Lord
   Can never, never fail!

3 Unfurl the Christian Standard now
   With firm and fearless hands!
For no pale flag of compromise
   With error's legion bands,
And no faint-hearted flag of truce
   With mischief and with wrong,
Should lead the soldiers of the cross,
   The faithful and the strong.

4 Now, who is on the Lord's side, who?
   Come, throng his battle-field;
Be strong, and show that ye are men!
   Come forth with sword and shield!
The Lord of Hosts, in whom alone
   Our weakness shall be strong,
Shall lead us on to conquest with
   A mighty battle-song!

Frances R. Havergal.

291   *The Race for Glory.*

1 Awake, my soul, stretch every nerve,
   And press with vigor on;
A heavenly race demands thy zeal,
   And an immortal crown.
A cloud of witnesses around
   Hold thee in full survey;
Forget the steps already trod,
   And onward urge thy way.

2 'Tis God's all-animating voice
   That calls thee from on high;
'Tis his own hand presents the prize
   To thine aspiring eye:—
Blest Savior, introduced by thee,
   Have I my race begun;
And, crowned with victory, at thy feet
   I'll lay my honors down.

P. Doddridge.

292 The Mission of the Word. 7. 6. D.

W. C. GANNETT.
PLUMA M. BROWN.

1. It sounds a - long the a - ges, Soul an - swer - ing to soul;
2. From Si - nai's cliffs it ech - oed, It breathed from Buddha's tree,
3. It dates each new i - de - al,— It - self it knows not time:
4. It ev - 'ry-where ar - riv - eth: Recks not of small and great:

It kin - dles on the pa - ges, Of ev - 'ry bi - ble scroll;
It charmed in Ath - en's mar - ket, It gladdened Gal - i - lee:
Man's laws but catch the mu - sic Of its e - ter - nal chime;
It shapes the un - born at - - om, It tells the sun its fate:

The psalm - ists heard and sang it, From mar - tyr lips it broke.
The ham - mer-stroke of Luth - er, The pil - grim's sea - side pray'r,
It calls— and lo! new Just - ice; It speaks—and lo! new Truth;
The wing-beat of arch - an - gel It's boun - d'ry nev - er nears;

And proph - et tongues out - rang it, Till sleeping na - tions woke.
The or - a - cles of Con - cord, One ho - ly Word de - clare.
In ev - er no - bler stat - ure, And un - ex - haust-ed youth.
For - ev - er on it sound - eth The mu - sic of the spheres!

293   We should Hear the Angels.   8. 7. D.

French.

1. If we on - ly sought to bright-en   Ev-'ry path-way dark with care,
2. If we on - ly strove to cher - ish   Ev-'ry pure and ho - ly thought,
3. If it were our aim to pon - der   On the good that we might win,
4. If we on - ly did our du - ty, Thinking not what it might cost.

If we on - ly tried to light - en   All the bur-dens oth-ers bear:
Till with - in our hearts should per-ish   All that is with e - vil fraught:
Soon our feet would cease to wan - der   In for - bid - den paths of sin.
Then the earth would wear new beauty, Fair as that in E - den lost.

REFRAIN.

We should hear the an-gels sing - ing   All a-round us, day and night:

We should feel that they were wing-ing At our side their up-ward flight.

"If ye know these things, happy are ye if ye do them."—John 13; 17.

Beautiful hands are those that do
Work that is earnest, brave and true,
Moment by moment the long day through.

Beautiful feet are those that go
On kindliest ministries to and fro,
Down lowliest ways if God wills it so.

294 Whisper to the Hearts. 8. 7. D.

Middleton.—J. Arnold.

1. { Whis-per to the hearts in sor-row That so long have bowed in grief.—
{ That so long have yield-ed heav-en To the sin of wrong be - lief.—
D.C.—Who will give them joy for sor - row. And dis-pel their blighting fears.

That a Sav - ior reigns with-in them, Who will wipe a - way their tears.

2 He will fill their soul with gladness,
   If they but aspire to see
That sweet Spirit which sustains them,
   Which can set the captive free;
If they but unfold the petals
   Of their soul to heaven's light,
Which will nourish them to Christhood,
   And reclaim them from the night.

3 Sweeter than the breath of roses,
   Brighter than the noon-day sun,
Purer than the sparkling brooklets
   That below the mountains run,
Stronger than the Alpine torrents
   That beyond the mountains roll,
Softer than the flush of dawning,
   Is the Universal Soul.
                                L. H. H.

295 *Draw We Nearer Thee.*

1 Are we daily drawing nearer
   Thee, the Perfect, the Unseen?
Grows the pathway ever clearer,
   Stretching sense and God between?

Thine own messengers within us
   Wait, wherever we may be;
Earth and heaven are met to guide us
   Ever nearer unto thee.

2 In the web of beauty's weaving,
   In the picture and the song;
In our dreaming and believing,
   By our friendships borne along;
By our own hearts' human story,
   By the light on land and sea,
Glimpsing unimagined glory,
   Draw we ever nearer thee.

3 Brother hastening unto brother,
   Youth rewakening in our eyes,
Loving thee and one another,
   Find we our lost Paradise.
Where the heart is, there the treasure;
   Led by paths we cannot see
Unto heights no guess can measure,
   Draw we ever nearer thee!
                                LUCY LARCOM.

296 Awake! Arise! Away! P. M.

PLUMA M. BROWN.

1. A-wake! Awake! Put on thy strength! Thy Light has come to thee at length.
2. A-rise! A-rise! Stand in thy strength! Thy Life has come to thee at length.
3. A-way! A-way! Go forth in strength! Thy Lord has come to thee at length.

His ra-diance on thy brow doth shine: In slumbers thou shouldst not recline:
He comes with help to slay thy foes, And thou shouldst not at ease re-pose:
He bids thee bear the tidings grand All o-ver our be-lov-ed land:

A - wake! behold the glow divine. Awake! Awake! And all his brightness
A - rise! and in his might oppose. A-rise! A-rise! The vict'ry win ere
A - way! no lon-ger i-dle stand. A-way! A-way! The harvest white a-
                                        Awake!   Awake!

shall be thine.   Awake!   Awake!   And all his brightness shall be thine.
day shall close.   A-rise!   A-rise!   The vict'ry win ere day shall close.
waits thy hand.   A-way!   A-way!   The harvest white awaits thy hand.
                Awake!   Awake!

297 Drawing Nearer. 8. 7. D.

LUCY LARCOM.
D. BORTINANSKI.

1. With the foot-steps of the a - ges, We are draw-ing near-er thee:
2. O - ver fall - en tow'rs of er - ror, Laid by our own hands in dust:
3. Vain a se - cret hoard to car - ry From our ru - ined house of pride:
4. Dog - mas in - to truth trans-mut-ing, Fus - ing dif-f'ren-ces in love:

Beau - ti - ful up - on Time's pa - ges Will our name and rec - ord be.
Past the ghosts of doubt and ter - ror, Out of sloth's in - eat - ing rust.
Weights that hin - der, fiends that har - ry, Are the i - dols that we hide.
Creed and rite no more dis - put - ing, Clos-ing rank and file we move.

Year on year of wor-thier liv-ing, Add we to life's glo-rious sum;
From Go - mor -rah's lur - id smold'ring, Bor - ders of the drear Dead Sea;
Draw us rath - er by the sweet-ness Of thy breath in liv - ing things:
Leav-ing our dead past be - hind us, Turn-ing not, nor look - ing back:

Through our striv-ing, thy love-giv-ing, Lord, thy bless - ed king-dom come.
Graves where self - ish loves lie mold'ring, Fly we ev - er un - to thee.
To thy - self with un-clogged fleetness, Lift - ed, as on an - gel wings.
May no way-side glim - mer blind us To the one straight narrow track.

298   I Obey.   P. M.

ISABELLA G. GOULD.
PLUMA M. BROWN.

1. Speak! Lord, for thy serv-ant hear-eth. Glad-ly I o-bey:
2. As the Mas-ter, meek and low-ly, Min-is-t'ring to all.
3. In the si-lence wait-ing, list-'ning, For the "still small voice,"

Go I forth as one that serv-eth. Gird-ed thus al-way.
With a pur-pose high and ho-ly, Heed-ing Je-sus' call.
Seek-ing on-ly for its teach-ing, Thus will I re-joice.

REFRAIN.

"Go ye," in my name de-clar-ing God, the on-ly Good:

Won-drous love, its rich un-fold-ings Scarce-ly un-der-stood!

299   *Speak the Word.*

1 I've been longing that the shadows
    All might pass away.
Deeming not that I could send them
    Speeding on their way.
"Now, I bid you go, my children,
    You whom I have made!
Give your place to heaven-born treas-
    ures
That can cast no shade."

2 What are these, my new-found bless-
    ings?
Strength, and joy, and love:
Peace and rest in simply doing
    The sweet will of God.
"All my longing, my repining,
    Lord, I yield to thee."
Lo! my sun is brightly shining,
    All my shadows flee!

ELLEN M. DYER.

300 A Message. P. M. PLUMA M. BROWN.

1. If you have a task to do.   Let me whisper now to you,
2. If you have an-y-thing to love.   As a blessing from a-bove,
3. If you know what torch to light.   Guid-ing oth-ers thro' the night,
4. If you have an-y grief to meet.   At the lov-ing Fa-ther's feet,
5. Whether life is bright or drear.   There's a mes-sage sweet and clear,

Do it.   If you have an-y-thing to say,   True and need-ed,
Love it.   If you have an-y-thing to give,   That an-oth-er's
Light it.   If you have an-y debt to pay,   Rest you nei-ther
Meet it.   If you are giv-en light to see   What a child of
[Omit

D. C.

yea or nay,   Say it.
joy may live,   Give it.
night nor day,   Pay it.
God should be,   See it.   *Last verse only.*
] Whispered down to ev'ry ear,   Hear it.

TUNE—*I Obey.*

301   Love Makes Life.

1 Not a life so mean or lowly
    But, if love is there,
  Both ingrowing and outflowing,
    May be strong and fair.

CHORUS.—
    Love for every unloved creature,
        Lonely, poor or small;
    Christ was born to show how truly
    Love makes life for all.

2 Not a life so high in station
    But, without love's breath—

Neither giving nor receiving—
    Is a living death.

3 Love by love alone is ripened;
    Hearts through it grow true;
  Life is bounded, filled and rounded,
    By its power to do.

4 Having love, be sure to give it;
    Give it, having not;
  For in living through our giving
    Share we Christ's own lot.
ELLEN T. LEONARD.

302 Seed-Sowing. S. M.

Haydn.—Arr. fr. Haydn.

1. Sow in the morn thy seed: At eve hold not thy hand:

To doubt and fear give thou no heed, Broad - cast it o'er the land.

2 Beside all waters sow,
 The highway furrows stock:
Drop it where thorns and thistles grow,
 Scatter it on the rock.

3 The good, the fruitful ground,
 Not only here and there,
O'er hill and dale it may be found:
 Expect it everywhere.

4 Thou know'st not which shall thrive,
 The late or early sown;
Grace keeps the precious germ alive,
 When and wherever strown:

5 And duly shall appear,
 In verdure, beauty, strength,
The tender blade, the stalk, the ear,
 And the full corn at length.

6 Thou canst not toil in vain:
 Cold, heat, and moist, and dry,
Shall foster and mature the grain
 For garners in the sky.

    J. Montgomery.

303 *"Commit all thy ways unto the Lord."*

1 Commit thou all thy griefs
 And ways into his hands,
To his sure truth and tender care,
 Who earth and heaven commands;

2 Who points the clouds their course,
 Whom winds and seas obey,
He shall direct thy wandering feet,
 He shall prepare thy way.

3 Thou on the Lord rely,
 So safe shalt thou go on:
Fix on his work thy steadfast eye,
 So shall thy work be done.

4 No profit canst thou gain
 By self-consuming care:
To him commend thy cause: his ear
 Attends the softest prayer.

5 Leave to his sovereign sway
 To choose and to command,
So shalt thou wondering own his way,
 How wise, how strong his hand.

    Tr. by J. Wesley.

304 The Armor of God. S. M.   *Laban.*—L. MASON.

1. Sol-diers of Christ, a-rise, And put your ar-mor on: Strong in the strength which God sup-plies Thro' his e-ter-nal Son:

2 Strong in the Lord of hosts,
And in his mighty power,
Who in the strength of Christ shall trust,
Is more than conqueror.

3 Stand, then, in his great might,
With all his strength endued;
But take, to arm you for the fight,
The panoply of God:

4 That, having all things done,
And all your conflicts passed,
Ye may o'ercome through Christ alone,
And stand entire at last.

5 Leave no unguarded place,
No weakness of the soul;
Take every virtue, every grace,
And fortify the whole:

6 Indissolubly joined,
To battle all proceed;
But arm yourselves with all the mind
That was in Christ, your Head.
C. WESLEY.

305   All Work Divine.
1 Teach me, my God and King,
Thy will in all to see;
And what I do in anything
To do it as for thee;

2 To scorn the senses' sway,
While still to thee I tend;
In all I do be thou the way,
In all, be thou the end.

3 All may of thee partake:
Nothing so small can be
But draws, when acted for thy sake,
Greatness and worth from thee.

4 If done beneath thy laws,
E'en servile labors shine,
Hallowed is toil if this the cause;
The meanest work, divine.
C. WESLEY.

306   Let Us Go.
1 Come, brothers, let us go!
Our Father is our guide;
And be the way or bright or dark,
He journeys at our side.

2 The strong be quick to raise
The weaker, when they fall;
In love, and peace, and quiet go:
God's blessing keep us all!
Tr. fr. the German.

307 Lantern Lights. P. M.

CARRIE E. HALL.
PLUMA M. BROWN.

1. Let your light shine out, O Chris-tian, Do not fear to let the ray
2. Tho' the dis-tance may be short-ened That the trembling beam may thread,
3. Your own path will be the bright-er That you helped your friends in this:

Send a gleam of daz-zling brightness Thro' the dark-ness of the way.
Yet 'twill light the step be-fore thee.—Just the step you need to tread.
Guid-ed them in-to the shin-ing Of the Sun of Right-eous-ness:

Lan-tern-like 'twill pierce the shad-ows, Gold-en cir-cles round you throw,
And tho' small the space il-lum-ined, Yet, with-in its kind-ly glow,
Led the way to God's own cit-y, Where, with all the dark-ness riv'n,

Chase the gloom from off the path-way, Help you as you on-ward go.
Many a friend it may en-cir-cle, And to them the path-way show.
You have, with your friend, re-joic-ing, Come with-in the gates of heav'n.

Lantern Lights—Concluded.

REFRAIN.

Let your light so shine be - fore men, Let your light so shine be-fore men

that they may see your good works, and glorify your Father which is in heav'n.

308 The Lamp of Truth. S. M. *Silver Street.—I. Smith.*

1. Spir - it of man, a - wake! The bridegroom comes to-day; The vir - gin

lamp is shin - ing bright That lights the trav - ler's way.

2 The rays dispel the gloom,
   And show on what to tread;
The power of good, the truth, destroys,
   Where else the evil led.

3 Go preach the tidings glad,
   And works will follow thee;

As on thy way the spoken word
   Shall set the bondman free.

4 Lo, Light! the signal proofs
   Of truth, the restless world
Shall know, as free the suffering ones
   Thy way rejoicing go.

SARAH WILDER PRATT.

309   Work On, My Soul.   L. M.

Alsace — Arr. fr. Beethoven.

1. Work on, my soul, with voice and hand; Proclaim the truth thro' all the land,

Reach out to all with kind-er word; Let love in all thy tones be heard.

2 Hope on, my soul! all good is thine:
All strength is given, all power divine,
All wisdom, too, and happiness,
To shape thy life in true wholeness.

3 Trust on, my soul, in truth and love,
And life, which comes down from above.
The source is God; thro' us below
His words of love and healing flow.

4 Love on, my soul! give love divine
To all mankind in every clime.
Thy tho'ts have wings like those of dove,
And everywhere bring peace and love.
FELSON HISCOCK.

310   Life's Work.

1 It matters not so very much
Where the great work of life begins,
If only love shall lead the way,
Since love's grand law forever wins.

2 To follow up the high desire,
Nor falter by the wayside lone,
Truth's clear conviction guides aright;
Divinest gift true souls must own.

3 Truth's royalty will clothe with power
The soul's most pure, sublime ideal:
Earth will defend, and heaven will guard
Love's mightiest guest, the true, the
real.

4 Firm trust and patience oft renew
Their vigil watch for truth and right;
That life's immortal work may move
In love's full measure of God's light.

5 True love must underlie all work,
Must over-ride all doubt and fear;
Life's inspiration must be truth, [near.
Life's conquest gained when love is
CLARA E. CHOATE.

311   The Soul's Progress.

1 Awake, my soul, to higher thought!
The things of Truth cannot be bought;
That which is real comes rich and free,
If we but lift our souls to see.

2 Arise, my soul! cast off thy gloom;
There is no night, there is no tomb;
For all is light, and all is life,
And all is endless joy, not strife.

3 Stand up, my soul! thy birthright
claim;
A child of God, behold thy name!
Behind thee stands Omnipotence,
Who works thro' thee; arise, go hence!

4 Go forth, my soul, to nobler deed;
Along the path of duty speed;
For beautiful the feet of those
Which tidings good doth bring to foes.
ELINOR HISCOCK.

312 The Constant Pentecost. 7. 6 l.

Rock of Ages.—T. HASTINGS.

FINE.

1. Lord! thy church hath nev - er lost Fier - y tongues óf Pen - te - cost.
D.C.—Heart.and mind, and life may be Lit with fires of char - i - ty.

D. C.

Faith that works by love may claim Ev - er thy in - spir - ing flame:

2 All that holy angels feel,
  Through believing hearts may steal,
  Melting, with a sweet accord,
  All our being in the Lord;
  Till in mercy's path we move,
  Burning with the Savior's love.

3 May we all, from day to day,
  Follow thee, who art the way,
  Wresting from despair's embrace
  Brethren of our human race,
  Pouring in the oil and wine
  Of a Savior's love divine.

T. L. HARRIS.

313 *Following Christ.*

1 If thou wouldst like Jesus be,
    Shrine his image in the mind;
  Seek the inward harmony
    Of a soul from sense refined.

REFRAIN.—Journey eastward to the sun
    Till eternal life be won.

2 With a meek, heroic grace,
    Serving all thy fellow-men;
  His divinest pathway trace,
    For it leads to God again. —REF.

The Soul's Progress. L. M.

Panis Cœli.—J. BARNBY.

1. A-wake, my soul, to high-er tho't! The things of Truth can-not be bought:

That which is real comes rich and free, If we but lift our souls to see.

314   A Temple of Deeds.   L. M.

Loury.—J. E. SWEETSER.

1. Pour out thy inmost love like wine, If thou wouldst rise to life di-vine;

And let thy Sav-ior in thee plan, If thou wouldst be the Chris-tian man.

2 Tho' temples fall, and creeds decay,
Build faith and worship in the day;
Until thy deeds around thee stand,
Like angels at the Lord's right hand.

3 Work with a calm and patient trust;
Virtue shall blossom from the dust;
Her pyramid of toil shall be
A land-mark to eternity.
      T. L. HARRIS.

315   Long Life.

1 He liveth long who liveth well!
All else is life but thrown away:
He liveth longest who can tell
Of true things truly done each day.

2 Sow love, and taste its fruitage pure;
Sow peace, and reap its harvest bright;
Sow sunbeams on the rock and moor,
And find a harvest-home of light.
      H. BONAR.

"The present hour allots thy task;
For present strength and patience ask,
And trust his love whose sure supplies
Meet all thy needs as they arise."
      WM. H. BURLEIGH.

316   Following in Christ's Footsteps.

1 When, like a stranger on our sphere,
The lowly Jesus wandered here,
Where'er he went, affliction fled,
And sickness reared her fainting head.

2 The eye that rolled in irksome night,
Beheld his face,—for God is light;
The opening ear, the loosened tongue,
His precepts heard, his praises sung.

3 With bounding steps the halt and lame
To hail their great Deliverer came;
O'er the cold grave he bowed his head,
He spake the word, and raised the dead.

4 Despairing madness, dark and wild,
In his inspiring presence smiled;
The storm of horror ceased to roll,
And reason lightened through the soul.

5 Thro' paths of loving-kindness led,
Where Jesus triumphed we would tread;
To all, with willing hands dispense
The gifts of our benevolence.
      J. MONTGOMERY.

317 The Seed. L. M.   Jones.—Arr. fr. Mozart.

1. Now is the seed-time: God a - lone, Be-yond our vi-sion weak and dim.

Be-holds the end of what is sown: The har-vest time is hid with him.

2 Yet unforgotten where it lies,
Tho' seeming on the desert cast,
The seed of generous sacrifice
Shall rise with bloom and fruit, at last.

3 And he who blesses most is blest;
For God and man shall own his worth
Who toils to leave as his bequest
An added beauty to the earth.
J. G. WHITTIER.

318 Servants of Freedom.

1 Know, where our duty's task is wro't
In unison with God's great thought,
The near and future blend in one,
And whatsoe'er is willed is done!

2 Who calls the glorious labor hard?
Who deems it not its own reward?
Who, for its trials, counts it less
A cause of praise and thankfulness?

3 Be ours the grateful service whence
Comes day by day the recompense,—
The hope, the trust, the purpose stayed,
The fountain and the noon-day shade!
J. G. WHITTIER.

319 Our Armor.

1 Behold the Christian warrior stand
In all the armor of his God:
The Spirit's sword is in his hand:
His feet are with the gospel shod;

2 In panoply of truth complete,
Salvation's helmet on his head;
With righteousness a breast-plate meet,
And faith's broad shield before him
spread.

3 Undaunted to the field he goes:
Yet vain were skill and valor there,
Unless, to foil his seeming foes,
He takes the trustiest weapon, prayer.
J. MONTGOMERY.

320 The Christian's Cross.

1 From every cross of conquered pain,
A clearer view of heaven we gain:
How thrills the breast with holy fires!
What boundless love the heart inspires!

2 Our hearts embrace the inward cross,—
The fire that burns our being's dross:
By love we pass the golden gates
That ope to pure, celestial states.

321   Awake! Awake!   C. M.

Groton.—H. C. Zeuner

1. A-wake! a-wake! ye souls, a-wake! The hour has come at last;
The morning hour, when light doth break, Thro' a-ges o - ver-cast.

2 Arise, and cast aside the chains,
  The burdens that ye bear;
Remember that Jehovah reigns,
  And worship without fear.

3 Arise! go forth on mountain-peak,
  Away from church and spire,
There ye shall find the God ye seek,
  The truth that ye desire.

4 Come, train thy thoughts in purity,
  And cultivate thy will;
Oh! cast aside these bonds of clay,
  Bid carnal thoughts be still.

5 Seek God alone, and ye shall find
  Truths that to few are given;
Teach them with care and love combined,
  And make this earth as heaven.

McCARDELL.

322   The Healer.
TUNE—*Guide.*

1 So stood of old the holy Christ,
  Amidst the suffering throng;
With whom his lightest touch sufficed
  To make the weakest strong.

2 That healing gift is also theirs
  Who use it in his name;
The power that filled his garment's hem
  Is evermore the same.

3 For lo! in human hearts unseen,
  The Healer dwelleth still,
And they who make his temples clean,
  The best subserve his will.

4 The holiest task by heaven decreed,
  An errand all divine,
The burden of our common need
  To render less is thine.

5 So shalt thou be with power endued
  From him who went about
The Syrian hillsides doing good,
  And casting demons out.

6 That Good Physician liveth yet
  Thy friend and guide to be;
The Healer by Gennesaret
  Shall walk the rounds with thee.

J. G. WHITTIER.

323 The True Service. C. M.

Guide.—Arr. fr. Schubert.

1. Our Friend, our Brother, and our Lord, What may thy serv - ice be?

Nor name, nor form, nor rit - ual word, But sim - ply foll'wing thee.

2 Thy litanies, sweet offices
  Of love and gratitude;
Thy sacramental liturgies,
  The joy of doing good.

3 In vain shall waves of incense drift
  The vaulted nave around,
In vain the minster turret lift
  Its brazen weights of sound.

4 The heart must ring thy Christmas bells,
  Thy inward altars raise;
Its faith and hope thy canticles,
  And its obedience praise!
                        J. G. WHITTIER.

324 *More Reapers.*

1 Oh, still in accents sweet and strong
  Sounds forth the ancient word,
"More reapers for white harvest fields,
  More laborers for the Lord!"

2 We hear the call; in dreams no more
  In selfish ease we lie,
But, girded for our Father's work
  Go forth beneath his sky.

3 Where prophets' word, and martyrs'
    blood,
  And prayers of saints were sown,
We, to their labors entering in,
  Would reap where they have strown.
                        S. LONGFELLOW.

325 *No Work is Fruitless.*

1 Scorn not the slightest word or deed,
  Nor deem it void of power;
There's fruit in each wind-wafted seed,
  That waits its natal hour.

2 A whispered word may touch the heart,
  And call it back to life,
A look of love bid sin depart,
  And still unholy strife.

3 No act falls fruitless; none can tell
  How vast its power may be,
Nor what results infolded dwell
  Within it silently.

4 Work on, despair not, bring thy mite,
  Nor care how small it be;
God is with all that serve the right,
  The holy, true, and free.

326 Where shall I Sow My Seed? 8. 7.

Arr. fr. Mendelssohn.

1. "An-gel of the spring-time," said she, "Show me where to sow my grain:

Shall I plant it round my door-step, Or a-far there on the plain?"

2 "At thy feet!" the angel answered;
"Sow at once thy nearest field;
First thy dooryard, then beyond it;
Let new fields new furrows yield.

3 "Fill the nearest spot with gladness,
Fill thy home with goodness sweet;
Wider fields shall ask thy sowing,
If thou first sow at thy feet.

4 "Thus for thee shall widening harvests
Wave their manifolding grain,
Till the sixty-fold, the hundred,
Gild the door-yard and the plain."

327 Cast Thy Bread.

1 Cast thy bread upon the waters,
Thinking not 'tis thrown away;
God himself saith, thou shalt gather
It again some future day.

2 Cast thy bread upon the waters,
Wildly though the billows roll;
They but aid thee as thou toilest
Truth to spread from pole to pole.

3 Cast thy bread upon the waters;
Why wilt thou still doubting stand?
Bounteous shall God send the harvest,
If thou sow'st with liberal hand.

4 Give, then, freely of thy substance—
O'er this cause the Lord doth reign;
Cast thy bread, and toil with patience,
Thou shalt labor not in vain.
Mrs. P. A. Hannaford.

Tune—Innocents. p. 187.

328 True Freedom.

1 Justice in forgiveness lies,
Riches in self-sacrifice:
Own no rank but God's own Spirit,
Wisdom rule, and worth inherit.

2 Work for all and all employ;
Share with all and all enjoy;
God alike to all has given,
Heaven as earth and earth as heaven.
C. Kingsley.

Tune—Schumann. p. 199.

329 Teach Me, My God.

1 Teach me, my God and King,
In all things thee to see,
And what I do in anything,
To do it as of thee.

2 This is the famous stone
That turneth all to gold;
For that which God doth touch and own
Cannot for less be told.
G. Herbert.

330 Sow Thy Seed. 8. 7.
Worthing. — Arr. fr. Schulz.

1. Sow thy seed with gen-tle fin-gers; Love and mer-cy— let them lie
As the wheat germ in the meadow Waits the har-vest by and by.

2 Never fear! The soil lies hidden
Deep within the rocky pass;
Oft across the bristling ledges
Has there peeped a blade of grass.

3 If the birds should take thy treasures,
Do not count it loss or wrong,
For some tiny breast they nourish
That shall gladden thee with song.

4 Even should the rough winds scatter
Seeds that fall from out thy hand;
Even should relentless footsteps
Crush them idly in the sand.

5 Sow thy seed with gentle fingers;
Love and mercy—let them lie
As the wheat germ in the meadow
Waits the harvest by and by.
Tr. by CHARLOTTE H. COURSEN.

331 Be Never Weary.
1 Sow thy seed, be never weary,
Let no fears thy soul annoy;
Be the prospect ne'er so dreary.
Thou shalt reap the fruits of joy.

2 Soft descend the dews of heaven,
Bright the rays celestial shine;
Precious fruits will thus be given
Through an influence all divine.

3 Lo! the scene of verdure brightening,
See the rising grain appear;
Look again; the fields are whitening,
For the harvest time is near.

332 Psalm of Life.
1 Life is real! life is earnest!
And the grave is not its goal:
Dust thou art, to dust returnest,
Was not spoken of the soul.

2 Not enjoyment, and not sorrow
Is our destined end and way:
But to act that each to-morrow
Find us further than to-day.

3 Let us, then, be up and doing,
With a heart for any fate:
Still achieving, still pursuing,
Learn to labor, and to wait.
H. W. LONGFELLOW.

333   Thou Who art Strong to Heal.   6. 4.   *Tiroli.*—Wm. F. Sherwin.

Written for Rush Medical College.

1. O Fount of Be - ing's sea   For - ev - er   flow - ing free,

The One in all,— Thou whom no   eye e'er saw,   In - dwell-ing

Love and Law, To   thee we sup-pliant draw,   On   thee we   call.

Used by per. of Mrs. Wm. F. Sherwin.

2 Be consecrate to truth
In manhood as in youth,
    Our growing powers;
That we may read thy thought,
Nature and Life inwrought,
Thy perfect will be taught,
    And make it ours!

3 Thine image may we own
In man, creation's crown,
    These temples thine:
Holy our calling be,

From bonds of pain to free,
And bring the liberty
    Of life divine!

4 Thy presence still abide
Within these walls to guide,
    Inspire and bless;
Thou who art strong to heal,
The Christ-like touch reveal,
And in each spirit seal
    Thy tenderness.

                 F. L. Hosmer.

Tune—*Missionary Chant.* p. 191.

334   *In All the World.*

1 Behold! the heathen waits to know
The joy the gospel will bestow;
The exiled captive, to receive
The freedom Jesus has to give.

2 Speak, and the world shall hear thy
          voice:
Speak, and the desert shall rejoice:

Dispel the gloom of heathen night;
Bid every nation hail the light.

3 Where'er his hand hath spread the
          skies,
Sweet incense to his name shall rise;
And slave and freeman, Greek and Jew,
By sovereign grace be formed anew.

                 Mrs. Vokes.

335 Out of Self. 7.

Innocents.—Arr. by W. H. Monk.

1. What thou wilt, O Fa-ther, give! All is gain that I re-ceive:

Let the low-liest task be mine, Grate-ful, so the work be thine.

2 Let me find the humblest place
In the shadow of thy grace:
Let me find in thine employ
Peace that dearer is than joy.

3 Out of self to love be led,
And to heaven acclimated,
Until all things sweet and good
Seem my natural habitude.
J. G. Whittier.

336 *Loyalty to Christ.*

1 Now, like heaven's angelic bands,
Waiting for thine high commands,
All my powers shall wait on thee,
Captive, yet divinely free.

2 At thy word my will shall bow,
Judgment, reason, bending low;
Hope, desire, and every thought,
Into glad obedience brought.

3 Zeal shall haste on eager wing,
Hourly some new gift to bring;
Wisdom, humbly casting down
At thy feet her golden crown.
W. A. Muhlenberg.

Tune—*Guide.* p. 183.

337 *From Generation to Generation.*

1 O Light, from age to age the same,
Forever living Word,—
Here we have felt thy kindling flame,
Thy voice within have heard.

2 What visions rise above the years,
What tender memories throng,
Till the eye fills with happy tears,
The heart with grateful song!

3 Vanish the mists of time and sense;
They come, the loved of yore,
And one encircling Providence
Holds all forevermore.

4 Oh, not in vain their toil who wrought
To build faith's freer shrine,—
Nor theirs whose steadfast love and tho't
Have watched the fire divine.

5 Burn, holy fire, and shine more wide!
While systems rise and fall,
Faith, hope, and charity abide,
The heart and soul of all.
F. L. Hosmer.

338 Send Out the Sunlight. P. M.

ELLA DARE.
PLUMA M. BROWN.

1. Send out the sun-light, the sun-light of cheer, Shine on earth's sad-
2. Send out the sun-light, on rich and on poor, All need the sun-

ness till ills dis-ap-pear; Send out the sun-light in
light to strength-en and cure. Send out the sun-light—the

let-ter and word; Speak it and think it till hearts are all stirred.
spir-it's real gold! Give of it free-ly—this gift that's un-sold.

Send out the sun-light each hour and each day; Crown all the
Send out the sun-light as free as the air; Bless-ings will

years with its lum-in-ous ray; Send out the sun-light! 'tis
fol-low with none to com-pare; Send out the sun-light! you

Send Out the Sunlight—Concluded.

need-ed on earth, Bet-ter than gold is its wealth-giv-ing worth.
have it in you; Pray for its presence; your prayer will come true.

339   It is Time to be True.   P. M.   PLUMA M. BROWN.

1. It is time to be brave, it is time to be true, It is time to be
2. It is time to be kind, it is time to be sweet, To be scat-ter-ing
3. It is time to be low-ly and hum-ble of heart, It is time for the

find-ing the thing you can do; It is time to put by the
ros-es for some-bod-y's feet; It is time to be sow-ing, 'tis
lil-ies of meek-ness to start, For the heart to be white, the

dream and the sigh, And plead for the cause that is ho-ly and high.
time to be growing, It's time for the flow-ers of life to be blowing.
steps to be right, The hands to be wear-ing a gar-ment of light.

Copyright, 1896, by Pluma M. Brown.

340 Hail to the Brightness. 11. 10.　　L. MASON.

1. Hail to the brightness of Zi - on's glad morn-ing; Joy to the lands that in dark-ness have lain; Hushed be the ac - cents of sor - row and mourn-ing; Zi - on in tri - umph be-gins her mild reign.

2 Hail to the brightness of Zion's glad morning.
　Long by the prophets of Israel foretold;
　Hail to the millions from bondage returning;
　Gentiles and Jews the blest vision behold.

3 Lo! in the desert rich flowers are springing,
　Streams ever copious are gliding along;
　Loud from the mountain-top echoes are ringing,
　Wastes rise in verdure and mingle in song.

4 See! from all lands, from the isles of the ocean,
　Praise to Jehovah ascending on high;
　Fallen are the engines of war and commotion,
　Shouts of salvation are rending the sky.

5 Hail to the brightness of Zion's glad morning;
　Joy to the lands that in darkness have lain;
　Hushed be the accents of sorrow and mourning;
　Zion in triumph begins her mild reign.
　　　　　　　　　　　　T. HASTINGS.

341 Christ's Empire. L. M.

Missionary Chant.—H. C. Zeuner.

1. Je-sus shall reign where'er the sun Does his suc-cess-ive jour-neys run; His kingdom spread from shore to shore, Till moons shall wax and wane no more.

2 From north to south the princes meet,
To pay their homage at his feet;
While western empires own their Lord,
And savage tribes attend his word.

3 To him shall endless prayer be made,
And endless praises crown his head;
His name like sweet perfume shall rise
With every morning sacrifice.

4 People and realms of every tongue
Dwell on his love with sweetest song,
And infant voices shall proclaim
Their early blessings on his name.

I. Watts.

342 The Latter Day Glory.

1 Let thrones, and powers, and kingdoms be
Obedient, mighty God. to thee;
And over land. and stream. and main,
Now wave the scepter of thy reign.

2 Oh, let that glorious anthem swell;
Let host to host the triumph tell;
Till not one rebel heart remains.
But over all the Savior reigns.

3 Come. let us. with a grateful heart,
In this blest labor share a part:
Our prayers and offerings gladly bring
To aid the triumphs of our King.

Mrs. Vokes.

343 The Glorious Anthem.

1 From day to day, before our eyes,
Grows and extends the work begun;
When shall the new creation rise
O'er every land beneath the sun?

2 As sang the morning stars of old,
Shouted the sons of God for joy;
His widening reign while we behold,
Let praise and prayer our tongues
employ;

3 Till the redeemed from every clime,
Yea, all that breathe, and move, and
live.
To Christ. through every age of time,
The kingdom, power, and glory give.

J. Montgomery.

344 Light of Zion.

1 O light of Zion. now arise!
Let the glad morning bless our eyes;
Ye nations. catch the kindling ray.
And hail the splendors of the day.

2 That light shall shine on distant lands.
And wandering tribes, in joyful bands,
Shall come. thy glory. Lord. to see.
And in thy courts to worship thee.

L. Bacon.

345   The Light is Breaking.   7. 6. D.

Webb —G. J. WEBB.

1. The morn-ing light is break-ing; The dark-ness dis-ap-pears;

N:

The sons of earth are wak-ing To pen-i-ten-tial tears;
D.S.—Of na-tions in com-mo-tion, Pre-pared for Zi-on's war.

Each breeze that sweeps the o - cean Brings ti - dings from a - far

2 Rich dews of grace come o'er us
    In many a gentle shower,
And brighter scenes before us
    Are opening every hour;
Each cry to heaven going
    Abundant answers brings,
And heavenly gales are blowing
    With peace upon their wings.

3 Blest river of salvation!
    Pursue thine onward way;
Flow thou to every nation,
    Nor in thy richness stay—
Stay not till all the lowly
    Triumphant reach their home;
Stay not till all the holy
    Proclaim "The Lord is come."
                                        S. F. SMITH.

346   *Domestic Missions.*

1 Our country's voice is pleading,
    Ye men of God, arise!
His providence is leading,
    The land before you lies;

Day-gleams are o'er it brightening,
    And promise clothes the soil;
Wide fields, for harvest whitening,
    Invite the reaper's toil.

2 Go where the waves are breaking
    On California's shore,
Christ's precious gospel taking,
    More rich than golden ore;
On Alleghany's mountains,
    Through all the western vale,
Beside Missouri's fountains,
    Rehearse the wondrous tale.

3 The love of Christ unfolding,
    Speed on from east to west,
Till all, his cross beholding,
    In him are fully blest.
Great Author of salvation,
    Haste, haste the glorious day,
When we, a ransomed nation,
    Thy scepter shall obey!
                                        Mrs. M. F. ANDERSON.

347 Missionary Hymn. 7. 6. D.   L. Mason.

1. From Greenland's i-cy mountains, From India's coral strand; Where Afric's sunny foun-tains Roll down their golden sand; From many an an-cient riv - er, From many a palm - y plain, They call us to de - liv - er Their land from error's chain.

2 Shall we, whose souls are lighted
  With wisdom from on high,
Shall we to men benighted
  The lamp of life deny?
Salvation! O salvation!
  The joyful sound proclaim,
Till earth's remotest nation
  Has learned Messiah's name.

3 Waft, waft, ye winds, his story,
  And you, ye waters, roll,
Till, like a sea of glory,
  It spreads from pole to pole:
Salvation, O salvation!
  The joyful sound proclaim,
Till earth's remotest nation
  Has learned Messiah's name.
                        R. Heber.

348 *Hail to the Lord's Anointed.*

1 Hail to the Lord's Anointed.
  Great David's greater Son!
Hail in the time appointed,
  His reign on earth begun!
He comes to break oppression,
  To set the captive free,
To take away transgression,
  And rule in equity.

2 He shall descend like showers
  Upon the fruitful earth,
And love and joy, like flowers,
  Spring in his path to birth.
Before him, on the mountains,
  Shall Peace, the herald, go,
And righteousness in fountains
  From hill to valley flow.

3 For him shall prayer unceasing
  And daily vows ascend.
His kingdom still increasing—
  A kingdom without end.
The tide of time shall never
  His covenant remove;
His name shall stand forever:
  That name to us is Love.
                    J. Montgomery.

349) Truth is Victorious. P. M.

HANNAH MORE KOHAUS.
PLUMA M. BROWN.

1. Truth is vic-to-rious, Truth is vic-to-rious! Truth Om-ni-pres-ent
2. Truth is tri-um-phant, Truth is tri-um-phant! Om-nip-o-tent its
3. Truth is e-ter-nal, Truth is e-ter-nal! O bless-ed Truth that

all will make free. Er-ror no lon-ger chains us in bond-age,
pow-er to shield: Flee to its moun-tain, drink of its foun-tain,
bids er-ror flee! Break-ing the seem-ing, wak-ing the dream-ing,

Fet-ters our souls with il-lu-sion's de-vice; Truth all vic-to-rious,
Un-to its full-ness your souls now you yield; Sing of its tri-umphs,
In-to the re-al, the per-fect, the free; Truth is tri-um-phant,

ev-er-more glo-rious! Truth all vic-to-rious for-ev-er shall be.
sing of its triumphs, Bringing re-demp-tion, with vic-to-ry sealed!
Truth is e-ter-nal! Truth all vic-to-rious for-ev-er shall be.

350 The Day of Jubilee. 7. 6. D.   *Chenies.*—T. R. MATHEWS.

1. How beauteous on the mountains, The feet of him that brings, Like streams from living

fountains, Good ti-dings of good things; That pub-lish-eth sal-va-tion, And

ju-bi-lee re-lease, To ev-'ry tribe and na-tion, God's reign of joy and peace!

2 Lift up thy voice, O watchman!
　And shout, from Zion's towers,
Thy hallelujah chorus,—
　"The victory is ours!"
The Lord shall build up Zion
　In glory and renown,
And Jesus, Judah's lion,
　Shall wear his rightful crown.

3 Break forth in hymns of gladness,
　O waste Jerusalem!
Let songs, instead of sadness,
　Thy jubilee proclaim;
The Lord, in strength victorious,
　Upon thy foes hath trod;
Behold, O earth! the glorious
　Salvation of our God!
　　　　　　　　　B. GOUGH.

351　　*Truth in Splendor.*
1 The morn of Truth is breaking;
　Ten thousand notes of love
From tuneful souls are waking
　To swell the songs above.

Come, raise a glorious anthem
　Far over hill and plain,
For Truth in radiant splendor,
　Has come on earth to reign.

2 Oh, reign in every household,
　And where there's one soul sad,
Come as a radiant angel—
　A light to make it glad.
O Truth, shine on in splendor!
　Dispel these shades of gloom,
And where there seems a desert,
　The rose shall burst to bloom.

3 Come in, thou peaceful angel,
　And ope the gates of day;
With beams of living love-light,
　Chase all things false away.
Thou art that Light from heaven
　To glow in every soul;
Shine, thou, O Truth! in splendor,
　As age on ages roll.
　　　　　　　MARY E. BUTTERS.

352 Shout the Glad Tidings. P. M.

W. A. MUHLENBERG.
Avison.—C. Avison.

Shout the glad tidings, ex-ult-ing-ly sing... Je-ru-sa-lem triumphs, Mes-si-ah is King.

1. Zi-on, the mar-vel-ous sto-ry be tell-ing, The
2. Tell how he com-eth; from na-tion to na-tion, The
3. Chil-dren, your homage be grate-ful-ly bringing, And

Son of the Highest, how wondrous his birth; The brightest archangel in
heart-cheering news let the earth ech-o round; How free to the faith-ful he
sweet let the gladsome ho-san-na a-rise; Ye an-gels, the full bal-le-

Repeat 1st Chorus.

glo-ry ex-cell-ing, His truth now redeems thee. he reigns up-on earth.
of-fers sal-va-tion! How his people with joy ev-er-last-ing are crowned!
lu-jah be sing-ing: One cho-rus re-sound thro' the earth and the skies.

Chorus after last verse.

Shout the glad tid-ings, ex-ult-ing-ly sing;.. Je-

Shout the Glad Tidings—Concluded.

ru - sa-lem triumphs, Mes-si-ah is King, Mes-si-ah is King, Mes-si-ah is King.

353 Watchman, Tell Us of the Night. 7. D.

Wesley.—T. HASTINGS.

1. { Watchman, tell us of the night, What its signs of prom-ise are. }
   { Trav - 'ler, o'er yon mountain's height. See that glo - ry - beam-ing star! }

Watchman, does its beauteous ray Aught of joy or hope fore - tell?

Trav-'ler, yes: it brings the day, Prom-ised day of Is - ra - el.

2 Watchman, tell us of the night;
  Higher yet that star ascends.
Traveler, blessedness and light,
  Peace and truth, its course portends.
Watchman, will its beams alone
  Gild the spot that gave them birth?
Traveler, ages are its own;
  See! it bursts o'er all the earth.

3 Watchman, tell us of the night,
  For the morning seems to dawn.
Traveler, darkness takes its flight.
  Doubt and terror are withdrawn.
Watchman, let thy wanderings cease,
  Hie thee to thy quiet home.
Traveler, lo! the Prince of Peace,
  Lo! the Son of God is come!

J. BOWRING.

354   The Crowning Day.   P. M.

W. C. Gannett.
Pluma M. Brown.

1. The morn-ing hangs its sig-nal Up-on the mountain's crest,
2. A-bove the gen-er-a-tions The lone-ly prophets rise,
3. The soul hath lift-ed mo-ments A-bove the drift of days.
4. And in the sun-rise stand-ing, Our kin-dling hearts con-fess

While all the sleep-ing val-leys In si-lent dark-ness rest:
The Truth flings dawn and day-star With-in their glow-ing eyes;
When life's great mean-ing break-eth In sun-rise on our ways;
That no good thing is fail-ure, No e-vil thing suc-cess;

From peak to peak it flash-es, It laughs a-long the sky That the
From heart to heart it brightens, It draw-eth ev-er nigh. Till it
From hour to hour it haunts us, The vi-sion draw-eth nigh. Till it
From age to age it grow-eth, That ra-diant faith so high, And its

REFRAIN.

crowning day is com-ing, by and by!
crowneth all men thinking, by and by!
crowneth all men liv-ing, by and by!
crowning day is com-ing, by and by!

Oh, the crowning day is com-ing,

The Crowning Day—Concluded.

Is com - ing by and by: We can see the rose of morn - ing,

A glo - ry in the sky; And that splen - dor on the hill - tops

O'er all the land shall lie In the crowning day that's coming, by and by!

355 How Beauteous Their Feet! S. M.

Schumann.—R. Schumann.

1. How beauteous are their feet Who stand on Zion's hill, Who bring salvation

on their tongues, And words of peace reveal!

2 How charming is their voice!
How sweet the tidings are!
"Zion! behold thy Savior King;
He reigns and triumphs here."

3 How happy are our ears,
That hear this joyful sound,
Which kings and prophets waited for,
And sought, but never found!

4 The watchmen join their voice,
And tuneful notes employ;
Jerusalem breaks forth in songs,
And deserts learn the joy.

5 The Lord makes bare his arm
Through all the earth abroad;
Let all the nations now behold
Their Savior and their God.

I. Watts.

356 Apprehension. P. M.

Clara E. Choate.
Pluma M. Brown.

1. If the world could on - ly know us As we are, See the wholeness
2. Could we see the an - gel, he - ro, 'Neath the mask. Know the strug - gle
3. Could we know life's grandest pur - pose Is to love, Reach the high - est

of our natures Like the star: Could they feel our strong,deep heart-throbs,-
and the triumph,-Bit - ter task: Scorn and frown would cease for - ev - er,
as - pi - ra-tion Known a - bove, We would then win Christ's per-fec - tion,

Life of soul,—All the world would then be un - der Love's con - trol.
Love would reign, Glo - ry of the spheres ce - les - tial Come a - gain.
Self be - neath, Crowning ef - fort with a-chieve-ment, Lau - rel wreath.

If a - bove the fret and jan-gle, Pain, and sin, We could list - en
Could we see the light e - ter-nal Wait-ing near, Feel love's touch of
And e - ter - nal are the glo-ries All our own, Won by faith, in

Apprehension—Concluded.

to Love's mu-sic. Peace with - in; Feel up-borne by heav'n-ly pow-er,
strength im-mor-tal Ban - ish fear, We would soar a - bove the hu-man,
serv - ing, lov-ing Deeds were sown; All of earth must ring with glad-ness

Truth di - vine, Earth it - self would then be heav-en, Faith the shrine.
Trust sub-lime, Catch the soul's own in - spi - ra - tion, Will di - vine.
For such worth, All of heav'n bends low in prom-ise,—Wondrous birth.

357 The Invitation. S. M.

Arr. fr. Mozart.

!. Come to the land of peace; From shadows come a-way: Where all the sounds of

weeping cease, And storms no more have sway.

2 Fear hath no dwelling here;
But pure repose and love
Breathe thro' the bright, celestial air
The spirit of the dove.

3 Come to the bright and blest,
Gathered from every land;
For here thy soul shall find its rest,
Amid the shining band.

358 *Blessing of Friendship.*

1 Blest are the sons of peace
Whose hearts and hopes are one,
Whose kind designs to serve and please
Through all their actions run.

2 Blest is the loving band
Where zeal and friendship meet;
Their songs of praise, their mingled vows,
Make their communion sweet.

I. Watts.

359 The New Church. L. M.
Bera.—J. E. Gould.

1. Where is the church of God be-low? 'Tis where the ho-ly an-gels go, And find an hum-ble, trust-ing band Up-on the hills of wor-ship stand.

2 In love to God they all are one;
They glow like angels in the sun,
While mind, and heart, and life agree
In faith and use and charity.

3 They have no bond of party strife,
But each, in holiness of life,
Esteems his brother's good his own,
And makes his heart Messiah's throne.

4 The ancients of the "Age of Gold"
Encamp around that rising fold:
The Lord himself their truth inspires,
And dwells within their pure desires.

5 This was the church the Lord foreknew;
The first and last, the ever new,
Of every star the purest gem,
The beautiful Jerusalem.
T. L. Harris.

360 One Life.
1 I nothing am, can nothing be
Except a part, O God, of thee.
From thee I come, to thee I go,—
How we are one I do not know.

2 As stars that shine by single sun,
So life in each is life from one;

Each is for all, and all for each
In ways no finite thought can reach.

3 When Truth unveils this segment soul,
Unsevered part of God, the whole,
With God in Christ and Christ in man,
The circle ends where it began.

361 Brethren in Christ.
1 Brethren in Christ, and well beloved,
To Jesus and his servants dear,
Enter, and show yourselves approved;
Enter, and find that God is here.

2 Welcome from earth: lo! the right hand
Of fellowship to you we give!
With open hearts and hands we stand
And you in Jesus' name receive.

3 O Christ, attend; thyself reveal;
Are we not met in thy great name?
Thee in the midst we wait to feel:
We wait to catch the spreading flame.

4 Truly our fellowship below
With thee and with the Father is:
In thee eternal life we know,
And heaven's unutterable bliss.
C. Wesley.

362 Greeting. L. M.   *Ipswich.—J. B. Dykes.*

1. O Life. that mak-est all things new,—The blooming earth, the tho'ts of men!

Our pil-grim feet, wet with thy dew, In glad-ness hith-er turn a-gain:

2 From hand to hand the greeting flows,
From eye to eye the signals run,
From heart to heart the bright hope glows.
  The lovers of the Light are one.

3 One in the freedom of the Truth,
  One in the joy of paths untrod,
One in the soul's perennial youth,
  One in the larger thought of God;

4 The freer step. the fuller breath,
  The wide horizon's grander view,
The sense of life that knows no death.—
  The Life that maketh all things new!
             S. LONGFELLOW.

363 *Christ with His Disciples.*

1 Where those who love the Savior meet,
  His presence makes the place divine;
They kneel with Mary at his feet:
  With John upon his breast recline.

2 With fruits from heaven's immortal trees
  Attendant angels crown the board;
And each within his brother sees
  The beauteous image of the Lord.

3 While to his courts their feet repair.
  Their hearts outstrip them on the road;

And, clothed in raiment white and fair,
  They banquet on the love of God.

4 Free from the bonds of party strife
  They hear the Gentle Shepherd's call,
And. gathered in the fold of life,
  Messiah God is all in all.

364 *Fellowship in Christ.*

1 Giver of peace and unity.
  Send down thy mild, pacific Dove;
We all shall then in one agree.
  And breathe the spirit of thy love.

2 We all shall think and speak the same
  Delightful lesson of thy grace;
One undivided Christ proclaim.
  And jointly glory in thy praise.

3 Oh, let us take a softer mold,
  Blended and gathered into thee;
Under one Shepherd make one fold,
  Where all is love and harmony.

4 So shall the world believe and know
  That God hath sent thee from above,
When thou art seen in us below,
  And every soul displays thy love.
             C. WESLEY.

365 The Golden Chain. c. m.

Arcadia.—T. Hastings.

1. How sweet, how heav'nly is the sight, When those who love the Lord In one an-

oth-er's peace delight, And so ful-fill his word! And so ful-fill his word!

2 Let love, in one delightful stream,
  Through every bosom flow,
And union sweet, and dear esteem,
  In every action glow.

3 Love is the golden chain that binds
  The happy souls above;
And he's an heir of heaven who finds
  His bosom glow with love.
      J. SWAIN.

366 *Love, the Test of Discipleship.*

1 Our God is love; and all his saints
  His image bear below:
The heart with love to God inspired,
  With love to man will glow.

2 Teach us to love each other, Lord,
  As we are loved by thee;
None who are truly born of God
  Can live in enmity.

3 Heirs of the same immortal bliss,
  Our hopes and fears the same,
With bonds of love our hearts unite,
  With mutual love inflame.

4 So may the unbelieving world
  See how true Christians love:
And glorify our Savior's grace,
  And seek that grace to prove.
      T. COTTERILL.

367 *The Loadstone of His Love.*

1 Jesus, united by thy grace,
  And each to each endeared,
With confidence we seek thy face,
  And know our prayer is heard.

2 Still let us own our common Lord,
  And bear thine easy yoke,
A band of love, a threefold cord,
  Which never can be broke.

3 Make us into one spirit drink;
  Baptize into thy name;
And let us always kindly think,
  And sweetly speak, the same.

4 Touched by the loadstone of thy love,
  Let all our hearts agree,
And ever toward each other move,
  And ever move toward thee.
      C. WESLEY.

368 Work for To-day. C. M.

Chesterfield.—T. Haweis.

1. New words to speak, new thoughts to hear, New love to give and take:
Per-chance new bur-dens I may bear To-day, for love's sweet sake.

2 New hopes to open in the sun;
New efforts worth the will;
Or tasks, with yesterday begun,
More bravely to fulfill.

3 Fresh seeds for all the time to be
Are in my hand to sow,
Whereby, for others and for me,
Undreamed-of fruit may grow.

369 The Lord's Presence.

1 If thou hast dried the mourner's tear,
Or hushed the orphan's cry,
Inspired by mercy all sincere,
The Lord was standing by:

2 And tho' thou didst not own his name,
By outward sign or word,
That sweet and secret bosom-flame
Was kindled by the Lord.

3 Fling wide, fling wide the mystic doors
That ope within the breast!
He comes, whom every heaven adores,
To be our constant guest.

4 He comes, to make the heart his throne,
And pour his life abroad.
And all who live for love alone
Possess Messiah God.

T. L. Harris.

370 One Mind.

1 Our souls, by love together knit,
Cemented, mixed in one,
One hope, one heart, one mind, one voice,
'Tis heaven on earth begun.

2 Our hearts have often burned within,
And glowed with sacred fire,
While Jesus spoke, and fed, and blessed,
And filled the enlarged desire.

3 The little cloud increases still,
The heavens are big with rain;
We haste to catch the teeming shower,
And all its moisture drain.

4 A rill, a stream, a torrent flows!
But pour a mighty flood;
Oh, sweep the nations, shake the earth,
Till all proclaim thee God!

Miller.

371   Apostleship.   7.   *Last Hope.*—Arr. fr. Gottschalk.

1. Take thy brother's heart in thine; Hold it there by love di - vine;

So shall he the Lord re - ceive, And in per - fect faith be - lieve.

Used by arr. with Oliver Ditson Co., owners of copyright.

2 As the blooming rose exhales
   Fragrance to the summer gales,
   Breathe thy spirit thro' his breast;
   Love him from the land of rest:

3 Till that perfect love shall flow
   Filled with life to him below,
   And he owns the pure desires
   That Messiah God inspires.

372   *One in All.*

1 Lord, our fellowship increase;
   Knit us in the bond of peace;
   Join our hearts, O Father! join
   Each to each, and all to thine.

2 Move and actuate and guide,
   Diverse gifts to each divide;
   Placed according to thy will,
   Let us each his work fulfill.

3 Build us in one spirit up,
   Called in one high calling's hope,
   One the spirit, one the aim,
   One the pure baptismal flame; —

4 Sweetly may we all agree,
   Touched with softest sympathy;
   Kindly for each other care;
   Every member feel its share.

5 Many are we now and one,
   We who Jesus have put on;
   Names, and sects, and parties fall:
   Thou, O Christ, art all in all.

6 One the faith, and one the Lord,
   Whom, by heaven and earth adored,
   We our God and Father call;—
   O'er all, through all, with us all.
                              C. Wesley.

                  Tune—*Bera.* p. 202.
373   *Fellowship.*

   Wherever through the ages rise
   The altars of self-sacrifice,
   Where love its arms hath opened wide,
   Or man for man has calmly died,

2 We see the same white wings outspread
   That hovered o'er the Master's head;
   And in all lands beneath the sun
   The heart affirmeth, ''Love is one.''
                              J. G. Whittier.

374 We Welcome Thee. C. M.

Salzburgh.—Arr. fr. Haydn.

1. Come in, thou bless-ed of the Lord, Stran-ger nor foe art thou:

We wel-come thee with warm ac-cord, Our friend, our broth-er, now.

2 The hand of fellowship, the heart
Of love, we offer thee:
Leaving the world, thou dost but part
From lies and vanity.

3 Come with us; we will do thee good,
As God to us hath done;
Stand but in him, as those have stood
Whose faith the victory won.
J. Montgomery.

375 Harmony and Joy Unspeakable.

1 All praise to our redeeming Lord,
Who joins us by his grace,
And bid us, each to each restored,
Together seek his face.

2 He bids us build each other up;
And, gathered into one,
To our high calling's glorious hope,
We hand in hand go on.

3 The gift which he on one bestows,
We all delight to prove;
The grace through every vessel flows,
In purest streams of love.

4 E'en now we think and speak the same,
And cordially agree.

United all, through truth now known,
In perfect harmony.

5 We all partake the joy of one;
The common peace we feel;
A peace to sensual thought unknown,
A joy unspeakable.
C. Wesley.

376 The Bond of Love.

1 The glorious universe around,
The heavens with all their train,
Sun, moon, and stars, are firmly bound
In one mysterious chain.

2 In one fraternal bond of love,
One fellowship of mind,
The saints below and saints above
Their bliss and glory find.

3 Here, in their house of pilgrimage,
Thy statutes are their song;
There, through one bright, eternal age,
Thy praises they prolong.

4 Lord, may our union form a part
Of that thrice happy whole;
Derive its pulse from thee, the Heart,
Its life from thee, the Soul.
J. Montgomery.

Fellowship.

377 To a Friend. 10. D.

Elinor Hiscock.
Pluma M. Brown.

1. Send me, to-day, kind tho'ts, for tho'ts have wing, And soar as
2. Send me, to-day, sound tho'ts of strength and health: Of heav'n-ly
3. Send me, to-day, peace tho'ts, all calm, se-rene, To smooth the

high and far as birds that sing. Send me, to-day, great
treas-ures rare— the soul's true wealth. Send me, to-day, true
path of life and ways un-seen. Send me, to-day, grand

tho'ts where-e'er I roam: And send them all in love to glad-den home.
tho'ts that bless and heal, And work for good all things of woe or weal.
tho'ts of things sub-lime: Of love, that shall en-dure be-yond all time.

Send me, to-day, high tho'ts, so I can rest, And know what-
Send me, to-day, calm tho'ts of gen-tle deed, And pow'r di-
Send me, to-day, love tho'ts, all ho-ly, fair, Which make a

To a Friend—Concluded.

e'er may come, that all is best. Send me, to-day, right
vine to help an-oth-er's need. Send me, to-day, sweet
heav'n of earth and light-en care. Send me, to-day, pure

tho'ts to make me glad; That I may hap-py be, and no more sad.
tho'ts of peace and rest, And per-fect trust and faith, that make me blest.
tho'ts of love di-vine, Which comes from God, the source of yours and mine.

378 One in Christ. S. M.

Arr. fr. Rossini.

1. Dear Sav-ior! we are thine By ev-er-last-ing bands: Our names, our hearts, we

would resign, Our souls in-to thine hands.

2 Thy spirit doth unite
Our souls to thee, our head,
Doth form in us thine image bright,
That we thy paths may tread.

3 Since Christ and we are one,
Why should we doubt and fear?
If he in heaven hath fixed his throne,
He'll fix his members there.

379 One Church in Christ.

1 Let party names no more
The Christian world o'erspread;
Gentile and Jew, and bond and free,
Are one in Christ, their head.

2 Among the saints on earth,
Let mutual love be found;

Heirs of the same inheritance.
With mutual blessings crowned.

3 Thus will the church below
Resemble that above;
Where streams of pleasure ever flow,
And every heart is love.

B. Beddome.

380 Beyond. M. M.

Arr. fr. Abt.

1. Nev-er a word is said But trem - bles in the air,
2. Nev-er are kind acts done To wipe the weep - ing eyes,
3. There is no end to sky, And stars are ev - 'ry - where:

And tru - ant voice has sped To vi - brate ev - 'ry - where:
But like rays of the sun They sig - nal to the skies:
Time is e - ter - ni - ty: The here is o - ver there.

And far - off in e - ter - nal years, Ech - o may ring up -
And up a - bove the an - gels read How we have helped the
For com - mon deeds of com-mon day Are ring-ing bells in the

on our ears, Ech-o may ring up - on...... our ears.
sor - er need. How we have helped the sor - - er need.
far a - way, Are ring - ing bells in the far...... a - way.

381 Fellowship. C. M. 6 l.

ANNA L. WARING.
F. GLÜCK.

1. Wher-ev-er in the world I am, In what-so-e'er es-tate,
2. I ask thee for a thoughtful love, Thro' con-stant watching wise
3. In serv-ice which thy will ap-points, There are no bonds for me:

I have a fel-low-ship with hearts To keep and cul-ti-vate:
To meet the glad with joy-ful smiles, And wipe the weeping eyes;
My in-most heart is taught the truth That makes thy chil-dren free.—

A work of low-ly love to do, For him on whom I wait.
A heart at leis-ure from it-self, To soothe and sym-pa-thize.
A life of self-re-nounc-ing love Is a life of lib-er-ty.

382 *"Thy Kingdom Come."*
(Repeat last two lines.)

1 Thy kingdom come, with power and grace,
In every heart of man;
Thy peace, and joy, and righteousness
In all our bosoms reign!

2 The righteousness that never ends,
But makes an end of sin;

The joy that human thought transcends,
Now to our souls bring in!

3 The kingdom of established peace
Which can no more remove;
The perfect power of Godliness,
The omnipotence of Love!

C. WESLEY.

383 Prayer. 11, 10.

PLUMA M. BROWN.

1. We wait on God, with-in his tem-ple kneeling, De-scend, thou Spir-it,
2. Let char - i - ty in ev-'ry breast pre-vail-ing, Trans-form our lives in

on us like the dove! May each a Sav-ior's heart within him feel - ing,
D. S.—To - day, dear Lord, may strife and en-vy per - ish,
im-age of thine own: Help us to o - ver-come our ev - 'ry fail - ing,
D. S.—Lov - ing each oth-er, we shall love thee bet - ter,

FINE.

Blend with his breth-ren in fra - ter - nal love. Sweet are the ties that
Till we be - come one fam - i - ly be - low.
And in us fix thy ev - er - last - ing throne. Oh, strike from ev - 'ry
Till ev - 'ry chord of life in mu - sic rings.

D. S.

ho - ly an - gels cher-ish, And lov - ing hearts in Christ to-geth-er flow;
heart the i - cy fet - ter: A - wake the An - gel in the breast that sings:

384   The True Worship.   11. 10.

J. G. Whittier.
Pluma M. Brown.

1. O broth-er   man! fold to thy heart thy brother; Where pity dwells the
2.   Fol-low with rev'rent steps the great ex-am-ple Of him whose ho-ly

peace of God is there: To wor-ship right-ly is to love each oth-er. Each
work was "do-ing good;" So shall the wide earth seem our Father's temple, Each

smile a hymn, each kindly deed a prayer. For he whom Je-sus loved hath tru-ly
lov-ing life a psalm of grat-i-tude. Then shall all shackles fall; the stormy

spo-ken: The ho-lier wor-ship which he loves to bless Restores the lost, and
clan-gor Of wild war music o'er the earth shall cease; Love shall tread out the

binds the spir-it bro-ken, And feeds the wid-ow and the fath-er-less.
bale-ful fire of an-ger, And in its ash-es plant the tree of peace.

214

385 Communion. P. M.

JULIA ESTY SCHREINER.
FERD. SILCHER.

1. I hold you in tho't, dear broth - er, As I sit in the
2. I hold you in tho't, my sweet friend,—The seed of the
3. I hold you in tho't, my dear one, In the "truth that shall
4. I hold you in tho't, O World, The cre - a - tions of

si-lence a - lone, To gath - er from in - fi - nite full - ness The
truth you shall sow: All hearts shall be lift - ed and bet - ter, Wher-
make you free:" Your life shall be mould-ed by pur-est tho't. Your
God are blessed: Souls are as white as pur-est light; Be -

bless-ings I claim for my own: I hold for you earth's rich-est
ev - er your pres-ence shall go: With the "Sword of the Spir - it" you'll
heart ev - er rest - ful shall be; I claim for you all that's di-
lief in the Good giv - eth rest: Spir - it shall know and

treas - ures. I claim all that's God - like and true, And the
con - quer: God's grace shall en - fold you a - new, And the
vin - est, Each day shall your bless-ings re - new, And the
claim its power: Er - ror shall yield to truth; The

Communion—Concluded.

ten - der-est tho't my heart doth hold, Is the tho't that it holds for you.
Christ - love tho't my heart doth hold, Is the tho't that it holds for you.
ho - li - est tho't my heart doth hold, Is the tho't that it holds for you.
fruit-age of love to God and man, Is the tho't I hold, World, for you.

386 What is Prayer? 10.

Eventide.— W. H. MONK.

1. Prayer is the in - ward con-scious-ness of need, The thought which

caus - es strong de - sire to plead; The faith - ful - ness with

which our work is wrought Is prayer ac - cept-ed, while vain words are naught.

2 In every form that mortal mind appears,
Prayer is the watchword that will conquer fears.
Go hence, all error thoughts of time and sense—
This is the saving prayer—our soul's defense.

3 The tenderness which thinks of others first,
Is living prayer which satisfies our thirst;
Prayer is the harmony of righteous life,
Which lives above all discord and all strife.

ELIZABETH A. DOUGLAS.

387   My Prayer.   C. M.   Heber.   Geo. Kingsley.

1. I do not pray be-cause I would.—I pray be-cause I must;
There is no mean-ing in my prayer But thank-ful-ness and trust.

2 I would not have thee otherwise
  Than what thou still must be:
  Yea, thou art God, and what thou art
  Is ever best for me.

3 And thou wilt hear the thought I
      mean,
  And not the words I say;
  Wilt hear the thanks among the words
  That only seem to pray.
                    J. W. Chadwick.

388   Thanksgiving.
1 I thank thee that I am thy child,
  My heritage secure;
  Thine image stamped upon my heart,
  Forever shall endure.

2 I thank thee, Father, that thy love
  Extends to all my ways;
  And so I cannot fear nor doubt,
  But love and trust and praise.

3 I know for every human need
  Thou hast a full supply,
  And they who trust thy bounteous hand
  Need never strive nor cry.

4 And so my heart with thankfulness,
  Is willing more and more;

And so my cup with blessings deep,
  Is running o'er and o'er.
                    Jennie Wayne.

389   We Thank Thee.
1 Our thanks, Almighty God, we give
  To thee for all thy love
  Made known to us who in thee live—
  Who in thee live and move.

2 We thank thee for thy tender care
  To us so freely given:
  We find thy presence everywhere,
  In earth as well as heaven.

3 We thank thee for the fruits and
      flowers,
  And fields of golden grain.
  For sunshine and refreshing showers
  That bless the verdant plain.

4 For all the seasons with their wealth
  Of happiness untold—
  Sweet ministers of life and health,
  More dear than shining gold.

5 For all these precious gifts of thine
  Our gratitude we raise;
  O God, whose bounties are divine,
  Accept thy children's praise.
                    G. W. Crofts.

590 Prayer of the Soul. C. M.   *Byefield. T. Hastings.*

1. Prayer is the soul's sin-cere de - sire. Un - ut - tered or ex - pressed:

The mo - tion of a hid - den fire That trem-bles in the breast.

2 Prayer is the burden of a sigh,
   The falling of a tear.
   The upward glancing of an eye.
   When none but God is near.

3 Prayer is the simplest form of speech
   That infant lips can try:
   Prayer, the sublimest strains that reach
   The Majesty on high.
              J. Montgomery.

591   *Communion with God.*

1 Sweet is the prayer whose holy stream
   In earnest pleading flows:
   Devotion dwells upon the theme.
   And warm and warmer glows.

2 Faith grasps the blessing she desires:
   Hope points the upward gaze:
   And Love. celestial Love. inspires
   The eloquence of praise.

3 But sweeter far the still small voice,
   Unheard by human ear.
   When God has made the heart rejoice.
   And dried the bitter tear.

4 No accents flow. no words ascend;
   All utterance faileth there:
   But God himself doth comprehend
   And answer silent prayer.

592   *A Song of Faith.*

1 We pray no more. made lowly wise.
   For miracle and sign:
   Anoint our eyes to see within
   The common, the divine.

2 We turn from seeking thee afar
   And in unwonted ways.
   To build from out our daily lives
   The temples of thy praise.
              F. L. Hosmer.

593   *Best Prayer.*

1 He prayeth well who loveth well
   Both man and bird and beast.
   For he hath offered to the Lord
   Who giveth to his least.

2 He prayeth best who loveth best
   All things both great and small,
   For the dear Lord who loveth us
   He made and loveth all.
              S. T. Coleridge.

394   Pray Evermore.   S. M.

Gordon.   ARR. FR. BEETHOVEN.

1. Come at the morn-ing hour. Come, let us kneel and pray:

Prayer is the Chris-tian pil-grim's staff To walk with God all day.

2 At noon, beneath the Rock
    Of Ages, rest and pray;
Sweet is that shelter from the sun
    In weary heat of day.

3 At evening, in thy home,
    Around its altar, pray;
And finding there the house of God,
    With heaven then close the day.

4 When midnight veils ours eyes,
    Oh, it is sweet to say,
"I sleep, but my heart waketh, Lord,
    With thee to watch and pray."
             J. MONTGOMERY.

395   *Prayer-Answer.*

1 At first I prayed for Light:—
    Could I but see the way,
How gladly, swiftly would I walk
    To everlasting day!

2 And next I prayed for Strength:—
    That I might tread the road
With firm, unfaltering feet, and win
    The heaven's serene abode.

3 And then I asked for Faith:—
    Could I but trust my God,

I'd live enfolded in his peace,
    Though foes were all abroad.

4 But now I pray for Love:
    Deep love to God and man;
A living love that will not fail,
    However dark his plan;—

5 And Light and Strength and Faith
    Are opening everywhere!
God only waited for me till
    I prayed the larger prayer.
             Mrs. E. D. CHENEY.

396   *My Prayer*

1 One gift, my God, I seek,—
    To know thee always near;
To feel thy hand, to see thy face,
    Thy blessed voice to hear.

2 Where'er I go, my God,
    Oh, let me find thee there;
Where'er I stay, thou art with me,
    A presence everywhere.

3 Long listening to thy words,
    My voice shall catch thy tone,
And, locked in thine, my hand shall
       grow
All loving, like thine own.
             B. T.

397 Prayer, the Heart's Desire. S. M. *Vigil.—G. Paisiello.*

1. Prayer is the heart's de-sire: Prayer is the spir-it's cry:

The thought that leaps in liv-ing fire When God is pass-ing by.

2 Prayer is the lifted sword
   That smites the tempter down;
   In prayer we rise to meet the Lord:
   And win the victor's crown.

3 Prayer is the burning tree.
   And God within it stands;
   Through prayer, O Lord! we come to
   thee.
   And clasp our Savior's hands.

4 Prayer is the holy shrine
   Where angels with us meet:
   The path that leads thro' realms divine.
   Unto our Father's feet.

5 Prayer is our flame by night.
   Our moving cloud by day;
   And angels hold us in their sight.
   And guide us while we pray.
   T. L. HARRIS.

   Blest are the pure in heart.
   For they shall see our God;
   The secret of the Lord is theirs;
   Their soul is his abode.

398 *Silence.*

1 We sink into his love.
   And wait the spoken word
   That by our inner consciousness.
   Alone. is sweetly heard.

2 Telling of higher life
   Where love and peace shall reign:
   That error is a passing dream.
   And Truth shall banish pain.

3 All is divinest peace.
   And we are strengthened there.
   By that uplifting of the heart.
   That is the truest prayer.
   E. T. R.

399 *Heart-Speech.*

1 Help me, my God. to speak
   True words to thee this day;
   Real let my voice be when I praise.
   And trustful when I pray.

2 Thy words are true to me;
   Let mine to thee be true,
   The speech of my whole heart and soul,
   However low and few.
   H. BONAR.

400 From Every Stormy Wind. L. M.

Retreat. T. HASTINGS.

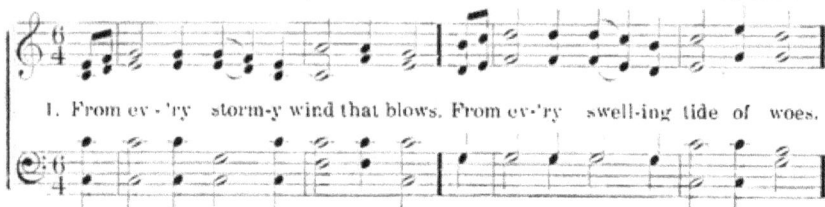

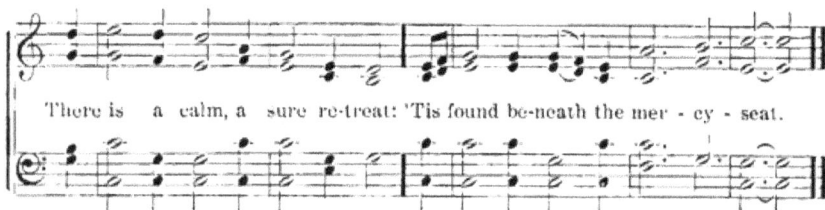

1. From ev-'ry storm-y wind that blows, From ev-'ry swell-ing tide of woes,

There is a calm, a sure re-treat: 'Tis found be-neath the mer - cy - seat.

2 There is a scene where spirits blend,
Where friend holds fellowship with
    friend;
Though sundered far, by faith they meet
Around one common mercy-seat.

3 There, there on eagle wings we soar,
And time and sense seem all no more,
And heaven comes down our souls to
    greet,
And glory crowns the mercy-seat.
                          H. STOWELL.

401   The Omnipresence of Christ.

1 Jesus, where'er thy people meet,
There they behold thy mercy-seat;
Where'er they seek thee, thou art found,
And every place is hallowed ground.

2 For thou, within no walls confined,
Dost dwell with those of humble mind;
Such ever find thee where they come,
Nor from thy presence can they roam.

3 Here may we prove the power of prayer
To strengthen faith, and sweeten care;
To teach our longing hearts to rise,
And bring all heaven before our eyes
                          WM. COWPER.

402   Prayer.

1 No words of labored prayer I know,—
I cannot seek my Father so:
It gushes up in sudden hours,
As sing the birds, as bloom the flowers.

2 And is it prayer? or is it praise?
I only know in loving ways,
When joy and gladness touch the springs,
To thee my spirit inly sings.

3 Away from forms I needs must turn;
No prayer have I that I must learn;
I ask but help to love thee more,
And thy dear will in peace adore.
                          MRS. L. J. HALL.

403   The Higher Level.

1 I am not glad till I have known
Life that can lift me from my own;
A loftier level must be won,
A mightier strength to lean upon.

2 And heaven draws near as I ascend;
The breeze invites, the stars befriend;
All things are beckoning to the Best,
I climb to thee, my God, for rest!
                          LUCY LARCOM.

404   The Hour of Prayer. 8. 4.   *Elliott.–J. B. DYKES.*

1. My God! is an-y hour so sweet, From blush of morn to ev-'ning star,

As that which calls me to thy feet, The hour of prayer?

2 Blest is the tranquil hour of morn,
And blest that solemn hour of eve
When, on the wings of prayer upborne,
   The world I leave.

3 No words can tell what sweet relief
Here for my every want I find,
What strength for warfare, balm for grief,
   What peace of mind.

4 Lord! till I reach that blissful shore,
No privilege so dear shall be,
As thus my inmost soul to pour
   In prayer to thee.
                    CHARLOTTE ELLIOTT.

405   *Divine Inflowings.*

1 The stream of love is deep and still,
Its fount eternity supplies;
It moves thro' all the silent will
   With breath of skies.

2 Pure from the source of primal day,
The waters of the spirit flow;
Wells in the world's dim desert they,
   That pilgrims know.

3 O stranger in the thirsty land,
Forlorn, with sense of care opprest,
Seeking, thro' wastes of burning sand,
   A calm, sweet rest:

4 Lo! Prayer, the angel, sits beside
The cooling well beneath the tree,
And fills her goblet from the tide,
   And gives to thee.
                    T. L. HARRIS.

TUNE—*Amsterdam.* p. 112.

406   *The Still, Small Voice.*

1 Open, Lord, my inward ear,
And bid my heart rejoice;
Bid my quiet spirit hear
   The comfort of thy voice:
Never in the whirlwind found,
   Or where earthquakes rock the place.—
Still and silent is the sound,
   The whisper, of thy grace.

2 From the world of sin and noise
   And hurry, I withdraw;
For the small and inward voice
   I wait with humble awe:
Silent I am now, and still,
   Would not in thy presence move;
To my waiting soul reveal
   The secret of thy love.
                    C. WESLEY.

407 O Holy Spirit, Come to Me. L. M.

Gordon.—PLUMA M. BROWN.

1. O Ho-ly Spir-it, come to me; Touch thou mine eyes that I may see

Thy wis-dom, pow'r, and maj-es-ty Re-vealed to man from sea to sea.

Copyright, 1896, by Pluma M. Brown.

2 O Holy Spirit, come to me:
Touch thou mine heart that I may feel
Thou wilt thyself, as Love, reveal
To every human child of weal.

3 O Holy Spirit, come to me;
Touch thou my hands that I may hold

In steadfast faith thy love untold.
For those whose tho'ts to thee unfold.

4 O Holy Spirit, come to me;
Touch thou my feet until I stand
Firm as the Rock in Beulah land,—
Building no more on shifting sand.

L. G. W.

408 Prayer for Light. 6. 4.

Righini.—VINCENZO RIGHINI.

1. Thou, whose al-might-y word Cha-os and dark-ness heard,
Hear us, we hum-bly pray, And where the gos-pel's day

and took their flight;
[Omit . . . . .] Sheds not its glo-rious ray, "Let there be light!"

409   Oh, Lead Me, Lord.   L. M.

Earl. PLUMA M. BROWN.

1. Oh, lead me, Lord, that I may lead The wand'ring and the wav'ring feet:

Oh, feed me, Lord, that I may feed Thy hung'ring ones with manna sweet.

2 Oh, strengthen me, that, while I stand
Firm on the Rock and strong in thee,
I may stretch out a loving hand
To wrestlers with the troubled sea.

3 Oh, teach me, Lord, that I may teach
The precious things thou dost impart;
And wing my words that they may reach
The hidden depths of many a heart.

4 Oh, give thine own sweet rest to me,
That I may speak with soothing power
A word in season as from thee
To weary ones in needful hour.

5 Oh, fill me with thy fullness, Lord,
Until my very heart o'erflow
In kindling thought and glowing word,
Thy love to tell, thy praise to show.

TUNE—*Righini.*

2 Thou, who dost come to bring
On thy redeeming wing
Healing and sight,
Health to the sick in mind,
Sight to the inly blind,—
Oh, now to all mankind
"Let there be light!"

3 Spirit of truth and love,
Life-giving, holy Dove,
Speed forth thy flight;

Move o'er the waters' face,
Bearing the lamp of grace,
And in earth's darkest place
"Let there be light!"

4 Blessed and holy three,
All-glorious Trinity,
Wisdom, Love, Might!
Boundless as ocean's tide
Rolling in fullest pride
Through the world, far and wide,
"Let there be light!"

J. MARIOTT.

410 Savior, Teach Me! 7.

Dijon.—J G. BITTHAUER.

1. Sav - ior! teach me, day by day, Love's sweet les - son to o - bey:

Sweet - er les - son can - not be. Lov - ing him who first loved me.

2 With a child-like heart of love,
At thy bidding may I move;
Prompt to serve and follow thee,
Loving him who first loved me.

3 Teach me all thy steps to trace,
Strong to follow in thy grace;
Learning how to love from thee,
Loving him who first loved me.

4 Love in loving finds employ—
In obedience all her joy;
Ever new that joy will be,
Loving him who first loved me.

5 Thus may I rejoice to show
That I feel the love I owe;
Singing, till thy face I see,
Of his love who first loved me.
JANE E. LEESON.

411 *Inspiration.*

1 Holy Spirit, Truth divine!
Dawn upon this soul of mine;
Word of God and inward Light,
Wake my spirit, clear my sight.

2 Holy Spirit, Love divine!
Glow within this heart of mine;

Kindle every high desire;
Perish self in thy pure fire.

3 Holy Spirit, Power divine!
Fill and nerve this will of mine;
By thee may I strongly live,
Bravely bear, and nobly strive.

4 Holy Spirit, Right divine!
King within my conscience reign;
Be my law, and I shall be
Firmly bound, forever free.

5 Holy Spirit, Joy divine!
Gladden thou this heart of mine;
In the desert ways I sing
"Spring, O Well! forever spring."
S. LONGFELLOW.

TUNE—*Brownell.*

1 "Not as I will!—The sound grows
sweet—
Each time my lips the words repeat.
Not as I will! the darkness feels
More safe than light when this thought
steals
Like whispered voice to calm and bless
All unrest and all loneliness."
H. H.

412 A Plea for Service. L. M. 6 l.

Brownell.—Arr. fr. Haydn.

1. O Christ divine, up-lift my sight, That I my no-bler self may see:
Give strength to the clear, in-ner light In which my soul doth wor-ship thee!
The "still small voice" I wait to hear, Thrill deep the silence, sweet and clear.

2 Attune my feeble, wandering thought,
That eager service it may yield;
On ever swifter pinions brought.
To labor in a vaster field:
To all humanity I'd bring
The treasure of thy love, my King!

3 Refine and elevate my faith
To feel thee in the smallest things;
O Love supreme! what finite breath

Speak joys that from thy great Heart
springs;
This heavenly river of delight
Flows not beyond our inner sight.

4 I crave the largeness of thy peace.
Which comforteth our earthly state;
One note to sound and never cease,
One will to do, early and late:
Give me, dear Lord, swift eagerness,
My lowly, common way to bless.

LYDIA WOOD BALDWIN.

TUNE—*Dijon.*

413 The Light of Stars.

1 Slowly, by God's hand unfurled.
Down around the weary world
Falls the darkness; oh, how still
Is the working of his will!

2 Mighty Spirit, here am I!
Work in me as silently;
Veil the day's distracting sights,
Show me heaven's eternal lights.

3 Living stars to view be brought
In the boundless realms of thought!
High and infinite desires,
Flaming like those upper fires!

4 Holy Truth, eternal Right,
Let them break upon my sight:
Let them shine serene and still,
And with light my being fill.

W. H. FURNESS

414 Spirit of God, Possess Me. 7. 6.

Sarah Wilder Pratt.
Pluma M. Brown.

1. Spir-it of God, pos-sess me: Fill ev-'ry wand'ring tho't
2. Spir-it of Love, pos-sess me: Guide ev-'ry dai-ly act:
3. Spir-it of Truth, pos-sess me: Fill ev-'ry sense with might:
4. Spir-it of God, pos-sess me: I then shall quick-ly own

With vi-sions of the beau-ty Thy might-y pow'r hath wrought.
To thee I look with long-ing; Thou art the on-ly fact.
I then shall prove the pow'r di-vine, That is my own birth-right.
That God, our heav'n-ly Fa-ther, And Christ and I a:e One.

Copyright, 1896, by Pluma M. Brown.

415 Unveil Thy Face. 6. 4.

Oliret.—L. Mason.

1. Fa-ther of world and soul, Changeless while a-ges roll, Boundless in grace!

{ Who, with thy strength and rest, }
{ Quick'nest and qui-et-est, } Now in each yearning breast Unveil thy face!

2 Word, whose creative thrill
Wakes in all Nature still
Life, light, and bloom!
Now, with resistless ray,

Chase all our clouds away.
And with thy heavenly day
Our souls illume!

C. T. Brooks.

416 Enlighten Me. 7. 8. 7.   Arr. fr. HAYDN.

1. Light of light! en-light-en me, Now a - new the day is dawn-ing:

Sun of grace! the shad-ows flee. Bright-en thou my Sab-bath morn-ing:

With thy joy-ous sun-shine blest. Hap-py is my day of rest.

2 Fount of all our joy and peace!
   To thy living waters lead me;
Thou from earth my soul release.
   And with grace and mercy feed me.
Bless thy word that it may prove
Rich in fruit that thou dost love.

3 Kindle thou the sacrifice
   That upon my lips is lying:
Clear the shadows from mine eyes.
   That. from every error flying.
No strange fire within me glow
That thine altar doth not know.

4 Let me with my heart to-day,
   Holy, holy, holy, singing.
Rapt awhile from earth away.

All my soul to thee upspringing.
Have a foretaste only given
How they worship thee in heaven.

5 Rest in me and I in thee.
   Build a paradise within me;
Oh, reveal thyself to me.   [me;
   Blessed Love! which now doth win
Fed from thine exhaustless urn.
Pure and bright my lamp shall burn.

6 Hence all care. all vanity.
   For the day to God is holy:
Now. thou glorious Majesty!
   Thou dost fill this temple lowly:
Naught to-day my soul shall move.
Simply resting in thy love.
               Tr. by CATHARINE WINKWORTH.

417 Earnest Longings. 6. 5.   *Magdalene.*—J. B. DYKES.

1. Pur-er yet, and pur-er I would be in mind, Dear-er yet and

dear-er Ev-'ry du-ty find; Hop-ing still, and trust-ing

God with-out a fear, Pa-tient-ly be-liev-ing He will make all clear.

2 Higher yet and higher
　Out of clouds and night,
Nearer yet and nearer
　Rising to the light—

Oft these earnest longings
　Swell within my breast,
Yet their inner meaning
　Ne'er can be expressed.
　　　　　J. W. von GOETHE.

418 Prayer for Oneness. C. M.   *Emanuel.*—S. WEBBE.

1. Spir-it of God, oh, move up-on The wa-ters of my soul!

Vi-brate its thou-sand liv-ing strings, And make me tru-ly whole.

419 Holy Spirit, Dwell with Me. 7. 6 l.

DIX.—CONRAD KOCHER.

1. { Gra-cious Spir-it, dwell with me,— I my-self would gra cious be: }
{ And with words that help and heal, Would thy life in mine re-veal: }

And, with ac-tions bold and meek, Would for Christ, my Sav-ior, speak.

2 Truthful Spirit, dwell with me,—
I myself would truthful be;
And with wisdom kind and clear,
Let thy life in mine appear;
And, with actions brotherly,
Speak my Lord's sincerity.

3 Tender Spirit, dwell with me.—
I myself would tender be:
Shut my heart up like a flower

At temptation's darksome hour;
Open it, when shines the sun,
And his love by fragrance own.

4 Holy Spirit, dwell with me,—
I myself would holy be;
With thy faithfulness I would
Choose and cherish all things good;
And whatever I can be
Give to him who gave me thee.

T. T. LYNCH.

TUNE—*Emanuel.*

2 Spirit of God, I open wide
My inmost self to thee;
Come in, come in; fore'er abide,
And make me wholly free.

3 Spirit of God, thou Thought divine,
With ceaseless action thrill
My being into oneness with
God-Life, God-Love, God-Will.

HANNAH MORE KOHAUS.

420 *Prayer for Knowledge.*
1 Spirit of Truth, oh, let me know
The love of Christ to me;

Its conquering, quickening power bestow,
To set me wholly free.

2 I long to know its depth and height,
To scan its breadth and length;
Drink in its ocean of delight,
And triumph in its strength.

3 Thy quickening power to me impart,
And be my constant Guide;
With richer gladness fill my heart;
Be Jesus glorified.

421 My Petition. 8. 7. D.

CLARA E. CHOATE.
F. Abt. arr. by CLARA H. SCOTT.

1. Lift me up, O heav'n-ly Fa-ther, Till I feel thy strength sublime:
2. Wake with-in my heart, O Giv-er Of di-vin-est good and gain,
3. Fill my soul with rev-e-la-tion, Yet a-wait-ing hu-man kind:

Let thy Spir-it be my spir-it, Let me have no will but thine.
A re-sponse for-ev-er quick-'ning In-to ac-tion, love's re-frain.
Teach me of thy bound-less lov-ing, How the Christ all men may find,

Let me have no will but thine. Bring in-to my life, O Fa-ther,
In-to ac-tion, love's re-frain. O-pen wide of thy hid treas-ure,
How the Christ all men may find. Breathe thro' me thine own per-fec-tion,

Just the mu-sic of thy soul; Make the ra-diance of thy pow-er
Priceless more than pearl of sea: Meet my earn-est, soul-ful long-ing
Till my heart no more shall see Aught but thy di-vine ex-press-ing

My Petition—Concluded.

All my words and deeds con-trol, All my words and deeds con-trol.
For thy truth, earth's mys-ter - y, For thy truth, earth's mys-ter - y.
Of love's grand e - ter - ni - ty, Of love's grand e - ter - ni - ty.

422 Give Us, O Lord. 11. 10. *Hanover.—Arr. fr. Mozart.*

1. Love of the world too long in chains hath bound us: Give us, O
Lord! while here our hearts a - dore, To see the heav'n - ly
wonders that surround us: Oh, lead us there thro' faith's trans-par-ent door.

2 Give us to run, with feet that cannot weary,
  Thro' the bright paths of loving use below,
Lighting the lamps of faith along the dreary
  Pathways of trial where the mourners go.

3 Give us, with all thy beautiful, pure angels,
  To hold communion, till we grow, like them,
Wise in the spirit of thy true evangels,
  And dwellers in thy "New Jerusalem."

423 For Joy and Peace. 8. 7. D.

Arr. fr. MOZART.

1. Ho - ly Spir - it, Source of glad-ness! Come with all thy ra-diance bright:

O'er our sense of toil and sad-ness Breathe thy life, and shed thy light:
D. S.—Rest up - on this con - gre - ga - tion, Spir - it of un - fail - ing joy!

Send us thine il - lu - mi - na - tion: Ban - ish all our soul's an - noy:

D. S.

2 Let the peace which knows no measure,
  Now in quickening showers descend,
Bringing us the richest treasure
  Man can wish or God can send:
Hear our earnest supplication;
  Every struggling heart release;
Rest upon this congregation,
  Spirit of untroubled peace!
                    Tr. fr. P. GERHARDT.

424 The Blessing of Peace.

While the midnight turns to morning,
  While the world forsakes its tomb,
Clothe us with divine adorning,
  Crown us with immortal bloom.
Breathe, O Lord! thy Spirit's blessing,
  Unconfined by time or space,
Let us all, thy peace possessing,
  Rest within thy love's embrace.

425 Be Thou with Us.

1 Welcome, days of solemn meeting;
  Welcome, days of praise and prayer;
Far from earthly scenes retreating,
  In your blessings we would share:
Be thou with us, blessed Savior,
  Still at morn and eve the same:
Give us faith that cannot waver;
  Kindle in us heaven's own flame.

2 Hush! be still! in silent sweetness,
  Rapt in prayer our hearts do bow;
And our circle finds completeness
  In the Lord's dear presence now.
Oh! tho' sorrow's chain hath bound us,
  All our grief hath passed away;
For the Father's hand hath crowned us,
  In his glorious courts to-day.
                    S. F. SMITH.

426 An Affirmation. 8. 7.

Wilmot.—Arr. fr. Weber.

1. Hear our prayer, O gra-cious Fa-ther, Au-thor of ce-les-tial good,

That thy laws, so pure and ho-ly, May be bet-ter un-der-stood.

2 As the dew before the sunlight,
  Quickly fadeth from our sight.
So may every doubt and error
  Fade before eternal light.

3 As the starry hosts of heaven
  Speak the wonders of our God,
So to us shall strength be given
  To proclaim his truth abroad.

4 Like the star of Bethlehem shining,
  Love will guide us all the way,
From the depths of error's darkness,
  Into truth's eternal day.
    HARRIET PARR.

427 *Blessed Spirit.*

1 Blessed Spirit, guide me, lead me,
  Thro' the pearly gates of Truth;
Let thy presence now infuse me
  With new life,—eternal youth.

2 I am one with Life Eternal,
  In my heart dwells only love,
Sacred flame, divine, supernal,
  Melt all dross—admit the Dove.
    E. NICHOLS.

428 *Our Prayer.*

1 Father, hear the prayer we offer!
  Not for ease that prayer shall be,
But for strength that we may ever
  Live our lives courageously.

2 Not forever in green pastures
  Do we ask our way to be;
But the steep and rugged pathway
  May we tread rejoicingly.

3 Not forever by still waters
  Would we idly quiet stay;
But would smite the living fountains
  From the rocks along our way

429 *For a Blessing on the Word.*

1 Come, thou soul-transforming Spirit,
  Bless the sower and the seed;
Let each heart thy grace inherit;
  Raise the weak, the hungry feed

2 Oh, may all enjoy the blessing
  Which thy word's designed to give;
Let us all, thy love possessing,
  Joyfully the truth receive.
    J. EVANS.

430 Invocation. P. M.

SARAH WILDER PRATT.
A. RUBENSTEIN, arr. by CLARA H. SCOTT.

Solo, or voices in unison.

1. O heav'nly Peace with pin-ions white, Roll back the dark-ness
2. O heav'nly Peace with pin-ions white, Dis-pel the dark-ness
3. O heav'nly Peace with pin-ions white, Dis-pel the dark-ness
4. O heav'nly Peace with pin-ions white, Trans-mute the dark-ness

of this night, And o'er the land by strife op-pressed,
of this night. And let the pow'r of God pro-claim
of this night! Spread o'er the trem-bling, troub-led world
of this night; Let all the earth in si-lence sleep

Pour thou the bless-ing of the blessed! O Pow'r Om-nip-o
The mighty heal-ing in his name! O Pow'r Om-nip-o
The banner of God's love un-furled, O Pow'r Om-nip-o-
Be-neath the watch that God doth keep, O Pow'r Om-nip-o-

Invocation—Concluded.

tent! O heav'n - ly Peace!.....
tent! O heav'n - ly Peace!.....
tent! O heav'n - ly Peace!.....
tent! O heav'n - ly Peace!.....

431 Guide Me, O Thou. 8. 7. 4.

W. WILLIAMS.
Oliphant.—P. M. BAILLOT.

1. Guide me, O thou great Je - ho - vah! Pil-grim thro' this bar - ren land;
2. O - pen now the crys - tal fount-ain Whence the heal - ing streams do flow;

I am weak, but thou art might-y, Hold me with thy pow'r-ful hand:
Let the fier - y, cloud - y pil - lar Lead me all my jour - ney through;

Bread of heav - en, Bread of heav-en, Feed me till I want no more.
Strong De - liv - 'rer, Strong De - liv-'rer, Be thou still my strength and shield.

432 The Soul's Home.   P. M.

HANNAH MORE KOHAUS.
PLUMA M. BROWN.

1. Up-ward and on-ward, ev-er as-pir-ing, Up-ward and on-ward to
2. See-ing and hear-ing on-ly true Be-ing, Feel-ing and know-ing

our des-tined goal: Clos-er and clos-er, high-er and high-er.
D. S.—Back to per-fec-tion, whence we have is-sued.

just what we are: Gen-tly ex-pand-ing larg-er and larg-er,
D. S.—Shar-ing his glo-ry, hon-or, and pow-er,

Till we are ris-en to the home of the soul. Un-to the Spir-it.
Will we be gathered to the soul's true home.
Till to the meas-ure of Christ we have grown: Till of his na-ture.
Dwell we for-ev-er in the soul's des-tined home.

D. S.

ho-ly, e-ter-nal. Un-to the change-less source whence we come:
true and up-right-eous, Filled to re-ple-tion, we nev-er-more want:

433   Aspiration.   P. M.

HELEN VAN ANDERSON.
PLUMA M. BROWN.

1. Oh, let me climb for - ev - er higher To the con - se - crat - ed height,
2. Oh, let me speak the lov - ing word,—Or send the lov - ing tho't,—
3. Oh, let me send the heal-ing pow'r To all who seek its wealth;

Where al - ways burns the al - tar - fire Of love's con - sum - ing light;
Wher-e'er there is a heart that's stirred With pain, or grief, or fraught
And tell them in each long - ing hour That "God a - lone is health."

Where self and earth are purged a-way, And Love's sweet incense clears the way
With help-less - ness, and wild - ly seeks Re-dress from an - y source that speaks
Oh, hear! ye sick and err-ing world,—Read this glad mes-sage wide unfurled,

For pu - ri - ty and truth,—For pu - ri - ty and truth.
Of hap - pi - ness or peace,—Of hap - pi - ness or peace.
"The truth shall set you free! The truth shall set you free!"

434　There is No Unbelief.　P. M.

BULWER-LYTTON,
PLUMA M. BROWN.

1. There is no un - be - lief; Who-ev - er plants a seed be-neath the sod.
2. There is no un - be - lief; Who-ev - er sees 'neath winter's field of snow,
3. There is no un - be - lief; The heart that looks on when the eye-lids close,

And waits to see it push a - way the clod, Trusts in God.
The si - lent har - vest of the fu - ture grow, God's pow'r must know.
And dares to live when life has on - ly woes, God's com - fort knows.

Who-ev - er says, when clouds are in the sky, "Be pa-tient, heart! light
Who-ev - er lies down on his couch to sleep, Con - tent to lock each
And day by day, and night un - con-scious - ly, The heart lives by that

break-eth by and by," Trusts the Most High, Trusts the Most High.
sense in slum - ber deep, Knows God will keep, Knows God will keep.
faith the lips de - ny: God know-eth why, God know-eth why.

435 Sometime, Somewhere. P. M.

R. BROWNING.
PLUMA M. BROWN.

1. Un-an-swered yet? Tho' when you first pre-sent - ed This one pe - ti - tion
2. Un-an-swered yet? But you are not un - heed - ed: The prom - is - es of
3. Un-an-swered yet? Nay, do not say un - an-swered, Perhaps your part is
4. Un-an-swered yet? Faith can-not be un - an-swered; Her feet are firm - ly

at the Fa-ther's throne. It seemed you could not wait the time of ask-ing,
God for - ev - er stand; To him our days and years a - like are e - qual:
not yet whol - ly done: The work be-gan when first your prayer was ut-tered,
plant-ed on the Rock; A - mid the wild-est storms she stands un-daunt-ed,

So anx-ious was your heart to have it done: If years have passed since
Have faith in God! it is your Lord's com-mand; Hold on to Ja - cob's
And God will fin - ish what he has be - gun. Keep in - cense burn-ing
Nor quails be-fore the loud - est thun-der - shock: She knows Om - nip - o -

then. do not de - spair, For God will an-swer you some-time, some-where.
an - gel, and your prayer Shall bring a bless-ing down some-time, some-where.
at the shrine of prayer, And glo - ry shall de-scend some-time, some-where.
tence has heard her prayer, And cries, "It shall be done." some-time. some-where.

436   I Only Know.   C. M.   Evangel.—Arr. fr. MENDELSSOHN.

1. I on - ly know that God is good. And I must look to him:

And if I trust, my cup he'll fill With blessings to the brim.

2 I only know that God is all,
  And error holds no sway;
And if I cling to good alone,
  The evil must give way.

3 I only know that love is heaven,
  And heaven is within,
Where, circled by his love, I stand
  Beyond the reach of sin.

4 I only know that God is rest,
  And if his work I do,
His blessed peace will fall on me,
  And all my strength renew.

5 I only know, dear hearts, dear hearts,
  My own does overflow
With love for him and love for you,
  Since his glad way I know.
        FANNIE ISABEL SHERRICK.

437   The Heritage.

1 Mine be the reverent listening love
  That waits all day on thee;
The service of a watchful heart
  Which no one else can see.

2 The faith that, in a hidden way
  No other eye may know,

Finds all its daily work prepared,
  And loves to have it so.

3 My heart is resting, O my God!
  My heart is in thy care;
I hear the voice of joy and praise
  Resounding everywhere!
        ANNA L. WARING.

438   In Thy Care.

1 My heart is resting, O my God!
  I will give thanks and sing;
My heart is at the secret source
  Of every precious thing.

2 I thirst for springs of heavenly life,
  And here all day they rise;
I seek the treasure of thy love,
  And close at hand it lies.

3 I have a certainty of love
  That sets my heart at rest;
A calm assurance for to-day
  That to be thus is best.

4 And a new song is in my mouth
  To long loved music set,—
Glory to thee for all the grace
  I have not tasted yet!
        ANNA L. WARING.

439 He Ordains Their Ways. S. M. 6 l. *Selvin.—Arr. by L. Mason.*

1. A - mid earth's chang-es. Lord, Its shad - ows and its fears,
Its bro - ken pledg-es, shat-tered plans, Its sor-rows and its tears,
Thy chil-dren trust thy own sure word, And wait th' e-ter - nal years.

2 There is no change in thee;
   Thyself art steadfast truth;
   There is no room for grief and care,
   No place for woe and ruth.
   With thee is ever joy and love,
   And blessedness and youth.

3 Oh. dearest trust in God,
   That lights our darkest days,
   Oh, sweetest calm that lifts a psalm
   Forever to God's praise!
   Glad are the pilgrims on the road
   That he ordains their ways.
           MARGARET E. SANGSTER.

440 *Be True, Thyself.*
1 Thou must be true thyself,
   If thou the truth would teach;
   Thy soul must overflow, if thou
   Another's soul would reach.
   It needs the overflowing heart
   To give the lips full speech.

2 Think truly, and thy thoughts
   Shall the world's famine feed:
   Speak truly, and each word of thine
   Shall be a fruitful seed;
   Live truly, and thy life shall be
   A great and noble creed.
           H. BONAR.

TUNE—*Evangel.*

441 *All as God Wills.*
1 All as God wills! who wisely heeds
   To give or to withhold,
   And knoweth more of all my needs
   Than all my prayers have told.

2 That more and more a Providence
   Of love is understood,

Making the springs of time and sense
   Bright with eternal good.

3 No longer forward or behind
   I look, in hope or fear;
   But, grateful, take the good I find,
   God's blessing, now and here.
           J. G. WHITTIER.

442 Have Faith in God. P. M.

HANNAH MORE KOHAUS.
PLUMA M. BROWN.

1. O lov - ing soul, di - vine and pure, If thou wouldst tru - ly know
2. If thou wouldst know the gra-cious rest, Which is a name-less peace.
3. Faith is the germ with - in the tho't Which builds new worlds so fair,
4. Faith is the hand which o - pens wide The gates a - jar, that we,

The life of im - mor-tal - i - ty Which thro' thee now doth flow,
From which all er - ror flies a - way, And mor-tal war-fares cease,—
And peo - ples them with liv - ing things Most beau - ti - ful and rare.—
E'en now, may feast our long - ing eyes, And heav'n-ly glo - ries see,—

Have faith in God. If thou wouldst sure - ly feel that love
Have faith in God. It is the pow'r which guides the hand
O won - drous faith! It is the main-spring of the truth
Have faith in God. It is that sub - stance so di - vine

Which pass-eth per-fect joy. And bring-eth hap - pi - ness com-plete
Stretched forth in dark-est night, To catch with - in its ea - ger grasp
That mak - eth man-kind free. Re - leas - ing them from bur-dens borne
That naught can make nor mar: It shin - eth till the per - fect day—

Have Faith in God—Concluded.

To   all,   with - out   al - loy,—   Have   faith   in   God.
The   great mys - te - rious   light,—   Have   faith   in   God.
Thro' car - nal slav - er - y.—   O   faith   sub - lime.
The   soul's bright morn - ing   star.—   Have   faith   in   God.

443 Art Thou Weary? 8. 5. 3.

Stephanos.—W. H. MONK.

1. Art   thou wea - ry,   art thou lan - guid, Art thou sore dis - tressed?

"Come   to   me." saith   One. "and, com - ing,   Be   at   rest."

2 If I still hold closely to him.
  What hath he at last?
  ··Sorrow vanquished, labor ended.
  Jordan past."

3 If I ask him to receive me.
  Will he say me nay?
  ··Not till earth and not till heaven
  Pass away."

J. M. NEALE.

444 *Trusting Jesus.*

1 I am trusting thee, Lord Jesus,
  Trusting only thee;
  Trusting thee for full salvation,
  Great and free.

2 I am trusting thee to guide me:
  Thou alone shalt lead!
  Every day and hour supplying
  All my need.

3 I am trusting thee for power;
  Thine can never fail!
  Words which thou thyself shalt give me,
  Must prevail.

4 I am trusting thee, Lord Jesus;
  And I ne'er can fall;
  I am trusting thee forever.
  And for all.

FRANCES R. HAVERGAL.

445 Trust. P. M.

HELEN MARSH FLETCHER.
Arr. fr. Mrs. C. BARNARD.

1. I know, O
2. The sun of
3. Thy voice is

Father, that tho' grief may come to-day. Thy love en-folds; I know, what-
peace shall never fail to shine for me In an - y place. For in the
call-ing in each sound that greets the ear Thro' ev'ry day; The call of

ev - er stone of stumbling blocks my way, Thine arm upholds. Thou dost not
light of each new day I still shall see The Fa-ther's face. The con-stant
hope, and health, and beauty, truth and cheer, The perfect way. And so this

Trust— Concluded.

on - ly send a mes-sage from a-bove In answered pray'r,   But thou dost
beau-ty of the ev-er-changing year, Each field and tree,   The dis - tant
life we seek to un-der-stand, contains No mys-ter - y,   For all thy

let me know thy nev - er - fail-ing love Is ev - 'ry-where.
mountain snows, the ti - ny flow-ers near, All speak of thee.
world can hold or give of joy or pain—Re - veal-eth thee.

TUNE—*Dijon.* p. 224.

446   *Faith and Obedience.*

1 When we cannot see our way.
Let us trust and still obey;
He who bids us forward go,
Cannot fail the way to show.

2 Though the sea be deep and wide.
Though a passage seem denied.
Fearless let us still proceed,
Since the Lord vouchsafes to lead.

3 Though it seems the gloom of night.
Though we see no ray of light.

Since the Lord himself is there.
'Tis not meet that we should fear.

4 Night with him is never night,
Where he is, there all is light;
When he calls us, why delay?
They are happy who obey.

5 Be it ours then, while here,
Him to follow without fear;
When he calls us, there to go,
What he bids us, that to do.

T. KELLY.

447　A Song of Trust.　c. m. d.

J. W. Chadwick.
Arr. fr. English Tune.

1. O Love Di - vine, of all that is The sweet-est still and best!
2. I pray not, then, be - cause I would,—I pray be - cause I must:
3. I would not have thee oth - er - wise Than what thou still must be:

Fain would I come and rest to - day Up - on thy ten - der breast:
There is no mean-ing in my prayer But thank-ful - ness and trust.
Yea, thou art God, and what thou art Is ev - er best for me.

And yet the spir - it in my heart says, "Wherefore should I pray
And thou wilt hear the thought I mean, And not the words I say:
And so, for all my sighs, my heart Doth sing it - self to rest.

That thou shouldst seek me with thy love, Since thou dost seek al - way?"
Wilt hear the thanks a - mong the words That on - ly seem to pray.
O Love Di - vine, most far and near, Up - on thy ten - der breast.

448   Give Me Faith.   L. M. 6 l.

Palestine. —J. MAZZINGHI.

1. None loves me, Savior, with thy love: None else can meet such needs as mine:

Oh! grant me, as thou shalt ap - prove, All that be - fits a child of thine!

From ev - 'ry fear and doubt re - lease. And give me con - fi-dence and peace.

2 Give me a faith shall never fail.
  One that shall always work by love;
And then, whatever foes assail,
  They shall but higher courage move
More boldly for the truth to strive.
And more by faith in thee to live.
                        Unknown.

3 Just as God leads me would I go:
  I would not ask to choose my way;
Content with what he will bestow.
  Assured he will not lead me stray.
So as he leads. my path I make.
And step by step I gladly take.
                        LAMPERTIUS.

TUNE—*A Song of Trust.*

449   *The Stream of Faith.*

1 From heart to heart, from creed to
  The hidden river runs;   [creed.
It quickens all the ages down.
  It binds the sires to sons.—
The stream of faith whose source is God.
  Whose sound, the sound of prayer.
Whose meadows are the holy lives
  Upspringing everywhere.

2 And still it moves. a broadening flood;
  And fresher. fuller grows
A sense as if the sea were near
  Towards which the river flows.
O thou, who art the secret Source
  That rises in each soul,
Thou art the Ocean. too,—thy charm.
  That ever deepening roll!
                        W. C. GANNETT.

450 Leading. 6. D.

L. M. Hopkins.
Pluma M. Brown.

1. Led at our dai - ly work, Led when our work is done,
2. On - ly to rest and trust, On - ly his hand to hold,—

By one un - err - ing Mind From morn till set of sun,
This is the gate of pearl, This is the street of gold:

In - to the paths of peace, Now and for - ev - er - more;
Led at our dai - ly work, Led when our work is done.

All doubts and fears laid by, All fruit - less wrest-lings o'er.
By one un - err - ing Mind. To vic - t'ry brave - ly won.

451   *Heaven is Here.*

1 "How far from here to heaven?
    Not very far, my friend.
A single, hearty step
    Will all thy journey end."
Teach me the step to take;
    Then, first, the way to clear.
Raise thou, this fallen one,
    'Tis done, and heaven is here?

2 How far does heaven extend?
    Keep on if thou wouldst know;
A good deed every step
    Will endless beauties show.
Will death await me here?
    Have ne'er a care, my friend;
Heaven counts thy good for aye.
    Naught, then, but good 'twill send.

452 Behind the Cloud. 8. 7. D.

EVA BEST.
PLUMA M. BROWN.

1. If   a cloud should come between us And the splen-dor of the sun:
2. If   we hold to wrong o - pin - ions Till they form a might-y wall:
3. Although pain, and sin, and sor - row Seem to dark - en earth-ly days,

If   the rays of   gold - en sun-light Should be hid-den, one by one:
If   we har - bor tho'ts of   er - ror, And for - get that Good is All:
We may learn a   sim - ple les - son From the sun's ob-struct-ed rays.

If   a - cross the stream and mead-ow, Sud - den - ly   a dark-ness came—
If   we live in mor - tal dark-ness, Are we   not ourselves to blame,
And tho' life it - self seem cloud-ed With the dark-ness of de - spair—

Should we ques-tion for a   mo-ment That the sun shone just the same?
When God's truth be-yond the shad - ow Shines in splen-dor just the same?
Just re - mem-ber that the shad - ow Proves the light is al - ways there.

453   I Have Faith.   P. M.

GERALDINE D. ROBINSON.
PLUMA M. BROWN.

1. I trust in Je - ho - vah! I can - not be moved. For
2. As Je - ru - sa - lem's cit - y is girt by her hills, En-
3. E - ter - nal and change-less this life that is mine, With

naught from the Fa - ther can sev - er; Like Zi - on's strong mountain, my
trenched in the moun-tain-ous fast-ness; My life rests se - cure in the
health, strength, and peace in com-plete-ness: I sat - is - fied rest in the

faith shall re - main, Un - shak - en and stead-fast for - ev - er.
All Fa - ther's love, En - com-passed and hid in its vast - ness.
knowledge of God: I rest know-ing love and its sweet - ness.

REFRAIN.

Oh, strong as Mount Zi - on I stand, Up - held by the Father's own hand;

I Have Faith—Concluded.

Held by love—held by love, Up-held by Om - nip - o - tent love.

454 Promise to Faith. H. M.

Murray.—German.

1. Faith is the po - lar star That guides the Chris-tian's way, Di -

rects his wand'rings far To realms of end - less day: It points the

course wher-e'er he roam, And safe - ly leads the pil - grim home.

2 Faith is the rainbow's form
  Hung on the brow of heaven,
The glory of the storm,
  The pledge of mercy given;
It is the bright, triumphal arch
Thro' which the saints to glory march.

3 The faith that works by love.
  And purifies the heart,
A taste of joys above
  To us will now impart:
It bears us thro' all sense of strife.
And triumphs in eternal life.

F.

455 Denial.   L. M.   *Canonbury.*—R. Schumann

1. The heal-ing stream for-ev - er flows, A cleansing tide of liv-ing Truth:

And he who bathes, like Naaman, finds Re - turn-ing health, re-viv-ing youth.

2 Seven times, the mystic number given,
  Seven washings, and the leprous stain
Fades swift away, and, like a child's,
  The flesh grows soft and fresh again.

3 Seven times the mind shall bathe within
  Denial's potent, cleansing tide;
And from its waters shall arise
  From error free, all purified.

4 The vain imaginings of sin,
  Material creeds and doubts and fears.
Sickness and pain all washed away.
  God's child divinely fair appears.
              GERALDINE D. ROBINSON.

456   *Healing Waters.*

1 River of Eden from the skies.
Stream of celestial harmonies,
The Lord has made thy wave divine.
And turned thy crystal flood to wine.

2 Flow thro' us, in us rest, and lave
Our every act with sacred wave;
In heart and sense, in deed and will,
Flow with angelic music still.

3 River of life! the trees that grow
In angel-bowers thy virtues know:
The gardens of the soul above
Drink life and virtue from thy love.

4 From land to land roll on, till we
Behold, on earth, each human tree
With blossoms crowned, with fruit sup-
  plied,
And nourished by thy healing tide.

457   *The Living Bread.*

1 O Christ, thou joy of loving hearts!
  Thou Fount of life! thou Light of men.
From the best bliss that earth imparts.
  We turn, unfilled, to thee again.

2 Thy truth unchanged hath ever stood:
  Thou savest those that on thee call;
To them that seek thee, thou art good.
  To them that find thee, all in all.

3 We taste thee, O thou Living Bread.
  And long to feast upon thee still;
We drink of thee, the Fountain Head,
  And thirst, our souls from thee to fill!
           Tr. by R. PALMER.

458   Baptism.   P. M.

GERALDINE D. ROBINSON.
PLUMA M. BROWN.

1. Bap - tize   me now,   O Christ di - vine! With spir - it   and with fire;
2. The wa - ters clear   of   Jor-dan's stream Can nev - er cleanse the soul:
3. Im-mersed in   thee,   O   bless - ed Truth! My works shall fit - ly prove

Make clean my life, with-out, with - in, From sense of sick-ness, death. and sin.
The words of Life, and Truth, and Love, On their pure tide bear me a - bove
That I am thine, as thou art mine, My life and be - ing all di - vine;

Oh, pu - ri - fy   each tho't of mine From worldly, vain de - sire.—
The   er-rors of   this mor - tal dream, And I   am clean and whole.—
For - ev - er one with Christ in God, For - ev - er one with Love.—

Oh, pu - ri - fy   each tho't of mine From world-ly, vain de - sire.
The er - rors of   this mor-tal dream, And I   am clean and whole.
For - ev - er one with Christ in God. For - ev - er one with Love.

459   Bread of Life.   P. M.

MARY A. LATHBURY.
WM. F. SHERWIN.

1. Break thou the bread of life, Dear Lord, to me, As thou didst
2. Bless thou the truth, dear Lord, To me, to me, As thou didst

break the loaves be - side the sea. Be - yond the sa - cred page
bless the bread by Gal - i - lee: Then shall all bond - age cease,

I seek thee, Lord: My spir - it pants for thee, O liv - ing Word!
All fet - ters fall, And I shall find my peace, My All in All!

Used by arr with J. H. Vincent, owner of copyright.

460   Life of Life.   8. 7.

St. Sylvester.—J. B DYKES.

1. No more lab'ring, heav-y la - den,— Thou sup-pli - est all our need,

Sat - is - fy - est all our hun-ger: "Bread of Life!" on thee we feed.

461 **The Living Bread.** 7. 6. D.

Bolton.— J. Walsh.

1. O Bread to pilgrims giv-en, O food that an-gels eat, O man-na sent from heav-en, For heav'n-born natures meet! Give us, for thee long pin-ing, To eat till rich-ly filled: Till, earth's delights resigning, Our ev-'ry wish is stilled.

2 O Water. life-bestowing.
   From out the Sav-ior's heart!
A fountain purely flowing.
   A fount of love thou art:
Oh, let us. freely tasting.
   Our burning thirst assuage!
Thy sweetness. never wasting,
   Avails from age to age.

3 O Christ! this feast receiving,
   We thee unseen adore;
Thy faithful word believing.
   We take. and doubt no more;
Give us, thou true and loving!
   On earth to live in thee;
Then. faith the vail removing,
   Thy glorious face to see.
   Tr. by R. Palmer.

Tune—*St. Sylvester.*

2 Thirsting for the springs of water.
   That by love's eternal law,
From the stricken Rock are flowing.
   "Well of Life!" from thee we draw.

3 In the land of cloud and shadow.
   Where no human eye can see,
Light to those who sit in darkness.
   "Light of Life!" we walk in thee.

4 Sick of sense's vain deceivings,
   Crumbling round us into dust;
Strong alone in faith's believings.
   "Word of Life!" in thee we trust.

5 Thou the "Grace of life" supplying.
   Thou the "Crown of life" wilt give;
No more sighing, no more dying.
   "Life of Life" in thee we live.
   J. S. B. Monsell.

462 All to Thee.   7. 6 l.

Rosefield.—C. Malan.

1. { Fa - ther, Son, and Ho - ly Ghost, One   in Three, and Three in One. }
   { As   by   the   ce - les - tial host, Let   thy will   on earth be done; }

Praise by   all   to   thee   be giv'n, Glo-rious Lord   of earth and heav'n.

2 Take my soul and body's powers;
  Take my memory, mind, and will;
All my goods, and all my hours;
  All I know, and all I feel;
All I think, or speak, or do;
Take my heart, but make it new.

3 Now, O God, thine own I am;
  Now I give thee back thine own;
Freedom, friends, and health, and fame.
  Consecrate to thee alone:
Claim me for thy service, claim
All I have, and all I am.

C. Wesley.

463 The True Supply.   s m.

Inverness.—L. Mason.

1. Oh, bless - ed they   who know Thine un - seen pres - ence true,

Where, in the king-dom of   thy   grace. Thou mak - est all things new.

464 True Bread of Life. 10. Ernan.—L. Mason.

1. True Bread of life, in lov - ing mer - cy giv'n, Long fam-ished souls to strengthen and to feed; Christ Je - sus, Son of God, true Bread of heav'n, Thy flesh is meet, thy blood is drink in - deed.

2 I cannot famish, though this earth should fail,
  Though life through all its fields should pine and die;
  Though the sweet verdure should forsake each vale,
  And every stream of every land run dry.

3 True Tree of life! Of thee I eat and live,
  Who eateth of thy fruit shall never die;
  'Tis thine the everlasting health to give,
  The youth and bloom of immortality.

4 Feeding on thee, all weakness turns to power,
  This sickly soul revives, like earth in spring;
  Strength floweth on and in, each buoyant hour,
  This being seems all energy, all wing.
                                          H. Bonar.

TUNE—Inverness.

2 Here by thy loving hand
    Thy people now are fed;
  Thou art the Cup of blessing, Lord,
    And thou the Heavenly Bread.

3 Oh, may that grace be ours,
    In thee for aye to live,
  And drink of those refreshing streams
    Which thou alone canst give.
                                          H. W. Beadon.

465 Alone with Thee. 11. 10.

Berlin.—Arr. fr Mendelssohn.

1. Still, still with thee, when pur-ple morn-ing break-eth, When the bird wak-eth and the shad-ows flee: Fair-er than morn-ing, love-lier than the day-light, Dawns the sweet con-scious-ness. I am with thee.

2 Alone with thee, amid the mystic shadows,
   The solemn hush of Nature newly born;
Alone with thee, in breathless adoration,
   In the calm dew and freshness of the morn.

3 So shall it be at last, in that bright morning
   When the soul waketh, and the shadows flee;
Oh, in that hour, fairer than daylight dawning,
   Shall rise the glorious thought, I am with thee.

4 I cannot lose thee. Still in thee abiding,
   The end is clear, how wide, soe'er I roam;
The law that holds the worlds, my steps is guiding,
   And I must rest at last in thee, my home.

Mrs. H. B. Stowe.

The Holy Supper is kept, indeed,
In whatso we share with another's need;
Not what we give, but what we share—
For the gift without the giver is bare;
Who gives himself with his alms feeds three—
Himself, his hungering brother, and Me.

J. R. Lowell.

466 Consecration. 7. D.

FRANCES R. HAVERGAL.
Arr. fr. CONCONE.

1. Take my life. and let   it   be   Con - se - crat - ed. Lord. to   thee:
2. Take my voice, and let   me sing   Al - ways, on - ly,   for   my   King:
3. Take my will and make it thine: It   shall be   no   long - er   mine;

Take my mo-ments and my days: Let them flow   in   cease-less praise.
Take my lips. and let them be   Filled with mes - sa - ges from thee.
Take my heart, it   is thine own: It   shall be   thy   roy - al throne.

Take my hands and   let them   move   At   the im - pulse of   thy love:
Take my sil - ver   and my   gold: Not   a   mite would I   with-hold:
Take my love: my   Lord. I   pour   At   thy feet   its treas - ure store:

Take my feet. and let them   be   Swift and beau - ti - ful   for   thee.
Take my in - tel - lect, and   use   Ev - 'ry pow'r as   thou shalt choose.
Take my-self, and I   will   be   Ev - er, on - ly,   all   for thee.

467   **Bread of Heaven.**   P. M.   J. CRAMER

1. Fa - ther e - ter - nal!—Life pure and un - de - filed, Food for the
ree - on - ciled, O liv - ing bread! Bread with all sub-stance rife.
Heal-ing all pain and strife, Breath of e - ter - nal Life. O liv - ing bread!

2 Father supernal!—
Thou never failing Love.
Coming from realms above
    O living bread!
Bread with all wholeness fraught.
Fragrant with holy thought.
On angels' pinions brought.
    O living bread!

3 Father Almighty!—
Swiftly our souls arise,
To that which satisfies,
    O living bread!
Radiant its light shall be,
Shining eternally,
With us in unity,
    O living bread!
             HANNAH MORE KOHAUS.

TUNE.—*Waiting in Thy Presence.*

468   *The Everlasting Arms.*

1 I am resting, surely resting
   In "the everlasting arms,"
Baffling thus and safely breasting,
   Waves of every threatening harm.

2 No more buffeted and moulded
   By vain show of outward strife;

In the unseen arms enfolded.
   Here I find the one true Life.

3 Life unchanging. life unbounded,
   Love's great mystic "open sea."
Only by Truth's measure sounded.—
   Truth that made, and makes us free
             MRS. MARSH.

469 **Waiting in Thy Presence.** 8. 7. Arr. fr. Mrs. C. Barnard.

1. Sim - ply wait - ing in thy Pres-ence. Sim-ply standing in the glow

That the glo - ry of thy Be - ing Nev - er ceas - es to be - stow.

2 Pain there is not—pain nor sorrow,
  They have vanished as the dew
Where the morning sunlight glimmers
  From the bosom of the blue.

3 Fear I know not—like the shadows
  That take wing before the day—
In the brightness of thy Being
  All my fears have passed away.

4 Simply waiting in thy Presence,
  All the strength belongs to me:
Life that cometh from the Father,
  Frail or helpless cannot be.

5 Standing in thy fadeless Glory,
  All my life is glorified.
I am strong and true and mighty,
  Lord, thy child is satisfied.
                    J. C. MACY.

Let thy soul walk softly in thee,
  As a saint in heaven unshod;
For to be alone with silence
  Is to be alone with God.
                    S. M. HAGEMAN.

470   *Trust the Spirit.*

1 Trust, oh, trust the gentle Spirit!
  Let it lead your eyes to see
The pure spring, where you inherit
  Life and immortality.

2 Never care nor fear of trouble
  Dims the mirror of your soul,
That reflects the good, good only,
  When to Good you give control.

3 Overcome the seeming shadow;
  Step upon it, high above,
On the unseen Spirit ladder,
  Into realms of life and love.

4 Trust, oh, trust the gentle Spirit;
  For the substance and the soul,
That is worth the claim of merit,
  Vital life is, and the whole.
                    MARY E. BUTTERS.

"Everywhere the gate of beauty
  Fresh across the pathway swings,
As we follow truth or duty
  Inward to the heart of things."
                    W. C. GANNETT.

471 The Song Victorious. P. M.

PLUMA M. BROWN.

1. I stand in the great for - ev - er, I lave in the
2. In the death-less glo - ry of spir - it, That knows no de-
3. Oh, I stand in the great for - ev - er, All things are to
4. Ye pil - grims of va - ried pro - ba - tions, Ye teach-ers and
5. Oh, the glo - ry and joy of liv - ing! To know we are

o - cean of truth, I bask in the gold - en sun - shine
struc - tion or fall, From im - mor - tal fires of heav - en
me di - vine: I eat of the heav'n-ly man - na,
sav - iors of men, To your heav'n-born rev - e - la - tions
one with God— 'Tis an ar - mor of might to the spir - it.

Of end - less love and youth. And God is with-in and a-
To the plains of earth I call. Who is this "I" that is
I drink of the heav'n-ly wine. A glo - ri - ous song of re-
My spir - it shall an - swer "A - men." With you in the great for-
'Tis a blos - som that crowns the sod! I gaze thro' the dawn of the

round me, All good is for - ev - er mine; To all who
speak-ing? This be - ing so won-drous in might? 'Tis one with the
joic - ing In my in - ner-most spir - it I hear, And it sounds like
ev - er With the chil-dren of earth I stand, And this light flow - ing
morn-ing, And I dream 'neath the stars of night, And I bow my

The Song Victorious—Concluded.

seek it is giv-en, And it comes by a law di-vine.
Prim-i-tive Es-sence, A ray of the In-fi-nite Light.
heav-en-ly voi-ces In a cho-rus di-vine and clear.
out like a riv-er Shall bless and re-deem the land.
head to the bless-ing Of this won-der-ful gift of light!

472 Silence before God. 7. 6 l.

Pilot.—J. E. Gould.

1. God of Love, thou art with me, I am ev-er one with thee;
D.C.—Child of earth, be still while he Life e-ter-nal speaks thro' thee.

And thy-self, the Christ with-in, Speaks thro' all the world-ly din:—

2 "It is I, be not afraid,
For my voice thou hast obeyed;
Lo! I come to heal and bless,
Guide thy steps in righteousness;
Lead thee into paths of peace,
Bid all fear and discord cease.

3 I am closer than the air
Breathed around you everywhere;
I am now your very love,

Life and substance from above;
And in me there is no death,
For my very life is breath."

4 Thus he speaks, and it is done
Through the one beloved Son.
Rise, O child of God, arise!
Shout this message to the skies,—
"God is Life, oh, hear the call,
God is ever All in All!"

Esther Marion.

473 Love's Message. P. M.

HANNAH MORE KOHAUS.
PLUMA M. BROWN.

1. There is One for-ev-er with you, Have no fear:
2. Love be-nef-i-cent will bear you, On its wings,
3. Light will o-pen now its por-tals Wide for you,
4. Truth, al-might-y to de-liv-er, Frees your soul.

One, but wait-ing now to heal you, Ev-er near:
When your soul with all its long-ings To it clings:
That your vi-sion may be-hold its Treas-ures true:
And the knowledge of its pow-er Makes you whole:

In the shel-ter of this Pres-ence, Close-ly held.
Un-der-neath you is the Sub-stance, Strong and sure:
That your soul with all its rich-es Now al-lied,
You shall feel its weight of glo-ry. By and by.—

Ev-'ry seem-ing fear and dan-ger Are dis-pelled.
And through-out e-ter-ni-ty it Will en-dure.
Shall a-wa-ken in God's like-ness, Sat-is-fied.
Spir-it whis-pers, "My be-lov-ed. It is I."

474 In the Secret Place. P. M.

HANNAH MORE KOHAUS.
Swiss Melody.

1. In the se-cret of thy pres-ence will we bide.
2. With the brightness of thy glo-ry will we shine,
3. With thy peace be-yond all meas-ure are we filled,
4. From the sa-cred truth of be-ing, all we bring,

In the shel-ter of thy pow-er will we hide:
In the lus-tre of thy ra-diance all di-vine:
With thy love that fail-eth nev-er are we thrilled:
To the one al-might-y Spir-it will we cling:

To thine Om-ni-pres-ence on-ly, swift we flee,
In thy ev-er-last-ing splen-dor will we wake,
All our be-ing is trans-port-ed by thy praise,
Lean-ing ful-ly on its fast-ness hour by hour.

Rest-ing, peace-ful rest-ing, fold-ed now in thee.
Know-ing, tru-ly know-ing, thou wilt ne'er for-sake.
Feel-ing, tru-ly feel-ing, thou wilt guide our ways.
Trust-ing, whol-ly trust-ing. Om-ni-pres-ent pow'r.

475   Precious Truth.   P. M.

HELEN VAN ANDERSON.
Arr. fr. FLOTOW.

1. O precious Truth, but thee I love, Heart and hand with thee I'll rove;
2. O precious Christ, my Truth's fair name, May I thy life and love at-tain:
3. O precious Truth, thou art to me The Key to joy's sweet minstrelsy:
4. O precious Christ, that peace of thine Steals o'er my soul—a rest sub-lime;

'Tis but with thee I take de-light, Thro' ev'ning, morning, noon, and night.
Thou art my in-spir-a-tion true, My strength, and health, and perfect view.
The Sun that gives life's radiant light. The Pow'r that gives tho'ts pinions flight.
Thy wondrous love, a might-y flood, Shall flow thro' all my tho'ts of Good.

REFRAIN.

Pre-cious Truth, thou art to me, The on-ly Guide o'er
life's great sea: I walk no more in doubt or fear, For thou, O
Truth, art ev-er near,—For thou, O Truth, art ev-er near

476 Realization. P. M.

GERALDINE D. ROBINSON.
PLUMA M. BROWN.

1. In the pres-ence of God I am stand-ing, And full-ness of
2. And I drink of the life-giv-ing foun-tain. The foun-tain of
3. Oh, the glad-ness of be-ing and know-ing! The glad-ness of

joy is now mine: For a great love per-vades all my be-ing,
truth fair and free: Till the mind that was known in Christ Je-sus
get-ting so still! That rich streams of the God-life flow thro' me,

And it fills me with peace that's di-vine.)
Thinks and speaks its sweet wis-dom thro' me. }
And I know but the Fa-ther's own will.)

REFRAIN.

In his pres-ence, in his pres-ence. In his pres-ence is full-ness of joy: Health now holds me, Love en-folds me, The sweet peace of his king-dom I know.

477 Life, Truth, Way. P. M.

MARY E. BUTTERS.
PLUMA M. BROWN.

1. I am the Life, the Truth, the Way,— En-ter there-in; I am the
2. I am the calm, un-troub-led Sea.— Peace-ful it flows; All that are
3. I am the Life, the Truth, the Way, To love's bright home; I am the

Gate to end-less day,—Free-dom from sin. I am the bright and
wea-ry come un-to me, Here find re-pose. Safe in the arms un-
Kingdom of peace al-way. Will you not come? Love that shall bid all

shin-ing Light, Nev-er to dim. The stars of glo-ry with-
bound-ed, deep, Lean on my breast: Storms of thy soul are
fear and doubt, All ills be gone, Sor-row and pain be

REFRAIN.

out a night Un-veiled in him!
lulled to sleep, Ev-er to rest. Come un-to me, O wea-ry soul!
all cast out In Love's bright sun.

Life, Truth, Way—Concluded.

Strength I will give; En-ter my realm of peace made whole,—Enter and live.

478 At-one-ment. 6. 4.

Scotch Air.

1. Spir - it om - nip - o - tent With us a - bides: Know-ing God

im - ma-nent, Naught ill be - tides: Fold - ed in Love's em - brace.

Feel-ing God face to face, Crowned with abundant grace, He that con - fides.

2 Deeply our inmost soul.
   Feels God alway;
Nor from this Presence sure
   Can it e'er stray;
O'ershadowed by its Power,
Guided from hour to hour,
Rich with unfailing dower,
   All who obey.

3 Spirit, O changeless One!
   Ever with thee;
Consciously now thine own,
   Would we all be;
Ever at-one we are,
Naught can this solace mar.
Naught can our souls debar
   From Deity.

HANNAH MORE KOHAUS.

For Realization.

479 Decree. P. M.

Mrs. Browning.
Pluma M. Brown.

Thy love shall chant its own be - at - i - tudes aft - er its

own life work-ing: A child - kiss set up - on the sigh-ing lips shall

make thee glad: A poor man served by thee shall make thee rich:

A sick man helped by thee shall make thee strong; Thou shalt be

served by ev - 'ry sense of serv - ice that thou ren - der - est.

480 The Life of Life. P. M.

PLUMA M. BROWN.

1. Om - ni-pres - ent Life of Life, Now all our be - ing fill - ing,
2. Om - ni-pres - ent Love di - vine, All doubt and fear dis - pel - ling:
3. Om - ni-pres - ent Peace of Christ, Source of our rest and glad -ness:

Life, Life, on - ly Life, Thro' all our sens - es thrill-ing. Now the
Love, Love, Love di - vine, All oth - er love ex - cel - ling. Spotless and
Peace, Peace, Rest and Peace, Balm for all care and sad - ness. Within thy

Word its pow'r re - veals, And life's mys-ter - y un - seals, Thro' all
pure, oh, lead thou me, Perfect in likeness, e'en like thee, Thro' all
light we dwell se - cure, Sheltered by thee, de-fense is sure Thro' all

e - ter - ni - ty; While we love and while we praise The Life of Life.
e - ter - ni - ty: While our love and while our praise Bids er - ror flee.
e - ter - ni - ty: While our love and while our praise Brings rest and peace.

481 The Silence of Spirit. 12.

HANNAH MORE KOHAUS.
PLUMA M. BROWN.

1. In the si - lence of Spir-it I pa - tient-ly wait Un - til there shall
2. In the si - lence of Spir-it I pause to be taught The les - sons of
3. In the si - lence of Spir-it I lin - ger to find The gar - ment of

o - pen the beau - ti - ful gate Of the tem - ple ce - les - tial, whose
life, with sin - cer - i - ty fraught,—How tru - ly to love, and how
life for the soul of man-kind; To re-ceive the new name in the

glo - ries, un - told, One aft - er an - oth - er to me will un - fold.
right-ly to live, How wise-ly with-hold, and how just - ly to give.
pu - ri - fied stone, Re-vealed to my in - ner-most be - ing a - lone.

DUET.

In the si - lence of Spir-it I list - en to hear The voice of all
In the si - lence of Spir-it I wait to be led In path-ways where
O sweet, hallowed si-lence of Spir - it di - vine! Up - on thy still

The Silence of Spirit—Concluded.

voi - ces to me the most dear: For it wak - ens my soul to an
on - ly the ho - ly may tread: Where blos-soms of mer - cy, the
bos - om I love to re - cline. Where, rest - ed. re-freshed, and re -

an - them of praise, As the rose to the sun all its beau - ty dis-plays.
fra-grance of grace. And the fruitage of love ev - 'ry foot-print doth trace.
vived thro' and thro', I come forth bap - tized for earth's struggles a - new.

482 Truth's Blessing. P. M.

Arr. fr. Schubert.

1. When hearts are full of love to God And to their fel - low - men,

But words of bless - ing will they speak. O - ver and o - ver a - gain.

2 When souls are thrilled with heavenly
bliss,
Which doth no sorrow ken,
They'll breathe on all this breath of life.
Over and over again.

3 When filled with wisdom. courage, faith.
Not many words can pen.

But songs of triumph will they sing.
Over and over again.

4 When souls vibrate with light divine,
And knowledge true. oh, then.
This gospel news they'll gladly sing.
Over and over again.

HANNAH MORE KOHAUS.

For Realization.

483 Know Thyself. P. M.

GERALDINE D. ROBINSON.
PLUMA M. BROWN.

1. Un - close, O soul of {man, / mine,} to know That Love is Lord; As
2. A - wake, O soul of {man, / mine,} to see That Truth is all: Bid
3. A - rise, O soul of {man, / mine,} to prove Your Life di - vine; Be

burst - ing bud your pet - als throw, For deep with - in doth gleam and glow
ig - no - rance and darkness flee. And in the name of Christ be free
your true self and you shall move Heav'n's gate by lev - er of that Love.—

The mys - tic word: As burst - ing bud your pet - als throw,
From er - ror's thrall; Bid ig - no - rance and dark - ness flee,
That Truth of thine: Be your true self and you shall move

For deep with - in doth gleam and glow The mys - tic word.
And in the name of Christ be free From er - ror's thrall.
Heav'n's gate by lev - er of that Love.—That Truth of thine.

484 At Rest. P. M.

WM. P. M'KENZIE.
PLUMA M. BROWN.

1. I am on-ly a child who is ly-ing On the bos-om of in-fi-nite love:
2. I am on-ly a child who is ly-ing On the bos-om of in-fi-nite love:

I speak not of liv-ing or dy-ing, I know not of sor-row or cry-ing.
I speak not of liv-ing or dy-ing, I know not of sor-row or cry-ing.

My tho'ts are dwelling a-bove. The spring of the life that is flow-ing
My tho'ts are dwelling a-bove. All I need with-out price I am buy-ing

Is hid-den with Christ in God: Not yet the mys-ter'-y know-ing.
By my trust in the good-ness a-bove: There's an end to my yearning and sighing.

I feel that the peace is grow-ing. As a riv-er grows deep and broad.
For just like a child I am ly-ing On the bos-om of in-fi-nite love.

485 Affirmation. P. M.

PLUMA M. BROWN.

1. Thou art here pres-ent with me, Thou hear-est my prayer to thee;

Thou art my Life and my Light; Thou art my Guide; Thou hast taught me,

helped me, com-fort-ed me: Thou hast healed me: I love thee. A - men.

Copyright, 1891, by Pluma M. Brown.

486 At Peace. C. M.

Evangel.—Arr. fr. MENDELSSOHN.

1. In the e-ter-nal Now I dwell, Se-cure from ev-'ry ill.

Be-cause I know God is su-preme, And doth cre-a-tion fill.

487 To Myself. P. M.

PAUL FLEMMING.
PLUMA M. BROWN.

SOLO.

1. Let noth-ing make thee sad or fret-ful, Or too re-gret-ful,
2. Why shouldst thou fill to-day with sor-row A-bout to-mor-row.
3. ✗ On-ly be stead-fast. nev-er wa-ver, Nor seek earth's fa-vor,

ACCOMP.

8va.

Be still; What God hath or-dered must be right,
My heart? One watch-es all with care most true,
But rest; Thou know-est what God wills must be

Then find in it thine own de-light, My will.
Doubt not that he will give thee, too, Thy part.
For all his crea-tures. so for thee. The best.

Copyright, 1891, by Pluma M. Brown.

TUNE—*Ecangel.*

2 There's naught to fear. for God is Love. And now I realize that peace
   Encircling me alway; God hath prepared for me.
And when this holy Name I speak.
   Doubt can no longer stay. 4 Let every shadow then depart.
   And leave my soul at rest:
3 There's naught to dread since God is For life and health. and strength and
   all bliss.
   That is. or e'er can be; Are my divine bequest.

HANNAH MORE KAHAUS.

488 My Song. L. M.   R. SCHUMANN.

1. I know my song, tho' simply sweet, Finds an-swer in some wea-ry heart,
Nor lost the ech-oes' soft refrain, Tho' heart and song seem worlds a-part.

2 The whisper of the soul divine
  In gentlest accents touches shore
With wave-beats of another soul
  Whose loving faith the message bore.

3 Unseen, unheard by human ears,
  Strains of celestial music weave
Their graceful symphony of dreams,
  Nor time, nor space can hold or leave.

4 The ocean, with its countless waves,
  Is naught beside this greater sea,
Whose mightier power outshines the stars,
  Or sings its song of ecstasy.

5 Beyond, anear, all things complete,
  For us awaiting yet to know
The vastness of the love that sleeps,
  The grandeur of life's overflow.

6 Divinest mystery of love,
  Thy secrets of the soul's domain
Wake raptures of the heavenly spheres,
  And crowns all earth with life again.
         CLARA E. CHOATE.

489   With Wider View.

1 With wider view come loftier goal!
  With broader light, more good to see!
With freedom, more of self-control,
  With knowledge, deeper reverence be!

2 Anew we pledge ourselves to thee,
  To follow where thy Truth shall lead;
Afloat upon its boundless sea,
  Who sails with God is safe indeed!
         S. LONGFELLOW.

490   Immutability.

1 The good is never of a day;
  Eternal verity doth live;
From everlasting ages on,
  The past doth to the future give.

2 Who loves the good, who loves the truth,
  Loves not a fleeting shadow dark;
Who loves the true, lives not in vain,
  But presses forward to the mark.

3 Our yesterday, to-morrow, now,
  But mean eternity begun;
So everlasting good, the truth,
  From ages back doth onward run.
         KATHERINE SMITH.

491 Beautiful Morning. 11.

German.

1. O beau-ti-ful morn-ing! thou day of de-light, That woke us from dream-ing, from er-ror's long night; O day when Truth's shin-ing lights all the dark way, Far back from earth's morning, to close of each day.

2 O day of rejoicing! when doubt and despair
Were vanquished by knowledge, so bright and so fair;
O day of rejoicing! when out of the night
Love woke us from error and showed us the light.

3 This beautiful morning will dawn for us all,
Who earnestly seek it, will come at our call,
Oh, turn from the darkness of error and sense,
Seek, seek for the treasure, make Love your defense!

4 O beautiful morning! far out of the night
Of ignorance hasten, on into Truth's light;
Come, hasten with gladness, Love calls you to-day,
Her treasures are waiting in bounteous array!

M. R. B.

492 Aspiration of the Soul. C. M. D.

HANNAH MORE KOHAUS.
PLUMA M. BROWN.

1. Spir - it of God, oh, move up - on The wa - ters of my soul:
2. Spir - it of Truth, oh, quick-en me With ev - er - last - ing life:

Vi - brate its thou-sand liv - ing strings, And make me tru - ly whole.
Then, new - ly born, I, too, shall be With quick'ning pow'r en - rife.

Spir - it of Love, I o - pen wide My in - most soul to thee;
Spir - it of Life, O breath di - vine, With cease-less ac - tion thrill

Come in, come in, and there a - bide, And make me whol - ly free.
My be - ing in - to one - ness with God - life, God-love, God - will.

Copyright, 1896, by Pluma M. Brown.

C. P. M.

Look up, look up, my soul, still higher!
On to the heavenly goal aspire.
   On God's love ever lean:
Burst this dull earth's control, and wing
Thy way where no clouds roll, and sing
   In deeps of God unseen.

A. E. EVANS.

493 Nearer I Cannot Be. C. M. D.

HANNAH MORE KOHAUS.
PLUMA M. BROWN.

1. How can I near-er be to God Than what I am to-day?
2. How can I near-er be to Love Than feel its glow and thrill,

In God I live, and move, and breathe, From God ex - ist al - way.
By be - ing filled with one de - sire, Love's mis-sion to ful - fill?

How can I near-er be to Truth Than in its am - pli - tude
How can I near-er be to Life Than with my think-ing pow'r:

Be close-ly fold-ed ev-'ry hour, Re-ceiv-ing on-ly good?
To breathe it in, and breathe it out, With ev-'ry pass-ing hour?

7. 6 l.
What thou shalt to-day provide,
Let me as a child receive;
What to-morrow may betide,
Calmly to thy wisdom leave.
'Tis enough that thou wilt care;
Why should I the burden bear?

J. NEWTON.

494   Infinite Majesty.   6. 4.

Bethany. — L. Mason.

1. In - fi - nite Maj - es - ty, To thee we bow, Know-ing thy

pres-ence here, We feel thee now. Deep in our hearts we hear

Soft spo-ken words of cheer. An-gels now hov-er near, Whis-per-ing low.

Used by arr. with Oliver Ditson Co., owners of copyright.

2 In thy deep tenderness
  We are at home;
To thy great heart of love
  Trusting we come;
We do not have to tread
By ways of fear and dread,
For thou our path hast made,
  Thou art our home.

3 Higher than heaven art thou,
  Dearest and best;
Father-love, mother-love,
  Thou art our rest;
With never-ending joy
Naught can our souls annoy;
Peace, ours—without alloy.—
  So are we blest.

SARAH E. GRISWOLD.

495   Nearer, my God, to Thee.

1 Nearer, my God, to thee,
  Nearer to thee!
E'en though it be a cross
  That raiseth me!
Still all my song shall be,
Nearer, my God, to thee,
Nearer, my God, to thee,
  Nearer to thee!

2 There let the way appear,
  Steps unto heaven;
All that thou sendest me,
  In mercy given:
Angels to beckon me
Nearer, my God, to thee,
Nearer, my God, to thee,
  Nearer to thee!

Mrs. S. F. ADAMS.

496 I Love Thy Words. P. M.

HANNAH MORE KAHAUS, English.

1. I love thy words, O Spir - it! I feed them to my soul;
2. I love thy words, O Spir - it! I speak them aft - er thee.

I know their per - fect fruit - age Will ev - 'ry whit make whole.
And lo! be - fore their pow - er How swift the shad - ows flee!

They are my guide whate'er be - tide, They are my stay in ev - 'ry way,
The clouds a - rise, the darkness hies, There's naught to fear, for thou art near,

Thy words are strength and light, Thy words are strength and light:
Thy words thy pres - ence bring, Thy words thy pres - ence bring;

I feed up - on them hour - ly, And prove their won - drous might.
I lean up - on them hour - ly, And un - to them I cling.

497 Open My Eyes that I may See. P. M.   CLARA H. SCOTT. By per.

1. O - pen my eyes that I may see Glimps - es of Truth thou
2. O - pen my ears that I may hear Voi - ces of Truth thou
3. O - pen my mouth and let me bear Glad - ly the warm Truth

hast for me; Place in my hands the won - der - ful key,
send - est clear, And, while the wave-notes fall on my ear,
ev - 'ry - where: O - pen my heart and let me pre - pare.

That shall un - clasp and set me free. Si - lent - ly now I
Ev - 'ry - thing false will dis - ap - pear. Si - lent - ly now I
Love, with thy chil - dren, thus to share. Si - lent - ly now I

wait for thee, Read - y, my God, thy will to see,
wait for thee, Read - y, my God, thy will to see.
wait for thee, Read - y, my God, thy will to see,

Open My Eyes that I may See—Concluded.

O - pen my eyes, il - lu - mine me, Spir - it di - vine.
O - pen my ears, il - lu - mine me, Spir - it di - vine.
O - pen my heart, il - lu - mine me, Spir - it di - vine.

498 The Hidden Life. S. M.

Mornington.—G. C. WELLESLEY.

1. Our life is hid with Christ, With Christ in God a - bove:

Up-ward our heart now turns to him, Know-ing his life is love.

499 *One Mind.*

2 He liveth, and we live!
  His life for us prevails;
  His fullness fills our mighty void,
  His strength for us avails.

3 Life worketh in us now,
  Life is for us in store;
  So death is swallowed up of life;
  We live forevermore.

4 Like him eternally
  Transformed and glorified;
  We recognize him as he is,
  And in his light abide.

H. BONAR.

1 Our God as Mind we know
  Divinely wise and kind;
  In him we live, and move, and are
  In omnipresent Mind.

2 One image fair in Mind,
  One likeness true and sweet:
  One Christ, the well-beloved Son,
  In whom all graces meet.

3 All one in Christ, the Son,
  As Christ with God is one.
  One Mind in all, and all in Mind.
  The Father's will is done.

GERALDINE D. ROBINSON.

For Realization.

500   Out and Into.   P. M.

PLUMA M. BROWN.

1. Out of my pov-er - ty, in - to his wealth; Out of my sick-ness and

in - to pure health: Out of the false, and in - to the true; Out of the

old man, in - to the new. Won-der-ful Love that has wrought all for me!

Won-der-ful work that has thus set me free! Won-der - ful ground up - on

which I have come! Won-der - ful ten - der - ness, wel - com - ing home!

501   The Song.   P. M.

ALICE E. FITTS.
PLUMA M. BROWN.

1. There is a song so thrill-ing, So far all songs ex-cel-ling, That
2. The love which it re-veal-eth All earth-ly sor-rows heal-eth, They

they who sing it, sing it oft a-gain; No mor-tal did in-vent it, But
flee like mist be-fore the break of day; When, O my soul, thou learnest That

God by an-gels sent it— So deep and earn-est, yet so sweet and plain.
song of songs in earn-est, Thy cares and sor-rows all shall pass a-way.

TUNE—*Out and Into.*

Nerve thee yet stronger, O resolute mind!
Let care no longer so heavily bind;
Rise on thy eagle wings gloriously free,
Till from material things pure thou shalt be!
Winds from the mountains of glory, now blow!
Life from the swells of the Infinite, flow!
Thy peace, O Love, the whole world now see!
Thy peace, O Love, descend upon me!

‖: Joy is the knowing that all is for best;
Peace is the showing that God is our rest;
Love is sweet trusting that all is now well;
Truth is the bursting of error's cloud vail. :‖

502   **And I will Heal Him.**   P. M.
Is. 57: 19.

GERALDINE D. ROBINSON.
PLUMA M. BROWN.

Peace, peace un-to him that's a-far, And peace un-to him that is near:

Peace, peace, by the Word cometh health. For the fruit of the lips God cre-ates.

Peace, peace un-to all that will hear,—Peace, peace un-to all that will hear.

INST.

Peace, peace, we a-wait now the heal-ing, We wait in the strong faith of

Copyright, 1896, by Pluma M. Brown.

And I will Heal Him—Concluded.

know-ing. We look to see health as the watch-man Looks for the

com-ing of morn-ing; And sure as the dawn and the sun - rise

Is the Truth of the Fa-ther that prom-ised. INST.

I wait on the Lord, and he bring-eth To

pass the swift word of my speak-ing,—I wait on the Lord. A - men.

503   I Would.   C. M.

Holy Trinity.—J. BARNBY.

1. O God, I would not fill my tho'ts With sad-ness, sin, and blight,

When thine e - ter - ni - ty of Love En-folds me like the light.

2 I would not let these little cares
  Waste all my strength away,
When thine eternity of Life
  Is mine for every day.

3 I would not let my vision droop
  Till only wrong I see.
When thine eternity of Truth
  Upbears the world to thee.

4 But I would have my daily tho't
  Illumined with thy love,
I would remember only thee,
  And in thy presence move.

5 I would regard the thrilling Life
  That fills the earth and air,
As but a likeness of my God,
  Whose power is everywhere.

6 I would be true in thought and act
  To that implanted Light
Which guides my footsteps in the way,
  Impelling to the right.

7 And since thy love surrounds my days,
  And moves in all I see,

I would make mine a life of praise,
  And joy, O God, in thee.

HELEN MARSH FLETCHER.

504   Our Father.

1 Our Father, thou which art in heaven,
  Thy hallowed name is dear:
Thy kingdom now is come to earth,
  Thy will is honored here.

2 Thou givest us our daily bread,
  Which here will magnify
Thyself in us from day to day,—
  Our beings deify.

3 There's naught to be forgiven; to us
  The past is all forgot:
Thy ways are ways of pleasantness,
  In sin, thou leadest not.

4 But from illusion's seeming toils,
  Deliverest as we call,
And recognize thee as thou art,—
  Our Father—All in All.

5 Since untold glory now is thine,
  And all the praise and power,
We will reveal thy nature true,
  By living thee each hour.

HANNAH MORE KOHAUS.

505   The Arm of Might.   C. M.

St. Agnes.—J. B. DYKES.

1. To yon-der hills I raise my sight Where all my suc-cor lies:

My help is in that arm of might, That made the earth and skies.

2 My hand from evil he shall keep,
 My foot from every snare;
His eyes shall slumber not, nor sleep
 While Israel needs his care.

3 His arm shall ever be my stay,
 A shade upon my right;
The sun shall neither smite by day,
 Nor changing moon by night.

4 My head from evil he shall screen,
 My soul preserve in peace;
My going out and coming in,
 Till time and nature cease.

506   *The Twenty-third Psalm.*

1 My Shepherd is the Lord, my God,
 There is no want I know;
His flock he leads in verdant meads,
 Where tranquil waters flow.

2 He doth restore my fainting soul,
 With his divine caress.
And, when I stray, he points the way
 To paths of righteousness.

3 Yea, though I walk the vale of death,
 What evil shall I fear?

Thy staff and rod are mine, O God,
 And thou, my Shepherd near!

4 Goodness and mercy shall be mine
 Unto my changing day;
There will I bide at his dear side
 Forever and for aye.

507   *Christ My All.*

1 Thy life in me, my life for thee,
 O Christ! thy will be done;
No earthly bliss compares with this—
 Thy love my life hath won.

2 My Savior dear, thy voice to hear
 And follow at thy call,
Gives joy divine, and hope sublime,
 Since thou art all in all.

3 Spirit of Power! each day and hour,
 More of thee would I know;
Filled with thy light, thy glory bright,
 More like thee would I grow.

4 Abide within and vanquish sin,
 Thou Conqueror Divine;
O'er pain and strife, o'er death and life,
 The victory is thine.

H. C. ADAMS.

508　What the Silence will Teach. 10 D.

ELLA DARE.
Arr. fr. BERTINI.

(May be sung to first half of music.)

1. List-en and learn what the si-lence will teach, A les-son that
2. Free-dom of spir-it in ec-sta-cy soars, Bear-ing its
3. Puls-ing and beat-ing in rhyth-mic-al time, All of the

pass-eth in won-der all speech. Splen-dors e-ter-nal, that,
brightness to far-ther-most shores. 'Tis in the si-lence the
u-ni-verse falls in-to line. Cur-rents of be-ing sweep

growing in grace, Flow from the in-ner to out-er-most place.
soul meets its own, Mounts to its height, and is crowned on its throne;
in and a-round, Lift-ing us up with-out jar-ring or sound.

Truth in its gran-deur here waits to im-part Needs of the
Finds in the bound-less no bars to de-feat, Drinks in a
Car-ing for us in the ten-der-est way, Heal-ing all

What the Silence will Teach—Concluded.

soul and needs of the heart. Hope, with its snow-y-white
peace that is per-fect and sweet; Feels in the vast-ness the
hurts as the In-fi-nite may. Sit in the si-lence that

pinions, pro-claims ¶ Res-cue of race from the thrall-dom of pains.
throb of a heart That is of its life the cen-ter-most part.
we may be-hold ¶ Life and its laws writ in let-ters of gold.

Tune—*The Song Victorious.* p. 262.

509 *I Thank Thee.*

1 For an eye of inward seeing,
 A soul to know and love;
For these common aspirations,
 That our high heirship prove;
For the hearts that bless each other,
 Beneath thy smile, thy rod;
For the amaranth saved from Eden,
 I thank thee, O my God!

2 For the hidden scroll o'erwritten,
 With one dear Name adorned;
For the heavenly in the human,
 The Spirit in the Word;
For the tokens of thy presence,
 Within, above, abroad;
For thine own great gift of being,
 I thank thee, O my God!

LUCY LARCOM.

Tune—*Fiat.* p. 65.

510 *Chimes of Soul.*

1 List to the sweet chime of song,
 Softer than bell on the air,
Caught above sun-waves of earth,
 Sung from heights of God's care.

2 Tenderest melodies drift
 Like sun rays into the heart;
Singing the glories of life
 In strains that ne'er depart.

3 Dreams of a Christ-song unsung,
 Visions of blessings unknown,
Waiting fulfillment of love,
 Shine on soul heights alone.

4 List to the soul chimes of God,
 Lingering soft on the ear;
Sounding in sweet tones of love
 Promise that Christ is near.

CLARA E. CHOATE.

511   **Life, Love, Truth.**   P. M.

Geraldine D. Robinson.
Pluma M. Brown.

1. In the Life of Om - ni - pres - ence Do I dwell.
2. In the Love of Om - ni - pres - ence Do I rest.
3. In the Truth of Om - ni - pres - ence Do I stand.
4. Life and Love and Truth, for - ev - er Thou art mine!

'Tis a - bove, a - round, with - in me, All is well;
Feel it fill - ing, thrill - ing thro' me, Bless - ed guest!
For the pow'r of the Al - might - y Holds my hand.
Glo - rious Trin - i - ty of heav - en, All - Di - vine.

Life Di - vine for - ev - er guid - ing All my ways,
Love Di - vine all dis - cord sooth - ing In - to peace,
Truth Di - vine, su - preme, un - chang - ing, All art thou!
Oh, my soul doth sing with rap - ture Hymns of praise,

Life Di - vine for - ev - er fill - ing All my days,
Love Di - vine in whose sweet pres - ence Pain doth cease.
Truth Di - vine, thy word is free - dom, Spo - ken now.
And my feet shall walk with glad - ness In thy ways.

512 The Presence of God. 7. D.

PLUMA M. BROWN.

1. Calm and still, calm and cool. Like a clear and crys - tal pool,
2. In - to that dear hand of thine, Ev - 'ry-thing I now re - sign,
3. Now, from ev - 'ry weight set free. Rest - ful, turns my mind to thee;
4. Thou in me, the source of pow'r. Thou for me, from hour to hour;

Make my spir - it now to be, So thy pow'r may work in me:
All my work and all my cares, All of those who need my prayers;
E'en as plant ab - sorbs the air, Drink I in the at - mos-phere
Thou the Light and Life di - vine, Meet-ing ev - 'ry need of mine;

All un - eas - i - ness al - lay, Care and fret take thou a - way,
Let - ting go my wea - ry hold Of the bur - dens man - i - fold
Of thy Pres-ence, which, in love, All a - round, with - in, a - bove,
Thou in king - ly maj - es - ty, Fa - cing ev - 'ry en - e - my;

Bid all rest - less - ness to cease, Hush my spir - it in - to peace.
That up - on my spir - it press, Tempt-ing me to care - ful - ness.
Press - es, fills, sus - tains, con - trols, In its ten - der - ness en - folds.
Thou, the pure e - ter - nal Word, In me sat - is - fy - ing God.

513   "These Three."   P. M.   J. BARNBY.

1. Star of Hope, Star of Hope, Shine in my soul to-night; Shine, shine,
2. Faith, sweet Faith, angel Faith, Fold me neath thy white wing; Close, close,

Star di-vine, Shine in my soul to-night. Her-ald of in-fi-nite
Her - - ald of
hold me close, Fold me 'neath thy white wing; Safe from the chill-ing
Safe from the

good thou art, Pic-tur-ing vi-sions of heaven in the heart, Beau-ti-ful
good thou art. Pic-turing heav-en in the heart,
fear of death, Safe in the life of fade-less truth, Un-to thee
fear of death, Safe in the fade-less truth,

star of light, Star so soft-ly bright, thro' my silent night shine........
now I cling: Fold me ten-der-ly, hold me steadfast and true........

"These Three"—Concluded.

3 Love divine, Love divine,
  Lord of my inmost thought;
Love, Love, born above,
  Lord of my inmost thought;
Whisper thy heavenly message sweet,
(Whisper thy message sweet)
Speak while my listening heart doth
  beat,
(Speak while my heart doth beat)
  Beat to the harmony caught
With the tender word, now so softly
  heard, breathed.

4 Full and sweet, full and sweet,
  Showeth my life to me;
Life, Life, abiding life,
  Now thou art perfect and free.
Wonderful bounty and good divine.
(Wonderful good divine)   [mine.
Promise and substance of Truth are
(Promise and Truth are mine)
  Hope, Faith, and Love, these three;
But the greatest is, but the sweetest is
  Love.

GERALDINE D. ROBINSON.

514 Thou art My All. P.M.

EMMA (CURTIS) HOPKINS.
PLUMA M. BROWN.

1. Thou art my All, my Theme, my In-spir-a-tion
2. Thou art my Strength in age, my rise from low

and my Crown; My soul's Am-bi-tion, Pleas-ure, Wealth, my World:
es-tate; E-ter-ni-ty too short to speak thy praise;

Thou art my Light in dark-ness and my Life in death.
Or fath-om thy pro-found of love to man.

515 **I am Waiting.** 8. 7. D.

CLARA H. SCOTT.
Arr. fr. English Melody.

1. I am wait-ing in the si - lence, Thy dear voice, my Lord, to hear,
2. As the lil - y - bud a - wak-ing From its dream on wa-ter's breast
3. All my soul I lay be - fore thee, Ev - 'ry se-cret thought make bare:
4. So I lis - ten in the si - lence Thy sweet voice, my Lord, to hear,

And its ac - cents sweet are fall - ing Gen-tly on my list-'ning ear.
Soft un-folds its snow - y pet - als At the ar - dent sun's re-quest:
En - ter, thou blest Pu - ri - fi - er, Cleanse and reign su-preme - ly there.
And my ear can catch the mu - sic Waft-ed from ce - les - tial sphere.

Lifts my heart with ea - ger long-ings Thy rich Truth to ful - ly grasp,
So my heart would loose its wrap-pings Clust'ring round our ev - 'ry day,
Lord thou art of this frail tem - ple, Thou hast made and called thine own;
Hush, my soul, bend low and list - en, 'Tis thy Mas - ter speaks to thee;

While from off my soul I glad - ly Earth's il - lu - sions swift un-clasp.
O - pen to the pre - cious Love-light Shin-ing o'er my path al - way.
In my heart's most sa - cred cen - ter Thou art Guest, and thou a - lone.
Yes, and this the gate of heav - en, Love it - self the per - fect key.

516 Song of the Beautiful. P. M.

Mary E. Butters.
Pluma M. Brown.

1. Beau-ti-ful words of love and life, Beau-ti-ful, beau-ti-ful
2. Beau-ti-ful tho'ts and deeds sub-lime, An-gels of love and
3. Beau-ti-ful realm o'er all the way, Beau-ti-ful, beau-ti-ful
4. Beau-ti-ful ships of pearl to sail, Beau-ti-ful, beau-ti-ful
5. Beau-ti-ful, peace-ful waves to roll, Beau-ti-ful, beau-ti-ful

things; Beau-ti-ful realm from pain and strife, Where the
peace: Beau-ti-ful land and beau-ti-ful clime, In the
night; Stars to guide on the heav-en-ly way
sea; Where storms ne'er wreck nor wind-y gale Blows
rest; Calm on the tran-quil life of soul For-

beau-ti-ful foun-tain springs. Ev-er, for-ev-er, there's
life that ne'er shall cease. Ev-er, for-ev-er, there's
In-to the beau-ti-ful light. Ev-er, for-ev-er, the
o-ver the great To-Be. Ev-er, for-ev-er, there's
ev-er be loved and blest. Ev-er, for-ev-er, the

no drop gone In the beau-ti-ful foun-tain flow-ing on.
no pulse stilled, In the beau-ti-ful life his love has filled.
morn comes in The beau-ti-ful heav'n of love with-in.
no pearl gone Where the beau-ti-ful ships of Truth sail on.
white sails move In the beau-ti-ful tide of heav'n and love.

517   Who Giveth His Love to Thee.   P. M.

MARY E. BUTTERS.
PLUMA M. BROWN.

1. Is there one heart that is sad and lone - ly, A - way from the
2. Is there one eye look - ing dim and blind - ly A - way from the
3. Is there one hand ly - ing still, not giv - ing Its help to the

pres - ence of one to love? Is there one voice, stilled in
foun - tain of Life and Light.—A - way from the All - see - ing
need - y, the land to free? Heark-en to him that's for -

sor - row on - ly, Far from the heav - en of glad-ness a - bove?
Eye that kind - ly Looks up - on all with Om - nis-cient Sight?
ev - er giv - ing: "To give to thy neigh-bor you give un - to me."

Come to the peace that en-folds thee,—Love that shall ev-er be - hold thee,
Come to the light that shall fill thee: Hear the sweet voice that shall still thee:
Safe in the love that en - folds thee, One on - ly Eye that be - holds thee

Who Giveth His Love to Thee—Concluded.

Whole, hap-py and free! Come to the Light of the liv-ing,
"Soul, lean up-on me! I am the Light of the liv-ing,
From all thy bond-age now free! Safe in the Light of the liv-ing,

Un-to the Heart of Love-giv-ing, Who giv-eth his love to thee.
I am the Voice of Love-giv-ing, And on-ly give love to thee."
Safe in the Heart of Love-giv-ing, Who giv-eth his love to thee.

Tune—*Aurelia.* p. 30.

518 *My Finding.*

1 I've found a joy in sorrow,
A secret balm for pain,
A beautiful to-morrow
Of sunshine after rain;
I've found a branch of healing
Near every bitter spring;
A whispered promise stealing
O'er every broken string.

2 I've found a glad hosanna
For every woe and wail,
A handful of sweet manna
When grapes of Eshcol fail;
I've found a Rock of Ages
When desert wells are dry;
And after weary stages
I've found an Elam nigh.

3 An Elam with its coolness
Its fountains, and its shade;
A blessing in its fullness.
When buds of promise fade.
O'er tears of soft contrition
I've seen a rainbow light,
A glory and fruition
That's not beyond our sight.

4 My Savior, thee possessing,
I have the joy, the balm,
The healing and the blessing,
The sunshine and the psalm;
The promise for the fearful,
The Elam for the faint;
The rainbow for the tearful,
The glory for the saint.

519 In Truth's Realm. P. M.

HANNAH MORE KOHAUS.
PLUMA M. BROWN.

1. Peace is now my dai-ly por-tion, Since the Truth I know;
2. Love pre-dom-i-nates my be-ing, As I do its will,
3. Liv-ing faith is now my sub-stance, And so well it feeds
4. Oh, the glo-ry of the knowl-edge Of this Truth of truths,

From an in-ex-haust-less foun-tain Will it ev-er flow;
And I feel its pure, white ra-diance All my puls-es thrill;
Ev-'ry hope and as-pi-ra-tion With life's ho-ly deeds,
With its won-drous bliss un-fail-ing, That all sor-row soothes;

And its rest-ful, tran-quil wa-ters Doth my soul em-balm,
In at-one-ment with its pow-er, Naught my soul can daunt,
That my soul is o-ver-flow-ing With its bound-less store,
With its wis-dom, strength, and wholeness, Which so sat-is-fies,

With a con-scious-ness, most ho-ly, Of ce-les-tial calm.
For I live with-in its Pres-ence, And can feel no want.
And would scat-ter of its bless-ings Ev-er more and more.
That the soul, deep from its cen-ter, God can re-al-ize!

520 The Fullness of God. 7. PLUMA M. BROWN.

1. Liv-ing God, we feel that thou, With thy full-ness heal-eth now;
And we tru-ly re-al-ize All the wholeness this im-plies.

Copyright, 1896, by Pluma M. Brown.

2 Thou dost give us now to eat
Of the finest of the wheat;
And with honey from the Rock,
Thou wilt feed thy waiting flock.

3 Thou hast given us holy peace,
Which will evermore increase,
Till our life-cup runneth o'er
With thy never ending store.

4 Thou hast given us holy love,
Rained upon us from above,
From that high and sacred place,
Where we shall behold thy face.
HANNAH MORE KOHAUS.

521 *Friend Divine.*
1 Heavenly Helper, Friend divine,
Friend of all men, therefore mine,
Let my heart as thy heart be!
Breathe thy living breath thro' me!

2 Only at thy love's pure tide
Human thirst is satisfied;
He who fills his chalice there,
Fills, with thirstier souls to share.

3 As a bird unto its nest,
Flies the tired soul to thy breast,
Let not one an alien be!
Lord, we have no home but thee!
LUCY LARCOM.

522 *One With Christ.*
1 One with God, as heart with heart,
Savior, lift us where thou art!
Join us to his life, through thine,
Human still, though all divine!

2 Teach us how to live by prayer;
Reverently thy plans to share!
More than echoes of thy voice,
Make us partners in thy choice.

3 Lift us up to catch from thee
World-encircling sympathy;
Ardor, strength, and courage give;
As thou livest, let us live!

4 Let our deeds be syllables
Of the prayer our spirit swells:
In us thy desire fulfill!
By us work thy gracious will!
LUCY LARCOM.

523 The Might of Jehovah. L. M.

Park Street.—F. M. A. VENUA.

1. The Lord our God alone is strong: His hands build not for one brief day: His wondrous

works, thro' ages long, His wisdom and his pow'r display, His wisdom and his pow'r display.

2 His mountains lift their solemn forms
To watch in silence o'er the land;
The rolling ocean, rocked with storms,
Sleeps in the hollow of his hand.

3 Thou sovereign God, receive this gift
Thy willing servants offer thee;
Accept the prayers that thousands lift,
And let these halls thy temple be.
C. T. WINCHESTER.

524 Dedication of a Church.

1 Deep in the heart thy hands have laid,
O Lord! the temple's corner stone;
Here shall thy love the soul pervade,
Here thy eternal Word be known.

2 When tho'ts to living acts have grown,
They rise in monumental stone;
And life's long act of tho't shall be
Rock-built into eternity.

3 The church that, like an infant, sleeps
Within its cradled fold, shall be
Vast as the heaven with all its deeps,
And strong as the unfettered sea.

525 The Corner-Stone.

1 Grant that all we who here to-day,
Rejoicing, this foundation lay,
May be in very deed thine own,
Built on the precious Corner-stone.

2 The heads that guide, endue with skill;
The hands that work, preserve from ill;
That we, who these foundations lay,
May raise the topstone in its day.
J. MASON NEALE.

526 The First Temple.

1 The perfect world, by Adam trod,
Was the first temple, built by God;
His fiat laid the corner-stone,
And heaved its pillars one by one.

2 He hung its starry roof on high,
The broad expanse of azure sky;
He spread its pavement, green and bright,
And curtained it with morning light.

3 The mountains in their places stood,
The sea, the sky; and all was good;
And when its first pure praises rang,
"The morning stars together sang."
N. P. WILLIS.

527 One Holy Church. C. M.

Boardman.—GEO. KINGSLEY.

1. One ho - ly Church of God ap-pears Thro' ev - 'ry age and race.

Un - wast - ed by the lapse of years. Unchanged by chang-ing place.

2 From oldest time, on farthest shores.
Beneath the pine or palm,
One Unseen Presence she adores.
With silence or with psalm.

3 Her priests are all God's faithful sons.
To serve the world raised up:
The pure in heart her baptized ones.
Love, her communion-cup.

4 The Truth is her prophetic gift.
The Soul her sacred page;
And feet on mercy's errand swift
Do make her pilgrimage.
S. LONGFELLOW.

528 *The City of God.*

1 City of God, how broad and far
Outspread thy walls sublime!
The true thy chartered freemen are.
Of every age and clime.

2 One holy church, one army strong.
One steadfast high intent.
One working band, one harvest-song.
One King Omnipotent!

3 How purely hath thy speech come down
From man's primeval youth!

How grandly hath thine empire grown
Of freedom, love. and truth!

4 In vain the surges' angry shock.
In vain the drifting sands:
Unharmed. upon the eternal rock.
The Eternal City stands.
S. JOHNSON.

529 *Dedication Hymn.*

1 Like stars upon a troubled sea
Shine out the altars fair.
Where longings of the centuries
Have voiced themselves in prayer.

2 We seek the good those altars held.
Yet read their message clear,
To loyally receive the light
God sends us now and here.

3 Within these walls may worship fill
Our waiting souls anew.
A present help within our lives
To make them pure and true.

4 Eternal Life, whose love divine
Enfolds us each and all.
We know no other truth than thine,
We heed no other call.

530　The Building of the Temple.　7. 6. D.

Webb —G. J. Webb.

The Corner-stone.

1. He laid his rocks in cours - es. His for - est crowned the hill,

He yoked the an - cient for - ces, And lent them to our will;

D.S. —He gave cre - a - tion beau - ty, And he the tem - ple wrought!

The heart he woke to du - ty. He graced the build-er's thought,

2 Now, Father, build within us
   The temple's counterpart,
Deep laid in holy purpose,
   Fair colored of the heart:
Its windows, heaven-lighted;
   Peace and good-will its plan:
Its towers, our faith and worship:
   Its doors, the love of man!

The Dedication.

3 To cloisters of the spirit
   These aisles of quiet lead:
Here may the vision gladden,
   The voice within us plead!
The songs we sing, be echoes
   Of unheard song within;
The prayers we pray, in hushes
   Of secret vow begin!

4 Here be no man a stranger:
   No holy cause be banned:
No good for one be counted
   Not good for all the land!
And here for prophet voices
   The message never fail.—
God reigns! His Truth shall conquer,
   And Right and Love prevail.

W. C. Gannett.

531	Our Country's Temple.	7. D.	LUCY LARCOM
Messiah. -Arr. by GEO. KINGSLEY.

1. Thanks to thee, O God most high, For the men, the days gone by!
2. Stand-ing where they stood, we turn Un - to thee, our way to learn:
3. But the con-quests of the past Pale be - fore the fu - ture vast:
4. Build - ed not by mor - tal hands, Ev - er-more thy tem - ple stands:

Thanks for all the fa-thers wrought: For their pa - tient toil of thought:
Let our in - ward pur - pose be Not to fol - low them, but thee!
Bright'ning on the east - ern sky, Lo! thy com - ing draw - eth nigh!
Ris - ing glo-rious from the clod, Man thy tem - ple is, O God!

For their faith which lit the land With a glo - ry clear and grand:
Heirs of many a har - vest field From the cloud - y dawn con-cealed,
Deep as in - most thought can sound, Wide as far - thest be - ing's bound,
Thro' him let thy Spir - it flow Till our world no night shall know.

For the vic-t'ries that they won Thro' the gos - pel of thy Son.
Toil - ing aft - er them, we share Thank-ful - ly their hope and prayer.
Earth and heav'n thy praise shall swell, Pres - ent God—Im - man - u - el!
And the heights and depths shall ring With the name of Christ, our King!

532   My Country, 'tis of Thee.   6. 4.

America.—Ad. by H. Carey.

1. My coun - try! 'tis of thee, Sweet land of lib - er - ty,
Of thee I sing; Land where my fa - thers died, Land of the
pil - grims' pride, From ev - 'ry moun - tain side Let free - dom ring!

2 My native country, thee—
  Land of the noble, free—
    Thy name I love;
  I love thy rocks and rills.
  Thy woods and templed hills:
  My heart with rapture thrills.
    Like that above.

3 Let music swell the breeze.
  And ring from all the trees
    Sweet freedom's song:
  Let mortal tongues awake;
  Let all that breathe partake:
  Let rocks their silence break,—
    The sound prolong.

4 Our father's God! to thee,
  Author of liberty,
    To thee we sing:
  Long may our land be bright
  With freedom's holy light;

Protect us by thy might.
  Great God, our King!

S. F. Smith.

533

1 God bless our native land!
  Firm may she ever stand
    Thro' storm and night:
  When the wild tempests rave,
  Ruler of winds and wave!
  Do thou our country save
    By thy great might.

2 For her our prayers shall be.
  Our fathers' God! to thee:
    On thee we wait!
  Be her walls, Holiness;
  Her rulers, Righteousness;
  Her officers be Peace;
    God save the state!

C. T. Brocks.

534 Fatherland. 6.4.

J. V. BLAKE.
PLUMA M. BROWN.

1. To thee, O Fa-ther-land, Bond of our heart and hand, From love deep,
2. And thou, O God of Right, The Lord whose arm of might, In storm and
3. Free as our riv-ers flow, Pure as our breez-es blow, Strong as our

pure and strong Rolls our high song. May all thy path-ways be
bat-tle roar, Our fa-thers bore,—Thou mad'st their chil-dren strong,
moun-tains stand, Be our broad land! Bright home of lib-er-ty,

Highways of Lib-er-ty, And jus-tice throned in thee, Reign a-ges long!
To break the chains of wrong, Till rang the freeman's song From shore to shore.
High hope of all the free—Our love thy watch-tow'r be, Dear Fa-ther-land.

TUNE—*Boardman.* p. 305.

535 One Law, One Life, One Love.
Parliament Hymn.

1 O Prophet souls of all the years,
Bend o'er us from above;
Your far-off vision, toils and tears
Now to fulfillment move!

2 From tropic clime and zones of frost
They come, of every name,—
This, this our day of Pentecost,
The Spirit's tongue of flame!

3 The ancient barriers disappear;
Down bow the mountains high;
The sea-divided shores draw near
In a world's unity.

4 One Life together we confess,
One all-indwelling Word,
One holy call to righteousness,
Within the silence heard:

5 One Law that guides the shining spheres
As on through space they roll,
And speaks in flaming characters
On Sinais of the soul:

6 One Love, unfathomed, measureless,
An ever-flowing sea,
That holds within its vast embrace
Time and eternity.

F. L. HOSMER.

536	Our Thanks We Pay.	L. M. 6 I.

Loving-Kindness.—Western Melody.

1. Lord of the har-vest! thee we hail! Thine an-cient prom - ise doth not fail:

The vary-ing sea-sons haste their round. With goodness all our years are crowned:

Our thanks we pay, this ho - ly day: Oh, let our hearts in tune be found.

2 If spring doth wake the song of mirth,
If summer warms the fruitful earth,
When winter sweeps the naked plain,
Or autumn yields its ripened grain,
 We still do sing to thee our King;
Thro' all their changes thou dost reign.

3 But chiefly when thy liberal hand
Bestows new plenty o'er the land,
When sounds of music fill the air,
As homeward all their treasures bear,
 We too will raise our hymn of praise,
For we thy common bounties share.

4 Lord of the harvest! all is thine,
The rains that fall, the suns that shine,
The seed once hidden in the ground,
The skill that makes our fruits abound:

New every year thy gifts appear;
New praises from our lips shall sound.
J. H. Gurney.

Tune—Promise.

537	To the God of Nations.

1 Great God of nations, now to thee
 Our hymn of gratitude we raise;
With humble heart, and bending knee,
 We offer thee our song of praise.

2 Thy name we bless, Almighty God,
 For all the kindness thou hast shown
To this fair land the pilgrims trod,—
 This land we fondly call our own.

3 We praise thee that the gospel's light
 Thro' all our land its radiance sheds;
Dispels the shades of error's night,
 And heavenly blessings round us
 spreads.

A. A. Woodhall.

538 God's Presence Sure. L. M.

Promise.—F. H. BARTHELEMON.

1. Great God, we sing that mighty hand. By which sup - port-ed still we stand:

The op'ning year thy mer-cy shows: Let mer-cy crown it till it close.

2 By day, by night—at home, abroad,
Still we are guarded by our God;
By his incessant bounty fed;
By his unerring counsel led.

3 With grateful hearts the past we own
The future—all to us unknown—
We to thy guardian care commit.
And peaceful leave before thy feet.
P. DODDRIDGE.

539 Psalm 65.

1 The loved of God! how safely led!
How surely kept! how richly fed!
Savior of all in earth and sea,
How happy they who rest in thee!

2 Thy hand sets fast the mighty hills,
Thy voice the troubled ocean stills;
Evening and morning hymn thy praise,
And earth thy bounty wide displays.

3 The year is with thy goodness crowned!
Thy clouds drop wealth the world around:
Through thee the deserts laugh and sing.
And nature smiles and owns her King.

4 Lord, on our souls thy Spirit pour;
The moral waste within restore;

Oh, let thy love our spring-tide be,
And make us all bear fruit to thee.
H. F. LYTE.

540 Spring.

1 A nobler Spring revives the soul
When God renews the loving heart,
And, yielding to that sweet control,
The wintry storms of self depart.

2 Then Jesus to the heart is near.
While, with adoring love. we sing.
"The Lord is here! the Lord is here!
Incarnate in immortal Spring."

541 Lord, Fill Our Hearts.

1 Lord, fill our hearts with inward
strength,
Make our enlargéd souls possess.
And learn the height, and breadth. and
length
Of thine eternal love and grace.

2 Now to the God whose power can do
More than our thoughts and wishes
know,
Be everlasting honors done.
By all the church. thro' Christ his Son.
I. WATTS.

542 We Plough the Fields. 7. 6. D.

Tr. by JANE M. CAMPBELL.
J. A. P. SCHULZ.

1. We plough the fields, and scat-ter   The good seed on the land, But it is
2. He   on - ly   is the Ma - ker   Of all things near and far; He paints the
3. We thank thee, then, O Fa - ther, For all things bright and good—The seed-time

fed and   wa-tered   By God's al-might-y   hand; He sends the   snow in
way-side   flow - er.   He lights the ev-'ning star; The winds and waves o-
and the   har - vest, Our life, our health, our food: Ac - cept the   gift we

win - ter. The warmth to swell the grain,   The breez-es and the   sun-shine,
bey   him, By   him the birds are fed; Much more to   us, his   chil-dren,
of - fer   For   all   thy love im - parts, And, what thou most de - sir - est,

REFRAIN.

And soft, refreshing rain. }
He gives our dai-ly bread. } All good gifts around   us Are sent from heav'n a-
Our humble, thankful hearts. }

We Plough the Fields—Concluded.

bove; Then thank the Lord—Oh, thank the Lord— For all..... his love!

543   Harvest Song.   7. 6. D.

1. The corn is ripe for reap-ing, Fields glow with ruddy grain, And we must now be

keep-ing Our harvest feast a - gain; With voice of joy and sing-ing, Our praise to

God shall rise. Who, whilst the seed was springing, Rained blessings from the skies.

2 The year, by thee anointed,
   Is now with goodness crowned,
Clad in the robes appointed,
   With gladness girded round.
We thank thee for the blessing
   Which meets us on our way.
And come, thy love confessing.
   With happy hearts to-day.

3 But whilst our lips are praising.
   Our lives to thee belong;
With them we would be raising
   A nobler, sweeter song;
One that may sound forever.
   Whilst earth's great harvest speeds.
A song of high endeavor
   Rung out in earnest deeds.

544   Sing to the Lord.   7. 6. D.

Arr. fr. Mozart.

1. Sing to the Lord of harvest! Sing songs of love and praise! With joyful hearts and

voi - ces Your hal - le - lu - jahs raise: By him the roll-ing sea - sons In

fruitful or - der move; Sing to the Lord of har - vest A song of hap-py love.

2 By him the clouds drop fatness,
  The deserts bloom and spring,
The hills leap up in gladness,
  The valleys laugh and sing!
He filleth with his fullness
  All things with large increase,
He crowns the year with goodness,
  With plenty and with peace.

3 To God, the gracious Father,
  Who made us "very good,"
To Christ, who, when we wandered,
  Reclaimed us with his love.
And to the Holy Spirit,
  Who doth upon us pour
His blessed dews and sunshine,
  Be praise forevermore.

J. S. B. MONSELL.

545   Another Year.

1 Another year is dawning!
  Dear Master, it shall be,
In working or in waiting,
  Another year with thee.

Another year of leaning
  Upon thy loving breast,
Of ever-deepening trusting,
  Of quiet, happy rest.

2 Another year of mercies,
  Of faithfulness and grace;
Another year of gladness
  In shining of thy face;
Another year of progress;
  Another year of praise;
Another year of proving
  Thy presence "all the days."

3 Another year of service,
  Of witness for thy love;
Another year of training
  For holier work above;
Another year is dawning!
  Dear Master, it shall be,
In working or in waiting,
  Another year with thee.

FRANCES. R. HAVERGAL.

551 Let All Rejoice. 6. 4.

St. Edmund. A. S. Sullivan.

1. The God of har-vest praise; Let all re-joice! In loud thanks-

giv-ing raise Hand, heart, and voice: The val-leys laugh and sing,

Forests and mountains ring, The plains their tribute bring, The streams rejoice.

2 Yea, bless his holy name
  Through all the earth!
And joyous thanks proclaim
  Through all the earth!
To glory in your lot
Is comely, but be not
God's benefits forgot
  Amidst your mirth.

3 The God of harvest praise:
  Bless ye the Lord!
Hands, hearts, and voices raise
  With one accord!
From field to garner throng
Bearing your sheaves along.
And in your harvest song
  Bless ye the Lord!

Arr. fr. J. Montgomery.

552 The Summer Days.   C. M. D.

S. LONGFELLOW.
Brattle Street.—I. PLEYEL.

1. The sum-mer days are come a-gain: Once more the glad earth yields
2. The sum-mer days are come a-gain: The birds are on the wing:

Her gold-en wealth of rip'ning grain, And breath of clo-ver-fields:
God's prais-es, in their lov-ing strain, Un-con-scious-ly they sing:

And deep'ning shade of sum-mer woods, And glow of sum-mer air.
We know who giv-eth all the good That doth our cup o'er-brim:

And wing-ing tho'ts, and hap-py words Of love, and joy, and prayer.
For sum-mer joy in field and wood We lift our song to him.

553   *Spring.*

1 The softened mould is brown and
    warm,
  The early blossoms break,
And loosened streams along their banks
  A mossy verdure make.

REFRAIN:—
  Awake, O heart, awake and learn
    The secret of the spring!

From winter-sleep it comes like
    light,
  Or as a bird on wing.

2 A dewy light broods o'er the earth,
  A sweetness new and rare,
And tumults of brook, bird, and breeze
  With music wake the air. —REF.

J. V. BLAKE.

554 **Another Year.** C. M. D.

J. W. CHADWICK.
Greenport.—Arr. fr. THALBERG.

1. An - oth - er year of set - ting suns, Of stars   by night re-vealed,
2. An - oth - er year of hap - py work, That bet - ter is than play;
3. An - oth - er year at Beau-ty's feast, At ev - 'ry mo-ment spread;

Of spring-ing grass, of ten - der buds By   win-ter's snow con-cealed.
Of sim- ple cares, and love that grows More sweet from day to day.
Of si - lent hours, when grow dis-tinct The voi - ces nev - er dead.

An - oth - er year of   summer's glow, Of   autumn's gold and brown,
An - oth - er year of   ba - by mirth, And childhood's bless-ed ways:
An - oth - er year to   fol - low hard Where bet - ter souls have trod;

Of wav - ing fields, and rud - dy fruit The branch - es weighing down.
Of think - er's tho't, and prophet's dream, And po - et's ten - der lays.
An - oth - er year of life's de-light: An - oth - er year of God!

555   The Unfailing Promise.   8. 7. D.

FRANCES R. HAVERGAL.
Hymn of Joy.—ARR. fr. BEETHOVEN.

1. "Cer-tain-ly I will be with thee!" Fa-ther, I have found it true:
2. "Cer-tain-ly I will be with thee!" Blessed Spir-it, come to me.
3. "Cer-tain-ly I will be with thee!" Star-ry prom-ise in the night!

To thy faith-ful-ness and mer-cy I would set my seal a-new.
Rest up-on me, dwell with-in me, Let my heart thy tem-ple be;
All un-cer-tain-ties, like shad-ows, Flee a-way be-fore its light.

All the year thy grace hath kept me, Thou my help in-deed hast been,
Thro' the track-less year be-fore me, Ho-ly One, with me a-bide!
"Cer-tain-ly I will be with thee!" He hath spo-ken: I have heard!

Mar-vel-ous the lov-ing-kind-ness Ev-'ry day and hour hath seen.
Teach me, com-fort me, and calm me, Be my ev-er-pres-ent Guide.
True of old, and true this mo-ment, I will trust Je-ho-vah's word.

556 Prayer for Power. S. M.

Thacher. —Arr. fr. Handel.

1. Lord God, the Ho - ly Ghost! In this ac - cept - ed hour, As on the day of Pen - te - cost, De - scend in all thy pow'r.

2 We meet with one accord
In our appointed place,
And wait the promise of our Lord,
The Spirit of all grace.

3 Like mighty rushing wind
Upon the waves beneath,
Move with one impulse every mind.
One soul, one feeling, breathe.

4 The young, the old, inspire
With wisdom from above,
And give us hearts and tongues of fire,
To pray, and praise, and love.
                        J. Montgomery.

557 Sweet is the Work.

1 Sweet is the work, O Lord!
Thy glorious name to sing,
To praise, and pray, to hear thy word,
And grateful offerings bring.

2 Sweet—at the dawning light,
Thy boundless love to tell,
And when approach the shades of night,
Still on the theme to dwell.

3 Sweet—on this day of rest,
To join, in heart and voice,
With those who love and serve thee best,
And in thy name rejoice.
                        Harriet Auber.

558 Benediction.

1 Lord, at this closing hour,
Establish every heart
Upon thy word of truth and power,
To keep us when we part.

2 Peace to our brethren give;
Fill all our hearts with love;
In faith and patience may we live,
And seek our rest above.

3 To God, the only wise,
In every age adored,
Let glory from the church arise
Thro' Jesus Christ our Lord!
                        E. T. Fitch.

559 The Eternal Sabbath.

1 Lord, in this sacred hour,
Within thy courts we bend,
And bless thy love, and own thy power,
Our Father and our Friend.

2 But thou art not alone
In courts by mortals trod;
Nor only is the day thine own
When man draws near to God:

3 Thy temple is the arch
Of yon unmeasured sky;
Thy Sabbath, the stupendous march
Of vast eternity.
                        S. G. Bulfinch.

560 Summer Suns are Glowing.   6. s.

W. W. How.
S. Smith.

1. Sum-mer suns are glow-ing O-ver land and sea: Hap-py light is
2. God's free mer-cy stream-eth O-ver all the world, And his ban-ner

flow-ing, Boun-ti-ful and free. Ev-'ry-thing re-joi-ces
gleameth Ev-'ry-where un-furled. Broad and deep and glo-rious,

In the mel-low rays; All earth's thousand voi-ces Swell the psalm of praise.
As the heav'n a-bove, Shines in might vic-to-rious His e-ter-nal love.

Year by Year More Perfect.

1 Speak a shade more kindly
   Than the year before;
  Pray a little oftener.
   Love a little more;

Cling a little closer
   To the Father's love;
  Life below shall liker
   Grow to life above.

Tune—*Mendebras.*

561   *Our Heart's Devotion.*

1 Thine holy day's returning,
   Our hearts exult to see;
  And with devotion burning,
   Ascend, O God, to thee!
  To-day with purest pleasure,
   Our thoughts from earth withdraw;
  We search for heavenly treasure,
   We learn thy holy law.

2 We join to sing thy praises,
   Lord of the Sabbath day;
  Each voice in gladness raises
   Its loudest, sweetest lay!
  Thy richest mercies sharing,
   Inspire us with thy love.
  By grace our souls preparing
   For nobler praise above.

R. Palmer.

567 Through Another Week. 7. D.

J. NEWTON.
Newton.—L. MASON.

1. Safe - ly thro' an - oth - er week God has brought us on our way;
2. Here we come thy name to praise; Let us feel thy pres-ence near:

Let us now a bless - ing seek, Wait - ing in his courts to - day;
May thy glo - ry meet our eyes, While we in thy house ap - pear;

Day of all the week the best: Em - blem of e - ter - nal rest,—
Here en - joy we, Lord, a taste Of our ev - er - last - ing feast,—

Day of all the week the best: Em - blem of e - ter - nal rest.
Here en - joy we, Lord, a taste Of our ev - er - last - ing feast.

568 *Hail Thou Sacred Morn.*

1 Hail thou bright and sacred morn,
  Risen with gladness in thy beams!
Light, which not of earth is born,
  From thy dawn in glory streams:
Airs of heaven are breathed around,
And each place is holy ground.

2 Great Creation! who this day
  From thy perfect work didst rest;
By the souls that own thy sway
  Hallowed be its hours and blest;
Cares of earth aside be thrown,
This day given to heaven alone.

Mrs. Julia Ann Elliott.

569 Vesper Hymn. L. M.   *Evening Hymn.*—T. TALLIS.

1. A - gain, as ev'ning's shad - ow falls, We gath-er in these hallowed walls;

And ves - per hymn and ves-per prayer Rise mingling on the ho - ly air.

2 May struggling hearts that seek release
Here find the rest of God's own peace;
And, strengthened here by hymn and
       prayer,
Lay down the burden and the care!

3 O God, our Light! to thee we bow;
Within all shadows standest thou:

Give deeper calm than night can bring;
Give sweeter songs than lips can sing.

4 Life's tumult we must meet again;
We cannot at the shrine remain;
But in the spirit's secret cell
May hymn and prayer forever dwell.

S. LONGFELLOW.

570 Day of Rest. 8. 4   Arr. fr. J. B. DYKES.

1. Hail! sa-cred day of earth-ly rest, From toil se - cure, and troub-le free:

Hail! qui - et spir - it, bring-ing peace And joy to me.

571 Twilight Hymn. 8. 7.

Dorrnance.—I. B. Woodbury.

1. Now on land and sea de-scend-ing, Brings the night its peace profound:

Let our ves - per hymn be blend - ing With the ho - ly calm a - round.

2 Soon as dies the sunset glory,
Stars of heaven shine out above,
Telling still the ancient story,
Their Creator's changeless love.

3 Now our wants and burdens leaving
To his care who cares for all,
Cease we fearing, cease we grieving,—
At his touch our burdens fall.

4 As the darkness deepens o'er us,
Lo! eternal stars arise;
Hope, and Faith, and Love rise glorious,
Shining in the spirit's skies.
S. Longfellow.

572   *Benediction.*

1 Lord, dismiss us with thy blessing;
Bid us now depart in peace;
Still on heavenly manna feeding,
Let our faith and love increase.

2 Praise the Father, earth and heaven;
Praise the Son, the Spirit praise;

As it was, and is, be given
Glory thro' eternal days.
R. Hawker.

573   *Part in Peace.*

1 Part in peace! is day before us?
Praise his name for life and light:
Are the shadows lengthening o'er us?
Bless his care who guards the night.

2 Part in peace! such are the praises
God our Maker loveth best;
Such the worship that upraises
Human hearts to heavenly rest.
Mrs. S. F. Adams.

574   *The Apostolic Benediction.*

1 May the grace of Christ our Savior,
And the Father's boundless love,
With the Holy Spirit's favor,
Rest upon us from above.

2 Thus may we abide in union
With each other and the Lord;
And possess, in sweet communion,
Joys which earth cannot afford.
J. Newton.

Tune.—Sabbath Rest.

2 A holy stillness, breathing calm
    And peace on all the world around,
Uplifts my soul, O God, to thee,
    Where rest is found.

3 No sound of jarring strife is heard
    As now the weekly labors cease;
No voice, but those that sweetly sing
    Their songs of peace.
Arr. fr. G. Thring.

575 All Glory to the King. S. M.

Luther.—T. Hastings.

1. Now let our songs a - rise, In new, ex-alt-ed strains: Let earth re - peat it

to the skies:—The Lord, the Savior reigns, The Lord, the Sav - ior reigns!

2 Sing to the Lord, our God,
  And bless his sacred name;
His great salvation, all abroad,
  From day to day proclaim.

3 Mid heathen nations place
  The glories of his throne;
And let the wonders of his grace
  Thro' all the earth be known.

4 Thro' earth, let every tribe,
  Let every nation sing:
Glory, and grace, and might ascribe
  To our eternal King.
              Wm. Goode.

576 The Name of Christ.

1 Thy name, Almighty Lord!
  Shall sound through distant lands:
Great is thy grace, and sure thy word;
  Thy truth forever stands.

2 Far be thine honor spread,
  And long thy praise endure,
Till morning light and evening shade
  Shall be exchanged no more.
              I. Watts.

577 Bless the Lord.

1 Stand up, and bless the Lord,
  Ye people of his choice;

Stand up, and bless the Lord your God
  With heart, and soul, and voice.

2 God is our strength and song,
  And his salvation ours;
Then be his love in Christ proclaimed
  With all our ransomed powers.

3 Stand up, and bless the Lord;
  The Lord your God adore:
Stand up, and bless his glorious name,
  Henceforth, forevermore!
             J. Montgomery.

578 Praise to the Trinity.

1 To God, the only wise,
  Who keeps us by his word,
Be glory now and evermore,
  Through Jesus Christ, our Lord.

2 Hosanna to the Word,
  Who from the Father came;
Ascribe salvation to the Lord,
  And ever bless his name.

3 The grace of Christ our Lord,
  The Father's boundless love,
The Spirit's blest communion, too,
  Be with us from above.
             I. Watts.

583   Invitation to Praise God.   L. M.

Old Hundred.—L. Bourgeois.

1. From all that dwell be-low the skies, Let the Cre-a-tor's praise a-rise:

Let the Re-deem-er's name be sung, Thro' ev-'ry land, by ev-'ry tongue.

2 Eternal are thy mercies. Lord;
Eternal truth attends thy word:
Thy praise shall sound from shore to
   shore.
Till suns shall rise and set no more.

3 Your lofty themes, ye mortals. bring;
In songs of praise divinely sing:
The great salvation loud proclaim.
And shout for joy the Savior's name.

4 In every land begin the song;
To every land the strains belong:
In cheerful sounds all voices raise.
And fill the world with loudest praise.
              J. WATTS.

584   *The Eternal God Exalted.*

1 Eternal God, celestial King,
Exalted be thy glorious name;
Let hosts in heaven thy praises sing.
And saints on earth thy love proclaim.

2 My heart is fixed on thee. my God;
I rest my hope on thee alone:
I'll spread thy sacred truths abroad.
   To all mankind thy love make known.

3 Awake, my tongue: awake. my lyre;
With morning's earliest dawn arise;
To songs of joy my soul inspire.
And swell your music to the skies.

4 With those who in thy grace abound,
To thee I'll raise my thankful voice;
Till every land, the earth around.
Shall hear, and in thy name rejoice.
           WM. WRANGHAM.

585   *Benediction.*

1 The peace which God alone reveals,
And by his word of grace imparts,
Which only the believer feels,
Direct, and keep, and cheer our hearts!

2 And may the holy Three in One.
The Father, Word. and Comforter,
Pour an abundant blessing down
On every soul assembled here!

3 Praise God. from whom all blessings
   flow:
Praise him, all creatures here below:
Praise him above, ye heavenly host:
Praise Father, Son, and Holy Ghost!
           J. NEWTON.

586   Praise to Thee.   8. 7. D.   Harwell.—L. Mason.

Praise to thee, O great Cre - a - tor, Praise be thine from ev - 'ry tongue;
Oh, let ev - 'ry liv - ing crea-ture Join the u - ni - ver - sal song!

Spir-it, Source of all our be-ing, Free e-ter - nal life is thine.
Spir-it, Source of all our be-ing, Free e - ter - nal life is thine.

Hail! the God of our sal - va - tion, Praise him, he is Love di - vine.

2 For ten thousand blessings given
     That he never could withhold,
Sound his praise, thro' earth and heaven,
     Let this Truth to men be told.
Joyfully on earth confess it,
     Till a heavenly song 'twill raise,
Till, enraptured, we perceive it,
     And are lost in love and praise.

587   *Blest be Thou.*

1 Blest be thou, O God of Israel,
     Thou, our Father, and our Lord!
Blest thy majesty forever!
     Ever be thy name adored.
Thine, O Lord, are power and greatness,
     Glory, victory, are thine own;
All is thine in earth and heaven,
     Over all thy boundless throne.

2 Riches come of thee, and honor,
     Power and might to thee belong;
Thine it is to make us prosper,
     Only thine to make us strong.
Lord, to thee, thou God of mercy,
     Hymns of gratitude we raise;
To thy name, forever glorious,
     Ever we address our praise!
                 H. U. Onderdonk.

588   *Spiritual Worship.*

1 Holy Lord! in pure devotion
     All the angels praise thy name,
In the loving heart's emotion
     All thy glorious deeds proclaim.
Changed from glory unto glory
     They delight to sing thy love,
Till the sweet and sacred story
     Fills the inmost heaven above.

589 Thy Glory Fills the Heaven.   8. 7. D.

R. Mant.
Faben. -J. H. Willcox.

1. Lord, thy glo-ry fills the heav-en; Earth is with its full-ness stored:
2. Ev-er thus in God's high prais-es, Brethren, let our tongues u-nite,

Un-to thee be glo-ry giv-en, Ho-ly, ho-ly, ho-ly Lord!
While our tho'ts his greatness rais-es, And our love his gifts ex-cite;

Heav'n is still with anthems ring-ing; Earth takes up the an-gels' cry;
Thus thy glo-rious day con-fess-ing, We a-dopt the an-gels' cry,

Ho-ly! ho-ly! ho-ly! sing-ing, Lord of hosts, thou Lord most high!
Ho-ly! ho-ly! ho-ly! bless-ing Thee, the Lord our God most high!

590   *Praise the Lord.*

1 Praise the Lord! ye heav'ns, adore him;
Praise him, angels in the height;
Sun and moon, rejoice before him;
Praise him, all ye stars of light.
Praise the Lord. for he hath spoken;
Worlds his mighty voice obeyed;
Laws which never can be broken.
For their guidance he hath made.

2 Praise the Lord! for he is glorious:
Never shall his promise fail;
God hath made his saints victorious,
Sin and death shall not prevail.
Praise the God of our salvation,
Hosts on high his power proclaim;
Heaven and earth and all creation
Laud and magnify his name.

R. Mant.

591   Hosanna.   L. M.   J. B. DYKES.

1. Lord God of Hosts, by all a-dored! Thy name we praise with one ac-cord;

The earth and heavens are full of thee, Thy light, thy love, thy maj-es-ty.

REFRAIN.

Ho-san-na, Lord! Ho-san-na in the high-est!

2 The holy church in every place
Throughout the world exalts thy praise:
Both heaven and earth do worship thee,
Thou Father of eternity!

3 From day to day, O Lord, do we
Highly exalt and honor thee;
Thy name we worship and adore,
World without end, forevermore.
                              F. GAMBOLD.

592   Universal Praise.
1 O holy, holy, holy, Lord!
   Bright in thy deeds and in thy name.
Forever be thy name adored,
   Thy glories let the world proclaim.

2 O holy Spirit from above,
   In streams of light and glory given,
Thou source of ecstacy and love,
   Thy praises ring thro' earth and heaven.

3 O God Triune, to thee we owe
Our every thought, our every song;

And ever may thy praises flow
   From saint and seraph's burning
      tongue.
                        J. W. EASTBURN.

593   Praise.
1 We are thy people, we thy care,
   Our soul and our immortal frame:
What lasting honors can we rear,
   Almighty Maker, to thy name?

2 We'll crowd thy gates with thankful
      songs!
   High as the heavens our voices raise!
And earth, with her ten thousand tongues,
   Shall fill thy courts with sounding
      praise.

3 Wide as the world is thy command!
   Vast as eternity thy love!
Firm as a rock thy truth shall stand,
   When rolling years shall cease to move!
                              I. WATTS.

594 Nations, Rejoice! L. M.   Anvern.—Arr. by L. Mason.

1. Ye nations round the earth, re-joice Before the Lord, your sov'reign King; Serve him with cheerful heart and voice; With all your tongues his glo-ry sing; With all your tongues his glo-ry sing.

2 Enter his gates with songs of joy;
With praises to his courts repair:
And make it your divine employ
To pay your thanks and honors there.

3 The Lord is good, the Lord is kind;
Great is his grace, his mercy sure;
And the whole race of man shall find
His truth from age to age endure.
I. WATTS.

595 *Welcome to the King of Glory.*
1 Lift up your heads, ye mighty gates!
Behold! the King of Glory waits;
The King of kings is drawing near,
The Savior of the world is here.

2 The Lord is just, a helper tried;
Mercy is ever at his side;
His kingly crown is holiness;
His sceptre, pity in distress.

3 Oh, blest the land, the city blest,
Where Christ, the ruler, is confessed!
O happy hearts, and happy homes
To whom this King of triumph comes!

4 Fling wide the portals of your heart;
Make it a temple, set apart
From earthly use for heaven's employ,
Adorned with prayer, and love, and joy.
G. WEISSEL.

596 *Praise Ye the Lord.*
1 Praise ye the Lord! let praise employ,
In his own courts, your songs of joy;
The spacious firmament around
Shall echo back the joyful sound.

2 Recount his works in strains divine,
His wondrous works—how bright they shine!
Praise him for all his mighty deeds,
Whose greatness all your praise exceeds.

3 Let all, whom life and breath inspire,
Attend, and join the blissful choir;
But chiefly ye, who know his word,
Adore, and love, and praise the Lord!
ANNE STEELE.

597 The Matchless Worth. C. P. M.   *Ariel.—Arr. fr. Mozart.*

1. Oh, could I speak the matchless worth, Oh, could I sound the glories forth,

Which in my Sav - ior shine! I'd soar and touch the heav'nly strings,

And vie with Ga - briel while he sings, In notes al - most di - vine,

In notes al - most di - vine.

2 I'd sing the characters he bears,
And all the forms of love he wears,
    Exalted on the throne;
In loftiest songs of sweetest praise,
I would to everlasting days
    Make all his glories known.
                S. Medley.

598   *The Faithful Comforter.*

1 To thee, O Comforter Divine,
For all thy grace and power benign,
    We sing Alleluia!
To thee, whose faithful power doth heal,
Enlighten, sanctify, and seal,
    We sing Allelulia!

2 To thee, by Jesus Christ sent down,
Of all his gifts the sum and crown,
    We sing Alleluia!
To thee, who art with God the Son,
And God the Father, ever One,
    We sing Alleluia!
          Frances R. Havergal.

599 O Zion, Tune Thy Voice. H. M.

Lenox.—L. Edson.

1. O Zi-on, tune thy voice, And raise thy hands on high: Tell all the earth thy joys, And boast sal - va - tion nigh: Cheerful in God, A-

Cheerful in God, A-rise and shine, While

rise and shine, While rays divine Stream all abroad, While rays divine Stream all abroad.

rays divine Stream all abroad, While rays di - vine Stream all a - broad.

2 He gilds thy mourning face
  With beams that cannot fade;
His all-resplendent grace
  He pours around thy head;
The nations round   │With lustre new
Thy form shall view,│Divinely crowned.

3 In honor to his name
  . Reflect that sacred light;
And loud that grace proclaim,
  Which makes thy darkness bright:
Pursue his praise   │ In worlds above,
Till sovereign love │ The glory raise.

P. DODDRIDGE.

600   *God in Creation.*

1 The Glory of the Lord
    The heavens declare abroad:

The firmament displays
  The handiwork of God;
Day unto day declareth speech.
And night to night doth knowledge teach.

2 Aloud they do not speak,
    They utter forth no word,
  Nor into language break—
    Their voice is never heard;
Their line through all the earth extends.
Their words to earth's remotest ends.

3 The fear of God is clean.
    And ever doth endure;
  His judgments all are truth
    And righteousness most pure;
To be desired are they far more
Than finest gold in richest store.

601　Our Grateful Praise.　7. 6 l.

F. S. PIERPOINT.
Pentecost.—English.

1. For the beau - ty of the earth, For the glo - ry of the skies,
2. For the won - der of each hour Of the day and of the night,

For the love which from our birth O - ver and a - round us lies:
Hill and vale, and tree and flow'r, Sun and moon, and stars of light:

Christ, our Lord, to thee we raise This our hymn of grate-ful praise.

Praise to Jehovah.　6. 4.

Dort.—L. MASON.

602 "Worthy the Lamb." 6. 4.   Italian Hymn.—F. GIARDINI.

1. Glo - ry to God on high! Let prais - es fill the sky;

Praise ye his name; An - gels! his name a - dore, Who all our

sor - rows bore; And saints! cry ev - er-more, "Wor-thy the Lamb!"

2 Join, all the human race!
Our Lord and God to bless;
  Praise ye his name:
In him we will rejoice,
Making a cheerful noise,
And say, with heart and voice,
  "Worthy the Lamb!"

3 What though we change our place,
Our souls shall never cease
  Praising his name;
To him we'll tribute bring,
Laud him our gracious King,
And through all ages sing,
  "Worthy the Lamb!"
                    JAS. ALLEN.

TUNE—Dort.

603   Praise to Jehovah.

1 Praise ye Jehovah's name;
Praise through his courts proclaim;
  Rise and adore;
High o'er the heavens above,
Sound his great acts of love,
While his rich grace we prove,
  Vast as his power.

2 Now let the trumpet raise
Sounds of triumphant praise,
  Wide as his fame;
There let the harp be found;

Organs with solemn sound
Roll your deep notes around,
  Filled with his name.

3 While his high praise you sing,
Shake every sounding string;
  Sweet the accord!
He vital breath bestows;
Let every breath that flows,
His noblest fame disclose,
  Praise ye the Lord.
                    WM. GOODE.

604   Nature's Praise.   C. M.

Bradford.—Arr. fr. Handel.

1. The harp at na - ture's ad - vent strung Has nev - er ceased to play:

The song the stars of morn-ing sung Has nev - er died a - way.

2 And prayer is made, and praise is
  By all things near and far: [given.
The ocean looketh up to heaven,
  And mirrors every star.

3 Its waves are kneeling on the strand,
  As kneels the human knee,
Their white locks bowing to the sand,
  The priest-hood of the sea!

4 The green earth sends her incense up
  From many a mountain shrine;
From folded leaf and dewy cup
  She pours her sacred wine.

5 The mists above the morning rills
  Rise white as wings of prayer;
The altar-curtains of the hills
  Are sunset's purple air.

6 The blue sky is the temple's arch,
  Its transept, earth and air;
The music of its starry march
  The chorus of a prayer.

7 So nature keeps the reverent frame
  With which her years began,
And all her signs and voices shame
  A prayerless heart in man.

              J. G. Whittier.

605   *Oh, Praise, My Tongue!*

1 Begin, my tongue, some heavenly
    theme,
  And speak some boundless thing,
The mighty works, or mightier name,
  Of our eternal King.

2 Tell of his wondrous faithfulness,
  And sound his power abroad,
Sing the sweet promise of his grace,
  And the performing God.

3 His very word of grace is strong,
  As that which built the skies;
The voice that rolls the stars along,
  Speaks all the promises.

4 Eternal Wisdom! thee we praise,
  Thee the creation sings;
With thy loved name, rocks, hills, and
    seas,
  And heaven's high palace, rings.

5 Infinite strength and equal skill
  Shine through the worlds abroad;
Our souls with vast amazement fill,
  And speak the builder, God.

              I. Watts.

606 Glory to God Alone. C. M.

Coronation.—O. Holden.

1. My soul doth mag-ni-fy the Lord, My spir-it doth re-joice

In thee, my Sav-ior and my God: I hear thy joy-ful voice;

In thee, my Sav-ior and my God: I hear thy joy-ful voice.

2 On me thy providence hath shone
   With gentle, smiling rays;
Oh, let my lips and life make known
   Thy goodness and thy praise.

3 I need not go abroad for joy,
   Who have a feast at home;
My sighs are turnéd into songs,
   The Comforter is come!

4 Down from on high the blessed Dove
   Is come into my breast,
To witness God's eternal love;
   This is my heavenly feast.

5 Glory to God the Father be,
   Glory to God the Son.
Glory to God the Holy Ghost—
   Glory to God alone!

WM. MASON.

607 Joy in God.

1 O God! our God! thou shinest here,
   Thine own this latter day;
To us thy radiant steps appear;
   Here beams thy glorious way!

2 On us thy Spirit hast thou poured.
   To us thy word has come;
We feel, we bless thee. quickening Lord,
   Thou shalt not find us dumb!

3 Bright garlands of immortal joy
   Shall bloom on every head;
While sorrow, sighing, and distress,
   Like shadows, all are fled.

4 March on in our Redeemer's strength;
   Pursue his footsteps still;
And let the prospect cheer our eyes
   While marching up the hill.

P. DODDRIDGE.

608   Praise God, the King Above.   P. M.

Brandon.—C. C. Smith.

1. Praise God, the King above, Give him your highest praise! He is the Au-thor
2. Lift high your voi-ces, sing! A-dore the God of peace! 'Tis he sup-plies your

of all good; He fills you with his boundless love, And blesses all your
ev-'ry need, Withholds from you no goodly thing, And makes your sorrows

days,—And bless-es all your days.
cease,—And makes your sorrows cease.

3 To God, the holy One,
    Let every creature bring
To Father,—Spirit,—Ruling power,—
To Blessed Christ,—Eternal Son,—
    The honors due our King,
    The honors due our King.

Copyright, 1896, by Piuma M. Brown.

609   Praise the Savior.   P. M.

German Melody.

1. Praise the Sav-ior, ye who know him: Who can tell how much we owe him?

Glad-ly let us ren-der to him All we are, and have!

610 Laudes Domini. P. M.   J. BARNBY.

1. When morn-ing gilds the skies, My heart, a - wak - ing. cries,
2. The night be-comes as day When from the heart we say.

"May Je - sus Christ be praised!" A - like at work and prayer,
"May Je - sus Christ be praised!" The claims of dark-ness fear

To Je - sus I re - pair: "May Je - sus Christ be praised!"
When this sweet chant they hear; "May Je - sus Christ be praised!"

3 In heaven's eternal bliss
The loveliest strain is this:
  "Let Jesus Christ be praised!"
Let earth and sea and sky
From depth to height reply:
  "May Jesus Christ be praised!"

4 Be this, while life is mine,
My canticle divine:
  "May Jesus Christ be praised!"
Be this th' eternal song
Through all the ages on:
  "May Jesus Christ be praised!"
E. CASWALL. Tr.

TUNE—*Praise the Savior.*
HEB. 13: 8.

2 With the Truth our God has bought us,
When we knew him not he sought us,
And from all our wanderings bro't us,
  His the praise alone.

3 Trust in him, ye saints, forever;
He is faithful, changing never.
Neither force nor guile can sever
  Those he loves from him.
T. KELLY.

4 Saints in glory, we together
Know the song that ceases never;
Song of songs thou art, O Savior,
  All this endless day.

5 Oh, th' unsearchable Redeemer!
Shoreless ocean, sounded never!
Yesterday, to-day, forever,
  Jesus Christ, the same.
N. ADAMS.

611   Evening Praise. P. M.

MARY A. LATHBURY.
WM. F. SHERWIN.

1. Day is dy - ing in the west, Heav'n is touching earth with rest;
2. Lord of life, be-neath the dome Of the u - ni-verse, thy home,

Wait and worship while the night Sets her ev'ning lamps alight Thro' all the sky.
Gath-er us who seek thy face, To the fold of thy embrace, For thou art nigh.

REFRAIN.

Ho - ly, ho - ly, ho - ly Lord God of hosts! Heav'n and earth are

full of thee! Heav'n and earth are praising thee, O Lord, Most High!

Used by arr. with J. H. Vincent, owner of copyright.

TUNE—*Manchester.* p. 22.

612   *A Psalm of Praise.* 10.

We praise thee, Lord, with early morn-
  ing ray,
We praise thee with the fading light of
  day: [land,
All things that live and move, by sea and
Forever ready at thy service stand.

Thy nations all are singing night and day,
"Glory to thee, the mighty God, for aye!
By thee, through thee, in thee, all beings
  are!"
The listening earth repeats the song afar.

FRANCK.

RESPONSIVE SERVICES.

Joy.

Make a joyful noise unto the Lord, all ye lands!
>Serve the Lord with gladness.

Come before his presence with singing!
>Be thankful unto him and bless his name!

For the Lord is good, his mercy is everlasting.
>And his truth endureth to all generations.

O come, let us sing unto the Lord; let us make a joyful noise to the Rock of our salvation.
>Let us come before his presence with thanksgiving and make a joyful noise unto him with psalms!

In his hand are the deep places of the earth; the heights of the hills are his also;
>The sea is his, and he made it; and his hands formed the dry land.

Let the sea roar, and the fullness thereof; the world and they that dwell therein.
>Let the floods clap their hands; let the hills be joyful together before the Lord!

With righteousness shall he judge the world, and the people with equity.

Gloria.

Glory be to the Father who is in heaven, The High and Ho-ly One.
As it was in the beginning, is now, and ev-er shall be: World with-out end, A-men.

The wilderness and the parched land shall be glad, and the desert shall rejoice and blossom as the rose.
>It shall blossom abundantly, and rejoice even with joy and singing.

The eyes of the blind shall be opened, and the ears of the deaf shall be unstopped:
>The lame man shall leap as an hart, and the tongue of the dumb sing.

In the wilderness shall waters break forth, and streams in the desert:
>And the parched ground shall become a pool, and the thirsty land springs of water.

There shall be joy and gladness, and sorrow and sighing shall flee away.

> *Glory be to the Father who | is in | heaven.*
> *The | High and | Holy | One!*
> *As it was in the beginning, is now, and | ever | shall be;*
> *World | without | end.   A- | men.*

The Ministry of the Holy Spirit.

And when the day of Pentecost was fully come, they were all with one accord in one place.

> And suddenly there came a sound from heaven as of a rushing mighty wind, and it filled all the house where they were sitting.

And there appeared unto them cloven tongues like as of fire, and it sat upon each of them.

> And they were all filled with the Holy Ghost, and began to speak with other tongues, as the Spirit gave them utterance.

1. O Ho-ly Spir-it, come to me: Touch thou mine eyes that I may see Thy wisdom, pow'r, and maj-es-ty Re-vealed to man from sea to sea.

Copyright, 1896, by Pluma M. Brown.

But the Comforter, which is the Holy Ghost, whom the Father will send in my name, he shall teach you all things,

> And bring all things to your remembrance, whatsoever I have said unto you.

Peace I leave with you, my peace I give unto you:

> Not as the world giveth, give I unto you.

Let not your heart be troubled, neither let it be afraid.

2. *O Holy Spirit, come to me;*
 Touch thou mine heart that I may feel
 Thou wilt thyself, as Love, reveal
 To every human child of weal.

And when he had said this, he breathed on them, and saith unto them, Receive ye the Holy Ghost.

Go ye therefore, and teach all nations, baptizing them in the name of the Father, and of the Son, and of the Holy Ghost.

Take no thought beforehand what ye shall speak, neither do ye premeditate:

But whatsoever shall be given you in that hour, that speak ye; for it is not ye that speak, but the Holy Ghost.

3. *O Holy Spirit, come to me;*
 Touch thou my hands that I may hold
 In steadfast faith thy love untold,
 For those whose thoughts to thee unfold.

Ye shall receive power, after that the Holy Ghost is come upon you:

And ye shall be witnesses unto me both in Jerusalem, and in all Judea, and in Samaria, and unto the uttermost parts of the earth.

Verily, verily, I say unto you, the works that I do shall ye do also.

Heal the sick, cleanse the lepers, raise the dead, cast out devils: freely ye have received, freely give.

Behold, I have given you power to tread on serpents and scorpions, and over all the power of the enemy:

And nothing shall by any means hurt you.

4. *O Holy Spirit, come to me;*
 Touch thou my feet until I stand
 Firm as the Rock in Beulah Land,
 Building no more on shifting sand.
 L. G. W.

But when the kindness of God our Savior toward man appeared, not by works of righteousness which we have done, but according to his mercy he saved us, by the washing of regeneration, and renewing of the Holy Ghost;

Which he shed on us abundantly through Jesus Christ our Savior;

That, being justified by his grace, we should be made heirs according to the hope of eternal life.

Therefore, being justified by faith, we have peace with God through our Lord Jesus Christ:

By whom, also, we have access by faith unto this grace wherein we stand, and rejoice in hope of the glory of God.

ALL:—The grace of the Lord Jesus Christ, and the love of God, and the communion of the Holy Ghost be with you all. Amen.

Be Still and Know.

PLUMA M. BROWN.

Be still, and know that I am God, O clamorous sense out-go-ing!

O rest-less tho'ts out-flow-ing! Be still, and know that I am God.

Copyright, 1896, by Pluma M. Brown.

God is Love.

Beloved, let us love one another: for love is of God; and everyone that loveth is born of God, and knoweth God.

> 2. *Be still, and know that I am Love,*
> *O mind that stirs with hating!*
> *O heart that aches with waiting!*
> *Be still, and know that I am Love.*

God is Peace.

Peace I leave with you, my peace I give unto you: not as the world giveth, give I unto you. Let not your heart be troubled, neither let it be afraid.

> 3. *Be still, and know that I am Peace.*
> *O tongue with thy complaining!*
> *O pain at pulses straining!*
> *Be still, and know that I am Peace.*

God is Light.

In him was life; and the life was the light of men. That was the true Light, which lighteth every man that cometh into the world.

> 4. *Be still, and know that I am Light.*
> *O eyes in darkness groping!*
> *O vision dulled with hoping!*
> *Be still, and know that I am Light.*

God is Life.

And we know that the Son of God is come, and hath given us an understanding, that we may know him that is true, and we are in him that is true, even in his Son Jesus Christ. This is the true God, and eternal life.

> 5. *Be still and know that I am Life,*
> *This knowledge is all freeing,*
> *That I am one with being!*
> *Be still, and know that I am Life.*

And he said unto me, It is done. I am Alpha and Omega, the beginning and the end. I will give unto him that is athirst of the fountain of the water of life freely. He that overcometh shall inherit all things; and I will be his God, and he shall be my son.

Strength.

Wait on the Lord; be of good courage and he shall strengthen thine heart; wait, I say, on the Lord.

The Lord is my strength and my shield: my heart trusted in him and I am helped.

Therefore my heart greatly rejoiceth, and with my song will I praise him.

It is God that guideth me with strength and maketh my way perfect.

The Lord liveth: and blessed be my rock: and let the God of my salvation be exalted.

The Lord is my light and my salvation, whom shall I fear?

The Lord is the strength of my life, of whom shall I be afraid?

Thine is the kingdom, O...... Lord,
All our blessings come from thee,
In thee is all power and might,
Therefore, O Lord, do we thank thee,

Thou art exalted, the Fa - ther o - ver all.
And thou dost care for all.
And thine it is to give strength un - to all.
And bless thy ho - ly name.

O Zion that bringest good tidings, get thee up into a high mountain.

O Jerusalem that bringest good tidings, lift up thy voice with strength: lift it up, be not afraid.

Say unto the cities of Judah, behold your God. Behold, the Lord God will come with strong hand, and his arm shall rule for him.

Behold, his reward is with him and his work before him. He shall feed his flock like a shepherd, he shall gather the lambs with his arm, and carry them in his bosom.

Hast thou not known? hast thou not heard, that the everlasting God, the Lord, the Creator of the ends of the earth, fainteth not, neither is weary?

He giveth power to the faint, and to them that have no might, he increaseth strength.

Even the youths shall faint and be weary, and the young men shall utterly fall:

But they that wait upon the Lord shall renew their strength;

They shall mount up with wings as eagles;

They shall run and not be weary; they shall walk, and not faint.

Finally, brethren, be strong in the Lord and in the power of his might.

ALL:—I can do all things through Christ which strengtheneth me.

Thine is the kingdom, | O | Lord,
Thou art exalted, the | Father | over | all.
All our blessings | come from | thee,
And | thou dost | care for | all.
In thee is all | power and | might,
And thine it is to | give strength | unto | all.
Therefore, O Lord, | do we | thank thee,
And | bless thy | holy | name.

Defense.

The Lord is good to all, and his tender mercies are over all his works.

The Lord is good, a stronghold in the day of trouble.

And he knoweth them that trust in him.

O Lord, my God, I cried unto thee and thou hast healed me.

Thou art my hiding place: thou shalt preserve me from trouble.

Thou shalt compass me about with songs of deliverance.

Thou wilt keep him in perfect peace whose mind is stayed on thee,

Because he trusteth in thee.

Fear thou not; for I am with thee: be not dismayed; for I am thy God:

I will strengthen thee; yea, I will help thee; yea, I will uphold thee with the right hand of my righteousness.

I will lift up mine eyes unto the hills from whence cometh my help.
He will not suffer thy foot to be moved: he that keepeth thee will not slumber.

My help cometh from the Lord which made heaven and earth.
Behold, he that keepeth Israel shall not slumber nor sleep.

Behold, all they that were incensed against thee shall be ashamed and confounded: they that war against thee shall be as nothing, and as a thing of naught.

For I, the Lord, thy God, will hold thy right hand, saying unto thee, Fear not: I will help thee.

I will instruct thee, and teach thee in the way thou shalt go: I will guide thee with mine eye.

And I will bring the blind by a way they know not: I will lead them in paths that they have not known.

I will make darkness light before them and crooked things straight. These things will I do unto them and not forsake them.

When thou passest through the waters I will be with thee: and through the rivers, they shall not overflow thee.

When thou walkest through the fire thou shalt not be burned: neither shall the flame kindle upon thee.

For I am the Lord thy God, the holy one of Israel, thy Savior.

The Lord is thy keeper; the Lord is thy shade upon thy | right | hand.
The sun shall not smite thee by day, nor the | moon by | night.
The Lord shall preserve thee from all evil: he shall pre- | serve thy | soul.
The Lord shall preserve thy going out, and thy coming in, from this time forth, and even forevermore. | A- | men.

God is our refuge and strength, a very present help in trouble.

Therefore will we not fear, though the earth be removed, and though the mountains be carried into the midst of the sea.

Though the waters thereof be troubled, though the mountains shake with the swelling thereof.

He shall deliver thee in six troubles: yea, in seven there shall no evil touch thee.

In famine he shall redeem thee from death: and in war from the power of the sword.

Thou shalt be hid from the scourge of the tongue: neither shalt thou be afraid of destruction when it cometh.

At destruction and famine thou shalt laugh: neither shalt thou be afraid of the beasts of the earth.

ALL:—For thou shalt be in league with the stones of the field: and the beasts of the field shall be at peace with thee.

Peace to the Nation.

God hath made of one blood all nations of men to dwell on all the face of the earth.

He maketh wars to cease unto the end of the earth:

He breaketh the bow and cutteth the spear in sunder;

He burneth the chariot in the fire.

Let men say among the nations, the Lord reigneth.

The Desire of all nations shall come, and he shall judge among the nations, and shall rebuke many people;

And they shall beat their swords into ploughshares, and their spears into pruning-hooks.

Nation shall not lift up sword against nation,

Neither shall they learn war any more.

In his days shall the righteous flourish;

And abundance of peace so long as the moon endureth.

He shall have dominion also from sea to sea,

And from the river unto the ends of the earth.

Yea, all kings shall fall down before him; All nations shall serve him.

All the ends of the earth shall remember and turn to the Lord.

And all the kindreds of the nations shall worship before thee.

The earth shall be filled with the knowledge of the glory of the Lord, as the waters cover the sea.

PLUMA M. BROWN.

Blessed be the   Lord God, And blessed be his glorious name for - ever:
Be still and know that I am God: I will be exalted a - mong   the heathen:

And let the whole   earth   be   filled   with his   glory.
I will be ex ·   · alt - ed   in   the   earth.

Rejoice ye with Jerusalem, and be glad with her. For thus saith the Lord, Behold, I will extend peace to her like a river,

And the glory of the Gentiles like a flowing stream.

Ye are a chosen generation, a royal priesthood, an holy nation, a peculiar people;

That ye should show forth the praises of him who hath called you out of darkness into his marvelous light.

Violence shall no more be heard in thy land, wasting nor destruction within thy borders;

But thou shalt call thy walls Salvation, and thy gates Praise.

And the Gentiles shall see thy righteousness, and all kings thy glory:

And thou shalt be called by a new name, which the mouth of the Lord shall name.

Thou shalt also be a crown of glory in the hand of the Lord,

And a royal diadem in the hand of thy God.

ALL:—Happy is that people, whose God is the Lord.

Blessed be the | Lord | God, | And blessed be his | glorious name for- | ever:
And let the whole | earth be | filled with his | glory.
Be still and know that | I am | God: | I will be exalted a- | mong the | heathen:
I will be ex- | alted | in the | earth.

Oneness with Christ.

There is one body, and one spirit, one faith, one baptism,

> One God and Father of all, who is above all, and through all, and in you
> all.

Know ye not that ye are the temple of God, and that the Spirit of God dwelleth
in you?

> The Lord is in his holy temple: let the earth keep silence before him.

I, a living soul, stand before the Lord with the light of his glory shining through
me, that it may fill his house with glory.

> We all, with unveiled face reflecting as a mirror the glory of the Lord,
> are transformed into the same image from glory to glory, even as
> from the Lord the Spirit.

This is the mystery which hath been hid from ages and from generations, but is
now made manifest....Christ in you the hope of glory.

> It pleased the Father that in Christ should all fullness dwell, and ye are
> complete in him.

Your life is hid with Christ in God.

> He that abideth in the doctrine of Christ, he hath both the Father and
> the Son.

ALL:—Therefore, let the same mind be in you which was also in Christ Jesus
our Lord.

PLUMA M. BROWN.

I. if I be lift - ed up, will draw all men un - to me.

I. if I be lift - ed up, will draw all men un - to me.

I am that I am, and beside me there is none other.

> He that hath seen me hath seen the Father.

Call no man your father, for One is your Father which is in heaven.

> That which is born of the Spirit is spirit.

The words that I speak are not mine, but the Father's in me.

And ye shall know that I am in the Father, and ye in me, and I in you.

I am the Way, the Truth, and the Life; no man cometh unto the Father but by me.

Ye have not chosen me but I have chosen you.

I am the vine, ye are the branches. He that abideth in me and I in him, the same bringeth forth much fruit; for without me ye can do nothing.

These things have I spoken unto you that my joy might remain in you, and that your joy might be full.

ALL:—Thanks be unto God for his unspeakable gift.

I, if I be lifted up, will draw all men unto me.

Unfailing Answer to Prayer.

Every good gift and every perfect gift is from above, and cometh down from the Father of Light,

With whom is no variableness, neither shadow of turning.

To us there is one God, the Father, from whom are all things, and we in him.

Thou shalt make thy prayer unto him, and he shall hear thee, and thou shalt pay thy vows.

Thou shalt also decree a thing, and it shall be established unto thee:

ALL:—And the light shall shine upon thy ways.

PLUMA M. BROWN.

And ye shall seek me and find me, When ye shall search for me with all your heart.

The Lord hath heard my sup-pli-cation: The Lord will re-ceive my prayer.

Verily, the Lord hath heard me; He hath attended un-to the voice of my prayer.

Thou shalt call, and the Lord shall answer; thou shalt cry, and he shall say, Here I am.

They shall call upon my name and I will hear them: I will say, It is my people: and they shall say, The Lord is my God.

And it shall come to pass, that before they call, I will answer;

And while they are yet speaking, I will hear.

When thou prayest, enter into thy closet, and when thou hast shut thy door,
    pray to thy Father which is in secret;
    And thy Father which seeth in secret shall reward thee openly.
But when ye pray, use not vain repetitions,
    For your Father knoweth what things ye have need of, before ye ask him.
And I say unto you, Ask, and it shall be given you; seek, and ye shall find;
    knock, and it shall be opened unto you:
    For every one that asketh, receiveth; and he that seeketh, findeth; and
    to him that knocketh, it shall be opened.
Therefore I say unto you, What things soever ye desire, when ye pray, believe
    that ye receive them, and ye shall have them.
    Verily, I say unto you, If ye have faith and doubt not, ... ye shall say
    unto this mountain, Be thou removed, and be thou cast into the
    sea; and it shall be done.
And all things, whatsoever ye shall ask in prayer, believing, ye shall receive.
ALL:—Now unto him that is able to do exceeding abundantly above all that we
    ask or think, according to the power that worketh in us, Unto
    him be glory throughout all ages, world without end.   Amen.

And ye shall | seek me and | find me,
When ye shall search for | me with | all your | heart.
The Lord hath heard my | suppli- | cation;
The Lord | will re- | ceive my | prayer.
Verily, the | Lord hath | heard me;
He hath attended | unto the | voice of my | prayer.

Eternal Life.

This is life eternal, that they might know thee the only true God, and Jesus
    Christ whom thou hast sent.
    Jesus said, I am the Resurrection, and the Life: he that believeth in me,
    though he were dead, yet shall he live:
And whosoever liveth and believeth in me shall never die.
    And ye shall know that I am in the Father, and ye in me, and I in you.
    Because I live, ye shall live also.
My sheep hear my voice, and I know them, and they follow me:
    And I give unto them eternal life; and they shall never perish, neither
    shall any pluck them out of my hand.
My Father, which gave them me, is greater than all; and no man is able to
    pluck them out of my Father's hand.
    I and my Father are one.
I am the Way, the Truth, and the Life: no man cometh unto the Father, but by
    me.
    I am the Bread of Life: he that cometh to me shall never hunger;

And he that believeth on me shall never thirst.

He that heareth my word, and believeth on him that sent me, hath everlasting life.

And shall not come into condemnation; but is passed from death unto life.

For as the Father hath life in himself; so hath he given to the Son to have life in himself;

And hath given him authority to execute judgment also, because he is the Son of man.

ALL:—Verily, verily, I say unto you, if a man keep my saying, he shall never see death.

PLUMA M. BROWN.

Incline your ear, and come unto me; hear, and your soul shall live;
I will give unto him that is a-} thirst of the fountain of the wa - ter of life.

And I will make an everlasting} covenant with you, Even the sure mercies of David.
He that overcometh shall in-} herit all things; {And I will be his God, and he shall} be my son.

This is the record, that God hath given to us eternal life, and this life is in his Son.

He that hath the Son hath life; and he that hath not the Son of God hath not life.

These things have I written unto you that believe on the name of the Son of God; that ye may know that ye have eternal life.

For the life was manifested, and we have seen it, and bear witness, and shew unto you that eternal life, which was with the Father, and was manifested unto us.

And we know that the Son of God is come, and hath given us an understanding, that we may know him that is true,

And we are in him that is true, even in his Son Jesus Christ. This is the true God, and eternal life.

ALL:—The law of the Spirit of life in Christ Jesus hath made me free from the law of sin and death.

Incline your ear, and | come unto | me; | hear, and your soul shall | live;
And I will make an everlasting | covenant with | you,
Even the sure | mercies of | David.
I will give unto him that is a- | thirst of the | fountain of the | water of | life.
He that overcometh shall in- | herit all | things;
And I will be his God, and he shall | be my | son.

He that hath an ear, let him hear what the Spirit saith unto the churches: To him that overcometh will I give to eat of the tree of life, which is in the midst of the paradise of God.

Behold, I make all things new. These words are true and faithful. I am Alpha and Omega, the beginning and the end.

I will give unto him that is athirst of the fountain of the water of life freely.

ALL:—He that overcometh shall inherit all things; and I will be his God, and he shall be my Son.

Light.

And God said, let there be light: and there was light.

God, who commanded the light to shine out of darkness, hath shined in our hearts also,

And given us the earnest of the Spirit within us whereby we lay hold of eternal life.

This is the light which lighteth every man who cometh into the world. God is Light and in him is no darkness at all.

The people that walked in darkness have seen a great light: they that dwell in the land of the shadow of death, upon them hath the light shined.

I am the light of the world; he that followeth me shall not walk in darkness, but shall have the light of life.

In him was life and the life was the light of man.

PLUMA M. BROWN.

With thee is the fountain of life: In thy light shall we see light.
Lead me, O Lord, in thy truth: The entrance of thy truth giveth light.

I am come a light into the world, that whosoever believeth on me should not abide in darkness.

Believe in the light that ye may be the children of light.

Ye are all children of light, and the children of the day. If thine eye be single, thy whole body shall be full of light.

Ye are a chosen generation, a royal priesthood, an holy nation, a peculiar people;

That ye should shew forth the praises of him who hath called you out of darkness into his marvelous light.

Thou shalt decree a thing and it shall be established unto thee.

ALL:—And the light shall shine upon thy ways.

> *With thee is the | fountain of | life:*
> *In thy light shall | we see | light.*
> *Lead me, O | Lord, in thy | truth;*
> *The entrance of thy | truth giveth | light.*

Arise, shine; for thy light is come, and the glory of the Lord is risen upon thee.

And the Gentiles shall come to thy light, and kings to the brightness of thy rising.

I will also give thee for a light to the Gentiles, that thou mayst be my salvation unto the ends of the earth.

A light of the Gentiles; to open the blind eyes, to bring out the prisoners from the prison, and them that sit in darkness out of the prison house.

If thou draw out thy soul to the hungry, and satisfy the afflicted soul;

Then shall thy light rise in obscurity, and thy darkness be as the noonday.

The sun shall be no more thy light by day; neither for brightness shall the moon give light unto thee;

But the Lord shall be unto thee an everlasting light, and thy God thy thy glory.

Thy sun shall no more go down; neither shall thy moon withdraw itself;

For the Lord shall be thine everlasting light, and the days of thy mourning shall be ended.

And thou shalt be as the light of the morning, when the sun riseth, even a morning without clouds.

As the tender grass springing out of the earth by clear shining after rain.

ALL:—And unto you that fear my name shall the Sun of righteousness arise with healing in his wings.

The Law of God.

This is the first and great commandment: Thou shalt love the Lord thy God with all thy heart, and with all thy mind, and with all thy strength.

And the second is like unto it: Thou shalt love thy neighbor as thyself. On these two commandments hang all the law and the prophets.

Owe no man anything but to love one another; for he that loveth his neighbor hath fulfilled the law.

Love is the fulfilling of the law.

PLUMA M. BROWN.

Open thou mine eyes that I may be-hold won-drous things out of thy law.

Open thou mine eyes that I may be-hold won-drous things out of thy law.

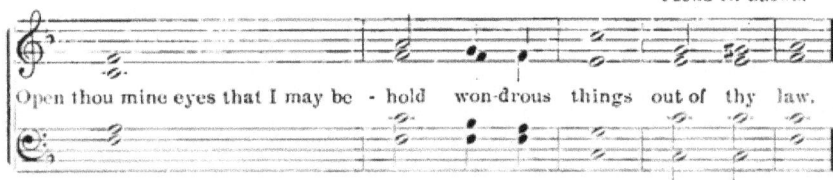

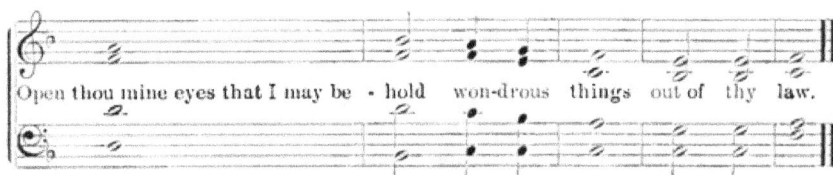

The law of the Lord is perfect, converting the soul.

The testimony of the Lord is sure, making wise the simple.

The statutes of the Lord are right, rejoicing the heart.

The commandment of the Lord is pure, enlightening the eyes.

The judgments of the Lord are true and righteous altogether.

More to be desired are they than gold, yea, than much fine gold.

Open thou mine eyes that I may be- | hold wondrous | things | out of thy | law.

Whoso looketh into the perfect law of liberty, and continueth therein, this man shall be blessed in his deed.

For Christ is the end of the law for Righteousness to every one that believeth.

The law of the spirit of life in Christ Jesus hath made me free from the law of sin and death.

Blessed is the man whose delight is in the law of the Lord.

Blessed are they whose ways are pure, who walk in the path of his commandments.

Blessed are they who keep his statutes, and who seek him with the whole heart.

Open thou mine eyes that I may be- | hold wondrous | things | out of thy | law.

The Word of God.

The entrance of thy words giveth light; it giveth understanding unto the simple.

Teach me, O Lord, the way of thy statutes. Make me to go in the path of thy commandments.

Then opened he their understanding, that they might understand the Scriptures.

Blessed are they that hear the word of God, and keep it.

Take fast hold of instruction; let her not go; keep her; for she is thy life.

Let the word of God dwell in you richly in all wisdom, so shall it be a lamp unto thy feet, and a light unto thy path.

Thine ears shall hear a word behind thee, saying, This is the way, walk ye in it.

Be ye doers of the word and not hearers only.

Keep my commandments and live. Bind them upon thy fingers, write them upon the table of thine heart.

My spirit which is upon thee, and my words which I have put in thy mouth, shall not depart out of thy mouth, nor out of the mouth of thy seed, nor out of the mouth of thy seed's seed, saith the Lord, from henceforth and forever.

The statutes of the Lord are right, re - - joicing the heart:
Teach me, O Lord, the way of thy statutes.
Let the words of my mouth and the meditations of my heart,

The commandments of the Lord are pure, giv-ing } light un - to the eyes.
Make me to go in the path of thy com - mandments.
Be acceptable in thy sight, O Lord, my strength and my re - deemer.

This commandment which I command thee this day is not hidden from thee, neither is it far off.

It is not in the heavens that thou shouldst say, Who will go up for us to the heavens and bring it to us, that we may hear it and do it?

Nor is it beyond the sea, that thou shouldst say, Who will go over the sea for us, that we may have it and do it?

But the word is very nigh to thee, in thy mouth and in thy heart, that thou mayst do it.

The anointing ye have received abideth in you and ye need not that any man teach you.

For I will give you a mouth and wisdom which all your adversaries shall
not be able to gainsay or resist.

Hold fast the form of sound words, which thou hast heard in faith and love
which is in Christ Jesus.

Their sound went into all the earth, and their words unto the ends of the
world.

So shall my word be that goeth forth out of my mouth;

It shall not return unto me void,

ALL:—But it shall accomplish that which I please, and it shall prosper in the
thing whereto I sent it.

Teach me, O Lord, the | way of thy | statutes.
Make me to go in the | path of | thy com- | mandments.
Let the words of my mouth and the meditations | of my | heart,
Be acceptable in thy sight, O Lord, my | strength and | my re- | deemer.

God Our Supply.

Every good gift and every perfect gift is from above, and cometh down from
the Father of lights,

With whom there is no variableness, neither shadow of turning.

Consider the lilies of the field, how they grow; they toil not, neither do they
spin: yet, Solomon in all his glory was not arrayed like one of
these.

Wherefore, if God so clothe the grass of the field, which to-day is, and
to-morrow is cast into the oven, shall he not much more clothe
you?

Take no thought, saying, What shall we eat? or, What shall we drink? or,
Wherewithal shall we be clothed?

For your heavenly Father knoweth that ye have need of all these things.

But seek ye first the kingdom of God and his righteousness.

And all these things shall be added unto you.

And I say unto you, Ask, and it shall be given you; seek, and ye shall find;
knock, and it shall be opened unto you.

For every one that asketh, receiveth; and he that seeketh, findeth; and
to him that knocketh it shall be opened.

PLUMA M. BROWN.

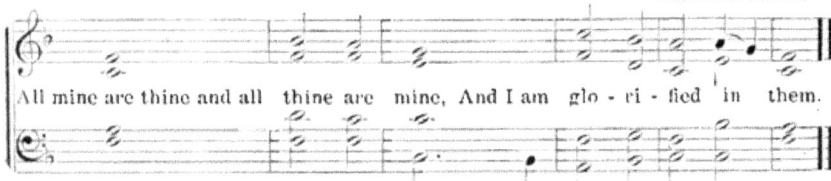

All mine are thine and all thine are mine, And I am glo - ri - fied in them.

If ye abide in me, and my words abide in you, ye shall ask what ye will and it
shall be done unto you.

My God shall supply all your need according to your riches in glory by Christ Jesus.

Whatsoever ye shall ask in my name, that will I do, that the Father may be glorified in the Son.

Every place that the sole of your foot shall tread upon, (that you stand squarely and firmly upon) that have I given you.

ALL:—In Christ all things are mine.

All mine are thine, and all | thine are | mine. And I am | glori- | fied in | them.

Immanuel.

The sceptre shall not depart from Judah, nor a lawgiver from between his feet until Shiloh come;

And unto him shall the gathering of the people be.

And there shall come forth a rod out of the stem of Jesse,

And a branch shall grow out of his roots,

And the spirit of the Lord shall rest upon him;

The spirit of wisdom and understanding,

The spirit of counsel and might,

The spirit of knowledge and of the fear of the Lord;

And righteousness shall be the girdle of his loins.

And faithfulness the girdle of his reins.

And in that day there shall be a root of Jesse which shall stand for an ensign of the people;

To it shall the Gentiles seek; and his rest shall be glorious.

And he shall set up an ensign for the nations,

And shall assemble the outcasts of Israel, and gather together the dispersed of Judah from the four corners of the earth.

PLUMA M. BROWN.

In his days shall the right - eous flourish;
His dominion shall be from sea unto sea,

And abundance of peace as long as the moon en - dureth.
And from the river even un - to the ends of the earth.

They shall call his name Immanuel, which being interpreted is, "God with us."

He shall be great, and shall be called the Son of the Highest; and of his kingdom there shall be no end.

His name shall endure forever; his name shall be continued as long as the sun; And men shall be blessed in him; all nations shall call him blessed.

The government shall be upon his shoulder; and his name shall be called Wonderful, Counselor, The Mighty God, The Everlasting Father, The Prince of Peace.

Every valley shall be exalted, and every mountain and hill shall be made low;

And the crooked shall be made straight, and the rough places plain.

Of the increase of his government and peace there shall be no end, upon the throne of David, and upon his kingdom, to order it, and to establish it with judgment, and with justice from henceforth even forever. The zeal of the Lord of hosts will perform this.

Wherefore God also hath highly exalted him, and given him a name which is above every name:

That at the name of Jesus every knee should bow, of things in heaven, and things in earth, and things under the earth:

ALL:—And that every tongue should confess that Jesus Christ is Lord, to the glory of God the Father.

In his days shall the | righteous | flourish:
And abundance of peace as | long as the | moon en- | dureth.
His dominion shall be from | sea unto | sea,
And from the river even | unto the | ends of the | earth.

Encouragement.

God is our refuge and strength, a very present help in time of trouble.

A Father of the fatherless, a refuge for the oppressed.

Our dwelling place in all generations.

The confidence of all the ends of the earth, and of them afar off upon the sea.

He healeth the broken in heart and bindeth up their wounds.

He telleth the number of the stars; he calleth them all by their names.

Why art thou cast down, O my soul, and why art thou disquieted within me?

Hope thou in God: thou shalt yet praise him for the help of his countenance.

Hearken ye, all Judah. Thus saith the Lord unto you: Be not afraid nor dismayed by reason of this great multitude;

For the battle is not yours, but God's.

O Judah, fear not; but tomorrow go out against them, for the Lord will be with you.

ALL:—Ye shall not need to fight this battle; set yourselves, stand ye still, and see the salvation of the Lord with you.

PLUMA M. BROWN.

Hearken ye, all Judah,
Not by might nor by power,
We praise thee, we bless thee, we worship thee, we glori - fy thee.

For the battle is not yours, but God's.
But by my Spir - it saith the Lord.
We give thanks to thee for thy great glory.

Acquaint now thyself with God, and be at peace: thereby good shall come unto thee.

Receive, I pray thee, the law from his mouth, and lay up his words in thine heart.

Then shalt thou be built up, thou shalt put away iniquity far from thy tabernacles.

Thou shalt lay up gold as dust, and the gold of Ophir as the stones of the brooks.

Yea, the Almighty shall be thy defense, and thou shalt have plenty of silver.

For then thou shalt have thy delight in the Almighty, and shalt lift up thy face unto God.

If thou take away from the midst of thee the yoke, the putting forth of the finger, and speaking vanity;

And if thou draw out thy soul to the hungry, and satisfy the afflicted soul;

Then shall thy light rise in obscurity, and thy darkness be as the noonday:

And the Lord shall guide thee continually, and satisfy thy soul in drought, and make fat thy bones:

And thou shalt be like a watered garden, and like a spring of water, whose waters fail not.

And they that shall be of thee shall build the old waste places:

Thou shalt raise up the foundations of many generations;

And thou shalt be called, The repairer of the breach, The restorer of paths to dwell in.

If thou shalt honour the Lord, not doing thine own ways,

Nor finding thine own pleasure, nor speaking thine own words:

Then shalt thou delight thyself in the Lord; and I will cause thee to ride upon the high places of the earth, and feed thee with the heritage of Jacob thy father:

ALL:—For the mouth of the Lord hath spoken it.

> *Thy light shall break | forth as the | morning,*
> *And thine health shall | spring forth | speedi- | ly.*
> *Thy righteousness shall | go be- | fore thee;*
> *The glory of the | Lord shall | be thy re- | ward.*

Love.

Though I speak with the tongues of men and of angels and have not love, I am become as sounding brass or a tinkling cymbal.

Though I have the gift of prophecy and understand all mysteries and all knowledge, and though I have all faith so as to remove mountains,

And have not love, I am nothing.

Though I bestow all my goods to feed the poor, and though I give my body to be burned,

And have not love, it profiteth me nothing.

Love suffereth long and is kind;

Love envieth not;

Love vaunteth not itself;

Seeketh not its own;

Is not easily provoked, thinketh no evil;

Rejoiceth not in iniquity, but rejoiceth in the truth.

Love beareth all things, believeth all things, hopeth all things, endureth all things.

Love never faileth.

Now abideth faith, hope and love, these three;

But the greatest of these is love.   PLUMA M. BROWN.

Thanks be unto God for his unspeakable gift.

Oh, let all men bless his holy name, now and for-ev-er-more.

He that hath my commandments and keepeth them, he it is that loveth me:

> And he that loveth me shall be loved of my Father, and I will love him, and will manifest myself to him.

If a man love me, he will keep my words: and my Father will love him,

> And we will come unto him, and make our abode with him.

Eye hath not seen, nor ear heard, neither have entered into the heart of man, the things which God hath prepared for them that love him.

> But God hath revealed them unto us by his Spirit.

In all things we are more than conquerors through him that loved us.

ALL:—For I am persuaded that neither death, nor life, nor angels, nor principalities, nor powers, nor things present, nor things to come, nor height, nor depth, nor any other creature, shall be able to separate us from the love of God, which is in Christ Jesus our Lord.

> *Thanks be unto God for his un- | speakable | gift.*
>
> *Oh, let all men bless his | holy | name, now and for- | ever- | more.*

And this I pray, that your love may abound yet more and more in knowledge and in all judgment.

> Being filled with the fruits of righteousness which are by Jesus Christ, unto the glory and praise of God.

And beside this, add to your faith, virtue.

> And to virtue, knowledge.

And to knowledge, temperance.

> And to temperance, patience.

And to patience, godliness.

> And to godliness, brotherly kindness, and to brotherly kindness, charity.

That ye being rooted and grounded in love, may be able to comprehend with all saints

ALL:—What is the breadth, and length, and depth, and height; and to know the love of Christ, which passeth knowledge, that ye might be filled with all the fullness of God.

Fellowship.

Beloved, let us love one another; for love is of God, and every one that loveth is born of God and knoweth God.

> This is the message that we have heard from the beginning, that we should love one another.

If thou bring thy gift to the altar, and there rememberest that thy brother hath aught against thee, go thy way. First be reconciled to thy brother, then come and offer thy gift.

He that loveth not his brother whom he hath seen, how can he love God whom he hath not seen.

And this commandment have we from him, That he who loveth God love his brother also.

Bear ye one another's burdens, and so fulfill the law of Christ. Be of the same mind one toward another.

Love your enemies and bless them that persecute you, that ye may become the children of your Father in heaven.

For he maketh his sun to rise on the evil and the good, and sendeth rain on the just and the unjust.

PLUMA M. BROWN.

A new commandment I give unto you; As I have lov'd you, that ye al - so love one another.

Do unto others as ye would that they should do unto you; And so ful fill the law of Christ.

There is neither Jew nor Greek, there is neither bond nor free, there is neither male nor female: for ye are all one in Christ Jesus.

For the same Lord over all is rich unto all that call upon him.

Judge not, and ye shall not be judged: condemn not, and ye shall not be condemned: forgive, and ye shall be forgiven.

Give, and it shall be given unto you; good measure, pressed down, and shaken together, and running over, shall men give into your bosom.

For with the same measure that ye mete withal it shall be measured to you again.

Every one of us shall give account of himself to God.

Let us not therefore judge one another any more:

But judge this rather, that no man put a stumbling-block or an occasion to fall in his brother's way.

I therefore beseech you that ye walk with all lowliness and meekness, with long-suffering, forbearing one another in love;

Endeavoring to keep the unity of the Spirit in the bond of peace.

A new commandment I | give unto | you;
As I have loved you, that ye | also | love one | another.
Do unto others as ye would that they should | do unto | you;
And so ful- | fill the | law of | Christ.

We, being many, are one body in Christ, and every one members one of another.

And are built upon the foundation of the apostles and prophets, Jesus Christ himself being the chief corner-stone;

In whom all the building fitly framed together groweth unto an holy temple in the Lord.

In whom we also are builded together for an habitation of God through the Spirit.

Finally, brethren, Be perfect, be of good comfort, be of one mind, live in peace:

All:—And the God of love and peace shall be with us.

Supply.

Ho, every one that thirsteth, come ye to the waters,

And he that hath no money; come ye buy and eat;

Yea, come, buy wine and milk without money and without price.

Wherefore do ye spend money for that which is not bread? and your labor for that which satisfieth not?

Hearken diligently unto me, and eat ye that which is good, and let your soul delight itself in fatness.

The Lord shall guide thee continually, and satisfy thy soul in drought, and make fat thy bones:

And thou shalt be like a watered garden, and like a spring of water, whose waters fail not.

PLUMA M. BROWN.

The Lord is a Sun and a Shield; No good thing will he withhold from them that walk up-rightly.

He openeth his hand and sat - is - fieth The desire of ev - 'ry liv - ing thing.

Blessed is the man that feareth the Lord, that delighteth greatly in his commandments.

Wealth and riches shall be in his house: and his righteousness endureth forever.

He that walketh righteously, and speaketh uprightly;

He that despiseth the gain of oppressions,
That shaketh his hands from holding of bribes,
That stoppeth his ears from hearing of blood,
And shutteth his eyes from seeing evil;

He shall dwell on high; his place of defense shall be the munitions of rocks:
Bread shall be given him; his waters shall be sure.

My people shall dwell in a peaceable habitation, and in sure dwellings, and in quiet resting-places.
They shall be abundantly satisfied with the fatness of thy house: and thou shalt make them drink of the river of thy pleasures.

Trust in the Lord and do good; so shalt thou dwell in the land, and verily thou shalt be fed.
Delight thyself also in the Lord; and he shall give thee the desires of thy heart.

For of him and through him and to him are all things: to whom be glory forever. Amen.

Peace.

Mark the perfect man, and behold the upright: for the end of that man is peace.

Acquaint now thyself with God and be at peace: thereby shall good come unto thee.
Stand still and see the salvation of God which he will work for you.

The Lord shall fight for you, and ye shall hold your peace.
Rest in the Lord and wait patiently for him.

PLUMA M. BROWN.

Thou wilt keep him in per-fect peace, Whose mind is stayed on thee.
Peace be to thee, and peace to thine house, And peace unto all that thou hast.

The Lord will give strength to his people: The Lord will bless his people with peace.
Glory be to God in the highest, And on earth peace, good-will to men.

How beautiful upon the mountains are the feet of them that bringeth good
tidings of good, that publisheth peace, that saith unto Zion, Thy
God reigneth!

Blessed are the peacemakers: for they shall be called the children of
God.

Now in Christ Jesus ye who sometimes were far off are made nigh.

For he is our peace, who hath made both one, and hath broken down
the middle wall of partition between us; having abolished in his
flesh the enmity:

And came and preached peace to you which were afar off, and to them that were
nigh.

For through him we both have access by one Spirit unto the Father.

Therefore being justified by faith, we have peace with God through our Lord
Jesus Christ.

Let us therefore follow after the things which make for peace, and things
wherewith one may edify another.

Peace I leave with you, my peace I give unto you: not as the world giveth,
give I unto you.

Let not your heart be troubled, neither let it be afraid.

If a man love me, he will keep my words: and my Father will love him, and
we will come unto him, and make our abode with him.

Thou wilt keep him in | perfect | peace,
Whose | mind is | stayed on | thee.
The Lord will give | strength to his | people;
The Lord will | bless his | people with | peace.

Peace be to thee, and | peace to thine | house,
And | peace unto | all that thou | hast.
Glory be to | God in the | highest,
And on earth | peace, good- | will to | men.

Ye shall go out with joy, and be led forth with peace:

The mountains and the hills shall break forth before you into singing,
and all the trees of the field shall clap their hands.

Thou shalt be in league with the stones of the field: and the beasts of the field
shall be at peace with thee.

And thou shalt know that thy tabernacle shall be in peace; and thou
shalt visit thy habitation, and shalt not sin.

Lo this we have searched it, so it is; hear it, and know thou it for thy good;
and the peace of God which passeth all understanding shall keep
your hearts and minds through Christ Jesus.

Wisdom.

I, wisdom, the Lord possessed in the beginning of his way, before his works of old.

I was set up from everlasting, from the beginning, or ever the earth was.

When there were no depths, I was brought forth; when there were no fountains abounding with water.

Before the mountains were settled, before the hills, was I brought forth;

When he prepared the heavens, I was there: when he set a compass upon the face of the depth:

When he established the clouds above: when he strengthened the fountains of the deep:

When he gave to the sea his decree, that the waters should not pass his commandment: when he appointed the foundations of the earth:

Then was I daily his delight, rejoicing always before him; and my delights were with the sons of men.

Now, therefore, hearken unto me, O ye children: for blessed are they that keep my ways.

Hear instruction, and be wise, and refuse it not.

Blessed is the man that heareth me, watching daily at my gates, waiting at the posts of my doors.

ALL:—For whoso findeth me findeth life, and shall obtain favor of the Lord.

Ancient English.

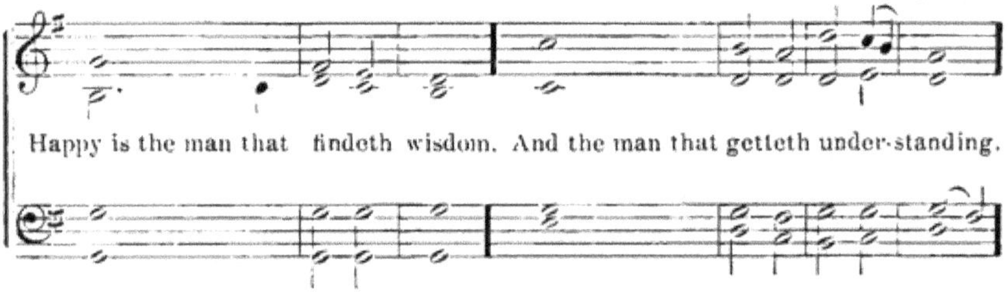
Happy is the man that findeth wisdom, And the man that getteth under-standing.

Her ways are ways of pleas - ant - ness, And all her paths are peace.

I, wisdom, call unto you, O men; and my voice is to the sons of man.

Hear; for I will speak of excellent things; and the opening of my lips shall be right things.

All the words of my mouth are in righteousness; there is nothing froward or perverse in them.

They are all plain to him that understandeth, and right to them that find knowledge.

Receive my instruction and not silver; and knowledge rather than choice gold.

For wisdom is better than rubies; and all the things that may be desired are not to be compared to it.

Counsel is mine, and sound wisdom: I am understanding; I have strength.

I love them that love me; and those that seek me early shall find me.

Riches and honor are with me, yea, durable riches and righteousness.

My fruit is better than gold, yea, than fine gold; and my revenue than choice silver.

I lead in the way of righteousness, in the midst of the paths of judgment;

That I may cause those that love me to inherit substance; and I will fill their treasures.

> *Hearken unto me, | O ye | children.*
> *And at- | tend to the | words of my | mouth.*
> *For they are life unto | those that | find them.*
> *And | health to | all their | flesh.*

Whence then cometh wisdom, and where is the place of understanding?

Seeing it is hid from the eyes of all living and kept close from the fowls of the air.

God understandeth the way thereof and he knoweth the place thereof.

And unto man he said, Behold the fear of the Lord, that is wisdom, and to depart from evil is understanding.

My son, attend to my words; incline thine ear unto my sayings.

Let them not depart from thine eyes; keep them in the midst of thine heart.

Then shalt thou walk in thy way safely, and thy foot shall not stumble.

When thou liest down thou shalt not be afraid; yea, thou shalt lie down and thy sleep shall be sweet.

Happy shalt thou be and it shall be well with thee.

The True Service.

Is not this the fast that I have chosen? to loose the bands of wickedness, to undo the heavy burdens, and to let the oppressed go free, and that ye break every yoke?

Is it not to deal thy bread to the hungry, and that thou bring the poor that are cast out to thy house?

When thou seest the naked, that thou cover him; and that thou hide not thyself from thine own flesh?

If ye know these things, happy are ye if ye do them.

Cast thy bread upon the waters: for thou shalt find it after many days.

In the morning sow thy seed, and in the evening withhold not thine hand: for thou knowest not whether shall prosper, either this or that, or whether they shall both be alike good.

Whatsoever a man soweth, that shall he also reap.

For he that soweth to his flesh, shall of the flesh reap corruption;

But he that soweth to the Spirit, shall of the Spirit reap life everlasting.

Then let us not be weary in well-doing: for in due season we shall reap if we faint not.

The fruit of the Spirit is love, joy, peace, long suffering, gentleness, goodness, faith, meekness, temperance: against such there is no law.

Let every man prove his own work, and then shall he have rejoicing in himself alone, and not in another.

RICHARD LANGDON.

Whatsoever ye would that men should do unto you, Do ye e - ven so unto them;
When men are cast down, Thou shalt say, there is lift - ing up.

Bear ye one an - - oth - er's burdens And so ful-fill the law of Christ.
He shall deliver the island of the innocent By the pure-ness of thine hands.

We preach not ourselves, but Christ Jesus the Lord; and ourselves your servants for Jesus' sake.

Giving no offense in anything, that the ministry be not blamed:

But in all things approving ourselves as the ministers of God, in much patience, in afflictions, in necessities, in distresses,

In stripes, in imprisonments, in tumults, in labors, in watchings, in fastings;

By pureness, by knowledge, by long suffering, by kindness, by the Holy Ghost, by love unfeigned,

By the word of truth, by the power of God, by the armor of righteousness on the right hand and on the left.

By honor and dishonor, by evil report and good report: as deceivers, and yet true;

As unknown, and yet well known; as dying, and behold, we live; as chastened, and not killed;

As sorrowful, yet alway rejoicing; as poor, yet making many rich; as having nothing, yet possessing all things.

Jesus said: Ye have not chosen me, but I have chosen you, and ordained you, that ye should go and bring forth fruit, and that your fruit should remain.

Therefore, labor not for the meat which perisheth, but for that meat which endureth unto everlasting life, which the Son of man shall give unto you.

Whatsoever ye would that men should | do unto | you,
Do ye | even | so unto | them.
Bear ye one an- | other's burdens
And so ful- | fill the | law of | Christ.

When men are | cast | down,
Thou shalt | say, there is | lifting | up.
He shall deliver the | island of the | innocent
By the | pureness | of thine | hands.

Be ye doers of the word and not hearers only, and whatsoever ye do, do it heartily, as to the Lord, and not unto men.

Rejoice with them that do rejoice, and weep with them that weep.

Be eyes to the blind and feet to the lame; loving not in word nor in tongue only, but in deed and in truth.

It is more blessed to give than to receive, and whoso giveth a cup of cold water only, shall not lose his reward.

Jesus said: He that doeth it unto one of the least of these my brethren, doeth it unto me; and he that receiveth me, receiveth him that sent me.

This is the work of God, that ye believe on him whom God hath sent.

Verily, I say unto you. Whatsoever ye shall bind on earth shall be bound in heaven:

And whatsoever ye shall loose on earth shall be loosed in heaven.

Go ye, therefore, and teach all nations, baptizing them in the name of the Father, and of the Son, and of the Holy Ghost:

Teaching them to observe all things whatsoever I have commanded you:

All:—And, lo, I am with you alway, even unto the end of the world. Amen.

Refuge.

The Ninety-first Psalm.

He that dwelleth in the secret place of the Most High shall abide under the shadow of the Almighty.

I will say of the Lord, He is my refuge and my fortress, my God; in him will I trust.

Surely he shall deliver thee from the snare of the fowler and from the noisome pestilence.

He shall cover thee with his feathers, and under his wings shalt thou trust.

His truth shall be thy shield and buckler.

Thou shalt not be afraid for the terror by night.

Nor for the arrow that flieth by day.

Nor for the pestilence that walketh in darkness.

Nor for the destruction that wasteth at noonday.

A thousand shall fall at thy side and ten thousand at thy right hand.

But it shall not come nigh thee.

Only with thine eyes shalt thou behold and see the reward of the wicked.

PLUMA M. BROWN.

The eternal God is our refuge; Underneath us are the ev-er-last-ing arms.
The Lord upholdeth all that fall, And raiseth up all that be bowed down.

The name of the Lord is a } strong tower: { The righteous runneth } in-to it and are safe.
In the midst of trouble he } will revive them: { None of them that put their } trust in him shall be desolate.

Because thou hast made the Lord, which is my refuge, even the Most High, thy habitation,

There shall no evil befall thee, neither shall any plague come nigh thy dwelling.

For he shall give his angels charge over thee to keep thee in all thy ways.

They shall bear thee up in their hands lest thou dash thy foot against a stone.

Thou shalt tread upon the lion and the adder.

The young lion and the dragon shalt thou trample under feet.

Because he hath set his love upon me, therefore will I deliver him.

I will set him on high because he hath known my name.

He shall call upon me and I will answer him.

I will be with him in trouble.

I will deliver him and honor him.

With long life will I satisfy him, and shew him my salvation.

The eternal God | is our | refuge;
Underneath us are the | ever- | lasting | arms.
The name of the Lord is a | strong | tower;
The righteous runneth | into | it and are | safe.

The Lord upholdeth | all that | fall,
And raiseth up | all that | be bowed | down.
In the midst of trouble he | will re- | vive them;
None of them that put their | trust in | him shall be | desolate.

Character

"Faithful in all things."

Lord, who shall abide in thy tabernacle?

He that walketh uprightly and worketh righteousness, and speaketh the truth in his heart. He that doeth these things shall never be moved.

Who shall ascend the hill of the Lord and stand in his holy place?

He that hath clean hands and a pure heart; who hath not inclined his soul to falsehood nor spoken deceitfully.

If a man be just, and do that which is lawful and right, and hath not oppressed . any, but hath restored to the debtor his pledge.

Hath spoiled none by violence, hath given his bread to the hungry, and hath covered the naked with a garment;

He that hath not given forth upon usury, neither hath taken any increase, that hath withdrawn his hand from iniquity.

Hath executed true judgment between man and man, hath walked in my statutes, and hath kept my judgments, to deal truly;

He is just, he shall surely live, saith the Lord God.

Pluma M. Brown.

Search me, O God. and know my heart: Try me and know my thoughts.
Blessed are the pure in heart, For they shall see God.

Create in me a clean heart O God, And renew a right spirit with - in me.
Let the words of my mouth, and the meditation } of my heart, { Be acceptable in thy sight, O Lord. my } strength and my re-deemer.

Wherewithal shall a young man cleanse his way?

By taking heed thereto according to thy word.

If any of you lack wisdom. let him ask of God. that giveth to all men liberally, and upbraideth not; and it shall be given him.

But let him ask in faith. nothing wavering. For he that wavereth is like a wave of the sea driven with the wind and tossed.

Let not that man think that he shall receive anything of the Lord.

Therefore, be ye steadfast, unmovable, holding fast the profession of our faith without wavering; (for he is faithful that promised.)

Present ye your bodies a living sacrifice. holy. acceptable unto God, which is your reasonable service.

And be not conformed to this world: but be ye transformed by the renewing of your mind, that ye may prove what is that good, and acceptable. and perfect will of God.

Let love be without dissimulation. Abhor that which is evil; cleave to that which is good.

Finally. brethren, whatsoever things are true. whatsoever things are honest, whatsoever things are just, whatsoever things are pure. whatsoever things are lovely. whatsoever things are of good report; if there be any virtue. and if there be any praise, think on these things.

Wherefore, beloved, seeing that ye look for such things, be diligent that ye may be found of him in peace, without spot, and blameless.

Search me, O God, and | know my | heart:
Try me and | know | my | thoughts.
Create in me a clean | heart, O | God,
And renew a right | spirit with- | in | me.

Blessed are the | pure in | heart,
For | they | shall see | God.
Let the words of my mouth, and the meditation | of my | heart,
Be acceptable in thy sight, O Lord, my | strength and | my re- | deemer.

Finally, my brethren, be strong in the Lord, and in the power of his might.

Put on the whole armor of God, that ye may be able to withstand in the evil day, and having done all, to stand.

Stand therefore, having your loins girt about with truth, and having on the breastplate of righteousness;

And your feet shod with the preparation of the gospel of peace;

Above all, taking the shield of faith, wherewith ye shall be able to quench all the fiery darts of the wicked.

And take the helmet of salvation, and the sword of the Spirit, which is the word of God:

Praying always with all prayer and supplication in the Spirit, and watching thereunto with all perseverance.

These are the things that ye shall do; speak ye every man the truth to his neighbor; execute the judgment of truth and peace in your gates.

And let none of you imagine evil in your hearts against his neighbor; and love no false oath: for all these are things that I hate, saith the Lord.

Study to shew thyself approved unto God, a workman that needeth not to be ashamed, rightly dividing the word of truth.

Seeing ye have purified your souls in obeying the truth through the Spirit unto unfeigned love of the brethren, see that ye love one another with a pure heart, fervently:

Being born again, not of corruptible seed, but of incorruptible, by the word of God, which liveth and abideth forever.

For whatsoever is born of God overcometh the world: and this is the victory that overcometh the world, even our faith.

ALL:—Him that overcometh will I make a pillar in the temple of my God, and he shall go no more out; and I will write upon him the name of my God.

382   Responsive Services.

The Word of the Lord is Health.

I am the Lord that healeth thee.

   I have heard thy prayer, I have seen thy tears: behold I will heal thee.

Unto you that fear my name shall the Sun of righteousness arise with healing
   in his wings.

PLUMA M. BROWN.

Then shall thy light break forth as the morning, And thine health shall spring forth speedi - ly:

Thy righteousness shall go be-fore thee: The glory of the Lord shall be thy re - ward.

Oh, that men would praise the Lord for his goodness, and for his wonderful
   works to the children of men.

   They cry unto the Lord in their trouble, and he saveth them out of their
      distresses.

He sent his word and healed them, and delivered them from their destructions.

   Why art thou cast down, O my soul? and why art thou disquieted within
      me?

Hope in God: for I shall yet praise him, who is the health of my countenance,
   and my God.

   I create the fruit of the lips; Peace, peace to him that is afar off, and to
      him that is near, saith the Lord; and I will heal him.

I will restore health unto thee, and I will heal thee of thy wounds.

   God be merciful unto us, and bless us; and cause his face to shine upon
      us.

That thy way may be known upon earth, thy saving health among the nations.

   Thy words are life to those that find them, and health to all their flesh.

Heal me, and I shall be healed; Save me, and I shall be saved: for thou art my
   praise.

   Thou art my hiding place; thou shalt preserve me from trouble;

Thou shalt compass me about with songs of deliverance.

ALL:—How excellent is thy loving-kindness, O God! therefore the children of
      men put their trust under the shadow of thy wings.

Bless the Lord, | O my | soul:
And all that is within me | bless his | holy | name.
Who forgiveth | all thine | iniquities,
Who | healeth | all thy | diseases.

Bless the Lord | , O my | Soul;
And for- | get not | all his | benefits.
Who redeemeth thy | life from de- | struction:
Who crowneth thee with loving | kindness and | tender | mercies.

Then he called his twelve disciples together, and gave them power and authority over all devils, and to cure diseases.

And he sent them to preach the kingdom of God, and to heal the sick.

And they departed, and went through the towns, preaching the gospel, and healing everywhere.

Afterwards the Lord appointed other seventy also, and sent them two and two before his face into every city and place, whither he himself would come.

And he said unto them, into whatsoever city ye enter, heal the sick that are therein, and say unto them, the kingdom of God is come nigh unto you.

And by the hands of the apostles were many signs and wonders wrought among the people;

Insomuch that they brought forth the sick into the streets, and laid them on beds and couches, that at the least the shadow of Peter passing by might overshadow some of them.

There came also a multitude out of the cities round about unto Jerusalem, bringing sick folks, and them which were vexed with unclean spirits: and they were healed every one.

To him who believeth, all things are possible.

[Repeat chant,—"Bless the Lord," etc.]

The prayer of faith shall save the sick, and the Lord shall raise him up; and if he have committed sins, they shall be forgiven him.

For all things are for your sakes, that the abundant grace might through the thanksgiving of many redound to the glory of God.

For which cause we faint not; but though our outward man perish, yet the inward man is renewed day by day.

For our light affliction, which is but for a moment, worketh for us a far more exceeding and eternal weight of glory;

While we look not at the things which are seen, but at the things which are not seen:

For the things which are seen are temporal; but the things which are not seen are eternal.

Judge not according to the appearance, but judge righteous judgment.

ALL:—Father, we thank thee that thou hast hidden these things from the wise and prudent and hast revealed them unto babes.

The Lord is my Shepherd.

Psalm 23.

LOWELL MASON.

The Lord is my Shepherd: I   shall not want.

He maketh me to lie down in green pastures: he leadeth me beside the still wa - ters. A - men.

He re- | storeth my | soul:
He leadeth me in the paths of righteousness for his | name's— | sake.
Yea though I walk through the valley of the shadow of death, I will | fear no |
     evil:
For thou art with me: thy rod and thy staff they | comfort | me.
Thou preparest a table before me in the presence of mine | ene- | mies,
Thou anointest my head with oil; my cup | runneth | over.
Surely goodness and mercy shall follow me all the | days of my | life,
And I will dwell in the house of the | Lord for | ever. | A- | men.

The Lord's Prayer.

Gregorian.

Our Father who art in heaven,   hal-lowed be thy name;
Give us this   day our dai - ly bread;
And lead us not into temptation. but de-   liv - er us from evil:

Thy kingdom come. thy will be done on   earth as it is in heaven.
And forgive us our debts, as   we for-give our debtors.
For thine is the kingdom, and the power, and the glory
     for ev - er, A - men.

Benediction.

The Lord be with you.

The Lord bless thee.

Ye shall go out with joy and be led forth with peace.

The Lord bless us and keep us: The Lord make his face to shine up - on us:

The Lord lift up the light of his countenance up-on us, And give us peace.

Benediction.

PLUMA M. BROWN.

The Lord bless thee, and keep thee: The Lord make his face

shine up - on thee, and be gra - cious un - to thee: The

Lord lift up his coun - ten-ance up - on thee, and give thee peace.

ALPHABETICAL INDEX OF TUNES.

METRICAL INDEX OF TUNES.

INDEX OF RESPONSIVE SERVICES.

INDEX OF AUTHORS, WITH HYMNS.

INDEX OF COMPOSERS, WITH TUNES.

INDEX OF FIRST LINES.

Index of First Lines. 399